JOSHUA, JUDGES,
and
RUTH
for
EVERYONE

OLD TESTAMENT FOR EVERYONE
John Goldingay

Genesis for Everyone, Part 1
Genesis for Everyone, Part 2
Exodus and Leviticus for Everyone
Numbers and Deuteronomy for Everyone
Joshua, Judges, and Ruth for Everyone
1 and 2 Samuel for Everyone
1 and 2 Kings for Everyone
1 and 2 Chronicles for Everyone
Ezra, Nehemiah, and Esther for Everyone

JOSHUA, JUDGES,
and
RUTH
for
EVERYONE

JOHN
GOLDINGAY

WESTMINSTER
JOHN KNOX PRESS
LOUISVILLE • KENTUCKY

© 2011 John Goldingay

First published in the United States of America in 2011 by
Westminster John Knox Press
100 Witherspoon Street
Louisville, KY 40202

First published in Great Britain in 2011 by
Society for Promoting Christian Knowledge
36 Causton Street
London SW1P 4ST

12 13 14 15 16 17 18 19 20—10 9 8 7 6 5 4 3 2

Unless otherwise indicated, Scripture quotations are the author's own translation.

Maps are © Karla Bohmbach and are used by permission.

Cover design by Lisa Buckley
Cover art: © istockphoto.com

Library of Congress Cataloging-in-Publication Data

Goldingay, John.
  Joshua, Judges, and Ruth for everyone : a theological commentary on
the Bible / John Goldingay.
      p. cm. — (The Old Testament for everyone)
  ISBN 978-0-664-23378-5 (alk. paper)
  1. Bible. O.T. Joshua—Commentaries.   2. Bible. O.T. Judges—Commentaries.
3. Bible. O.T. Ruth—Commentaries.   I. Title.
  BS1295.53.G66   2011
  222'.077—c22

                                                                    2010033593

Most Westminster John Knox Press books are available at special quantity
discounts when purchased in bulk by corporations, organizations, and special-
interest groups. For more information, please e-mail SpecialSales@wjkbooks.com.

CONTENTS

Maps		viii
Acknowledgments		xi
Introduction		1
Joshua 1:1–18	Just One River to Cross	7
Joshua 2:1–24	Meanwhile, in the Whorehouse	10
Joshua 3:1–17	On Getting Your Feet Wet	14
Joshua 4:1–5:1	Looking Forward and Backward	18
Joshua 5:2–15	Which Side Are You On? Neither	21
Joshua 6:1–21	Come Blow Your Horn	25
Joshua 6:22–7:15	Who Are the Real Canaanites?	29
Joshua 7:16–26	Coveting Can Kill	32
Joshua 8:1–21	The Importance of a Game Plan	36
Joshua 8:22–35	It's Over Even When It's Not Over	40
Joshua 9:1–21	How to Get Taken In	44
Joshua 9:22–10:11	How to Swallow Your Pride	47
Joshua 10:12–27	No Compromise	50
Joshua 10:28–43	Welcome to the Wild Wild West	54
Joshua 11:1–15	Welcome to the Wild Wild North	57
Joshua 11:16–12:24	Why Were They So Stupid?	61
Joshua 13:1–14:15	The Country That Remains to Be Possessed Is Very Great	64
Joshua 15:1–17:11	Living as Women in a Man's World	67
Joshua 17:12–19:21	Roots; or, Home Is Where Your Share Is	71
Joshua 20:1–21:43	Everything Came True	74
Joshua 22:1–34	The Universal and the Local	78

CONTENTS

Joshua 23:1–16	The Peril of Other People's Faiths	81
Joshua 24:1–33	"You Can't Serve Yahweh." "Yes We Can!"	85
Judges 1:1–36	Real Life Is More Complicated	88
Judges 2:1–3:4	The Power of Forgetting	92
Judges 3:5–31	Unlikely Saviors	95
Judges 4:1–24	Three Strong Women and Three Feeble Men (I)	99
Judges 5:1–31a	Three Strong Women and Three Feeble Men (II)	102
Judges 5:31b–6:24	On the Unimportance of Spiritual Insight	106
Judges 6:25–40	How to Be a Mixed-up Person	110
Judges 7:1–25	How to Increase the Odds against Yourself	113
Judges 8:1–35	I'm Not the Hero; the Hero Is God	117
Judges 9:1–57	The Man Who Would Be King	120
Judges 10:1–11:29	When God Finds It Hard to Be Tough	124
Judges 11.30–12:15	The Man Whose Promise Makes the Blood Run Cold	128
Judges 13:1–25	Entertaining Angels Unawares	131
Judges 14:1–15:20	Honey, We Solved the Riddle	134
Judges 16:1–21	Love Actually	138
Judges 16:22–31	But Samson's Hair Began to Grow Again	141
Judges 17:1–13	They All Did What Was Right in Their Own Eyes	145
Judges 18:1–31	Desperate Dan	149
Judges 19:1–30	The Story Reaches Its Lowest Point (I)	152
Judges 20:1–48	The Story Reaches Its Lowest Point (II)	156
Judges 21:1–25	How Not to Save the Situation	159
Ruth 1:1–9	How Naomi's Life Falls Apart	162
Ruth 1:10–19a	The Choice	166
Ruth 1:19b–2:9	She's A Moabite, for Goodness' Sake!	170

Contents

Ruth 2:10–23	The God of Coincidences	173
Ruth 3:1–18	How Not to Leave the Initiative to the Man	177
Ruth 4:1–10	How Not to Get Overextended in Real Estate	181
Ruth 4:11–22	How David Got His Grandfather	185
Glossary		189

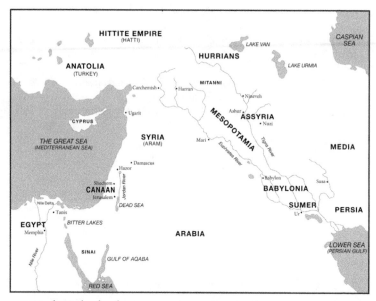

© *Karla Bohmbach*

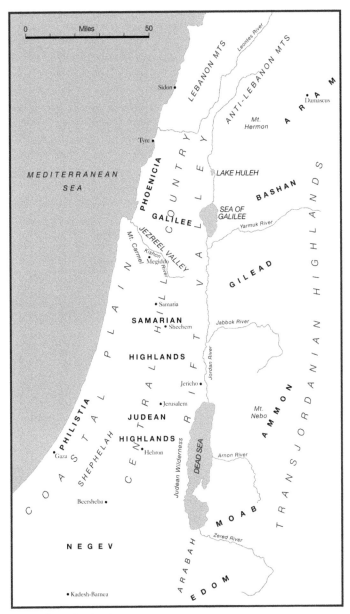

0   Miles   50

MEDITERRANEAN
SEA

Sidon

LEBANON MTS
Leontes River

ANTI-LEBANON MTS

Mt.
Hermon

A R A M

Damascus

Tyre

PHOENICIA

C O U N T R Y

LAKE HULEH

BASHAN

GALILEE

SEA OF
GALILEE

Yarmuk River

JEZREEL VALLEY

Mt. Carmel

Kishon River

Megiddo

R I F T   V A L L E Y

GILEAD

T R A N S J O R D A N I A N   H I G H L A N D S

Samaria

SAMARIAN

Shechem

Jabbok River

HIGHLANDS

Jordan River

Jericho

Jerusalem

JUDEAN

Mt.
Nebo

AMMON

HIGHLANDS

PHILISTIA

SHEPHELAH

Gaza

C O A S T A L   P L A I N

C E N T R A L   H I L L   C O U N T R Y

Hebron

Judean Wilderness

DEAD SEA

Arnon River

Beersheba

MOAB

A R A B A H

Zered River

N E G E V

EDOM

Kadesh-Barnea

© Karla Bohmbach

ix

ACKNOWLEDGMENTS

The translation at the beginning of each chapter of this book (and in other biblical quotations) is my own. I have stuck closer to the Hebrew than modern translations often do when they are designed for reading in church so that you can see more precisely what the text says. Although I prefer to use gender-inclusive language, I have let the translation stay gendered if inclusivizing it would make it unclear whether the text was talking in the singular or the plural. Sometimes I have added words to make the meaning clear, and I have put these words in square brackets. Space confines do not allow for including the whole of the biblical text; where there is insufficient room for the entire text, I make some general comments on the material I have had to omit. At the end of the book is a glossary of some terms that recur in the text (mostly geographical, historical, and theological expressions). In each chapter (though not in the introduction) these terms are highlighted in **bold** the first time they occur.

The stories that follow the translation often concern my friends as well as my family. None are made up, but to be fair to people, they are sometimes heavily disguised. Sometimes I have disguised them so well that when I came to read them again, it took me time to work out whom they described. In the stories, my wife, Ann, frequently appears. Just before I began writing this book, she died after negotiating with multiple sclerosis for forty-three years. Our shared dealings with her illness and disability over these years contribute to everything I write, in ways you will be able to see but also in ways that are less obvious. I thank God for her, and I am glad for her sake, though not for mine, that she can now sleep till resurrection day.

I am grateful to Matt Sousa for reading through the manuscript and pointing out things I needed to correct or clarify, and to Tom Bennett for checking the proofs.

INTRODUCTION

As far as Jesus and the New Testament writers were concerned, the Jewish Scriptures that Christians call the "Old Testament" *were* the Scriptures. In saying that, I cut corners a bit, as the New Testament never gives us a list of these Scriptures, but the body of writings that the Jewish people accept is as near as we can get to identifying the collection that Jesus and the New Testament writers would have worked with. The church also came to accept some extra books, the "**Apocrypha**" or "deuterocanonical writings," but for the purposes of this series, which seeks to expound the "Old Testament for Everyone," by the Old Testament we mean the Scriptures accepted by the Jewish community.

They were not "old" in the sense of antiquated or out-of-date; I sometimes like to refer to them as the "First Testament" rather than the Old Testament to make that point. For Jesus and the New Testament writers, they were a living resource for understanding God, God's ways in the world, and God's ways with us. They were "useful for teaching, for reproof, for correction, and for training in righteousness, so that the person who belongs to God can be proficient, equipped for every good work" (2 Timothy 3:16–17). They were for everyone, in fact. So it's strange that Christians don't read them very much. My aim in these volumes is to help you do that.

My hesitation is that you may read me instead of the Scriptures. Don't do that. I like the fact that this series includes much of the biblical text. Don't skip over it. In the end, that's the bit that matters.

An Outline of the Old Testament

The Jewish community often refers to these Scriptures as the Torah, the Prophets, and the Writings. While the Christian Old

1

Testament comprises the same books, it has them in a different order:

> Genesis to Kings: A story that runs from the creation of the world to the exile of Judahites to Babylon
>
> Chronicles to Esther: A second version of this story, continuing it into the years after the exile
>
> Job, Psalms, Proverbs, Ecclesiastes, Song of Songs: Some poetic books
>
> Isaiah to Malachi: The teaching of some prophets

Here is an outline of the history that lies at the background of the books (I give no dates for events in Genesis, which involves too much guesswork):

1200s	Moses, the exodus, Joshua
1100s	The "judges"
1000s	Saul, David
900s	Solomon; the nation splits into two, Ephraim and Judah
800s	Elijah, Elisha
700s	Amos, Hosea, Isaiah, Micah; Assyria the superpower; the fall of Ephraim
600s	Jeremiah, King Josiah; Babylon the superpower
500s	Ezekiel; the fall of Judah; Persia the superpower; Judahites free to go home
400s	Ezra, Nehemiah
300s	Greece the superpower
200s	Syria and Egypt, the regional powers pulling Judah one way or the other
100s	Judah rebels against Syrian power and gains independence
000s	Rome the superpower

Joshua

Joshua takes up the story from the end of Deuteronomy, where the Israelites were poised on the edge of their promised land;

Moses their leader had died, and Joshua had succeeded him as the person designated by God to take the Israelites into the land. The first half of the book of Joshua tells how he did so in a series of great victories but also with some reversals, and with many aspects of the task uncompleted. The book emphasizes the achievement, but between the lines it acknowledges the extent to which the Canaanites remain in control of the country. Archaeological discoveries occasionally indicate that somebody won a great victory in some part of the country, Hazor being the spectacular example (see Joshua 11), but they generally suggest that the emergence of Israel as a people and its becoming the dominant people in the area was a gradual process.

The second half of the book describes how Joshua allocated the country to the various twelve Israelite clans, again acknowledging between the lines that they are thus given quite a task in connection with entering into actual possession of their land. In its last pages the book closes rather in the way the Torah did, with the leader (now Joshua, not Moses) challenging Israel to commit itself in covenant to God for the future.

Many modern people don't like the way the book portrays Joshua's leading Israel in killing many Canaanites, but there is no indication that the New Testament shares this modern unease. The New Testament pictures Joshua as a great hero (see Hebrews 11) and portrays God's violent dispossession of the Canaanites as part of the achievement of God's purpose in salvation (see Acts 7). If there is a contradiction between loving your enemies and being peacemakers, on one hand, and Joshua's undertaking this task at God's command, on the other, the New Testament does not see it.

We need to separate two issues in considering the questions all this raises. One is that the Old Testament sees the Canaanites as under God's judgment for their wrongdoing. The idea that God judges people for their wrongdoing runs through both Testaments; Jesus is tougher about it as he pictures God sending people not merely to early death but to hell, where there is weeping and gnashing of teeth. In the context of modernity, we do not care for this idea, but we need to note its prominence in Jesus' thinking.

3

The other issue is that the Old Testament sees God as using the Israelites as the agents of judgment. I'm not sure why we don't like this idea, but the concern people often express is that it could become the basis or justification today for making war against other people. But Israel itself never saw God's commission to dispose of the Canaanites as a precedent for its relationships with other people. Nor does the book of Joshua imply that Joshua's action was a pattern for Israel's future practice. Occupying Canaan and being the means of bringing God's judgment on the Canaanites was a one-time event from the beginning of its story.

We do not know who wrote the book of Joshua or when it was written. As well as leading on from Deuteronomy, it leads into Judges, Samuel, and Kings. It resembles one season of a long-running TV series whose authors know they are leaving loose ends that they will need to tie up before the series finishes. Genesis to Kings as a whole takes Israel's story up to the exile and thus could not have been brought to completion (at least in a remastered version) before that time, though there might have been an earlier, more basic edition. In the boxed-set version, Deuteronomy sets the agenda for Joshua through Kings and provides readers with the clues for understanding why the story unfolds the way it does.

Judges

Judges comprises another season in this epic, taking Israel from the death of Joshua to the eve of Saul's emergence as Israel's first king. Its title comes from the form of leadership it describes, though the English word *judges* does not help a great deal in this connection. While the word for "judging" can denote fulfilling a role in the administration of justice, this activity is a subset of exercising authority or leadership in a broader sense, and *leaders* or *rulers* would be less misleading English equivalents to the Hebrew word. During the period from Joshua to Saul, Israel has no one ruling the entire people in the manner of Moses and Joshua, and then in the manner of Saul and David, but from time to time God causes "leaders" to arise to cope with particular crises in particular parts of the country. They all have leadership ability but for the most part have little moral or religious sensibility. There is little linear development in the narrative; it is generally a sequence of parallel stories of disobedience to God, chastisement, mercy, and restoration. It thus illustrates ways in which Deuteronomy's account of the potential dynamics of Israel's story works out in practice. In this sense, Deuteronomy provides the framework for Judges as it does for Joshua.

Judges is one of the most unpleasant books in the Bible, a dispiriting story of rebellion against God and violence among human beings, not least violence against women (and sometimes violence by women). It thus speaks especially powerfully in a world characterized by such violence. The story becomes more dispiriting the more you read, and by the end you may wish you had not bothered. Thus one reason it is important, and perhaps the reason God might have wanted such an unpleasant work in the Bible, is that it forces us to come to terms with the reality of how things are in the world, and often in the church. It epitomizes the way the Bible is not escapist literature, nor is it focused simply on me and my personal relationship with God.

The book's great dilemma is to know what can be done about the horror it analyzes. More precisely, its dilemma is that leadership is both the problem and the solution. On one hand, it knows that God is supposed to be Israel's king; thus a hero such as Gideon refuses to be turned into a king. On the other hand, the increasing social and moral collapse that accelerates towards the end of Judges happens in a context in which people are doing "what is right in their own eyes" because "there was no king in Israel." In this respect it prepares the way for the introduction of the monarchy, which comes in 1 Samuel.

Ruth

Ruth is the story of how a woman's life falls apart through famine, displacement, and the death of her husband and sons, and then how it is put back together through the extraordinary love of her foreign daughter-in-law and of a distant relative back home. It is a kind of sidebar to the story of Israel, the large-scale story running through Joshua, Judges, Samuel, and Kings. In other words, in the original series Judges led straight into 1 Samuel. In the order of books in the Jewish Bible the story of Ruth comes much later, in the company of some other shorter books such as Esther and the Song of Songs. This sequence likely suggests it was written later, in the same time after the exile as those other books. One aspect of its significance that would come home in that context is its portrait of a foreign woman's committing herself to her Israelite kin and to the God of Israel. While it does not question the idea that Israel needs to be wary of the influence of foreigners with their alien religion, it reminds Israel that its God wants to be the God of the whole world and that they need to be open to foreigners who want to join Israel and come to worship Israel's God.

The English Bible follows the order of the books when they were translated into Greek and moves Ruth to a different context that also makes sense, but in a different way. The first words of the story tell us that it takes place in the time when the "judges" ruled. (We have to keep reminding ourselves that the time to which a Bible story refers may be quite different from the time when it was written.) After the increasing horror of Judges, Ruth offers a much more encouraging portrait of Israel's life and takes away something of the bad taste in your mouth that Judges leaves. It also leads neatly into what follows in First and Second Samuel. It does so in two ways. Its more encouraging picture of everyday Israelite life (particularly women's lives) leads into the similar story of Hannah in 1 Samuel 1–2, and it closes by revealing that the son Ruth bears is none other than the grandfather of David.

JOSHUA 1:1-18

Just One River to Cross

[1]After the death of Moses, Yahweh's servant, Yahweh said to Joshua son of Nun, Moses' assistant: [2]"Moses, my servant, is dead. Up, now, cross over this Jordan, you and all this people, into the country I am giving to them, to the Israelites. [3]Every place on which you direct the sole of your foot I have given you, as I declared to Moses. [4]From the wilderness and Lebanon here, to the Great River, the river Euphrates, all the country of the Hittites, to the Great Sea on the west, will be your territory. [5]No one will take a stand before you all the days of your life. As I was with Moses, I will be with you. I will not fail you or abandon you. [6]Be strong, stand firm, because you will enable this people to possess this country that I promised to your ancestors to give them. [7]Simply be strong, stand very firm, taking care to act in accordance with all the teaching my servant Moses commanded you. Do not turn from it to the right or the left, so you may be successful everywhere you go. [8]This scroll of teaching is not to leave your mouth. Recite it day and night so you may take care to act in accordance with everything written in it, because then you will make your life go well, then you will be successful. [9]Haven't I commanded you, 'Be strong, stand firm'? Don't panic, don't be afraid, because Yahweh your God will be with you everywhere you go."

[10]So Joshua commanded the people's officials: [11]"Pass through the midst of the camp and command the people, 'Get provisions ready for yourselves, because in three days you are going to cross over the Jordan here, to go in to take possession of the country Yahweh your God is giving you to take possession of.'" [12]To the Reubenites, Gadites, and the half-clan of Manasseh, Joshua said, [13]"Be mindful of the thing Moses, Yahweh's servant, commanded you, 'Yahweh your God is letting you settle and is giving you this country.' [14]Your wives, your young people, and your livestock can stay in the country Moses gave you across the Jordan, but you are to cross over, organized into companies ahead of your brothers, all the fighting men. You are to help them [15]until Yahweh lets your brothers settle like you and they also take possession of the country Yahweh your God is giving them. Then you may return to the country that you are to possess and take possession of it, the country that

Moses, Yahweh's servant, gave you across the Jordan, to the east." [16]They answered Joshua: "All you have commanded us we will do, and everywhere you send us, we will go. [17]Just as we listened to Moses, so we will listen to you. Simply, may Yahweh be with you as he was with Moses. [18]Any person who rebels against what you say and does not listen to your words with regard to everything you command him is to be put to death. Simply be strong and stand firm."

As I write, I listen to CDs, or rather I half-listen. I do not pay too much attention to the words, though sometimes they catch me out. One day the title phrase of Jimmy Cliff's "Many Rivers to Cross" caught my attention, and I listened more carefully. The song speaks of there being all these rivers to cross and of its being only the singer's will that keeps him alive. Maybe he survives only because of his pride. He says, "The loneliness won't leave me alone" because the person he once loved is gone, and all sorts of temptations assail him, and he just has to keep looking for ways to cross the rivers. I found myself in tears because it described my life at the time. It now makes me think about a student who was describing her life to me this week. She has one or two medical issues that she needs to have investigated, and she is supposed to be finalizing applications for a PhD program, and she has the regular demands of her program at the seminary, and she has the work that makes it possible for her to pay her school fees. She has many rivers to cross.

Joshua and Israel have just one. In literal terms it is not very impressive. For much of the year the Jordan as it draws near the Dead Sea is a shallow, muddy affair. But symbolically, it is a big deal. On the other side of it are all those **Canaanites**, whose large size struck the Israelite spies a generation ago (see Numbers 13–14). Historically, they are indeed a much stronger and more sophisticated people than the Israelites. Two and a half of Israel's twelve clans have looked at the country east of the Jordan where Israel is camped at the moment ("across the Jordan" from the perspective of the people telling the story later). They have spotted that it is rather good and have asked that they might settle there. One can imagine that the other nine-and-a-half clans might be wondering whether there is room for them

8

there, too. Yet the real promised land lies west of the Jordan. There is a river to cross.

God focuses on Joshua (the "you" in verses 3–4 is plural and refers to Israel, but the "you" in verses 5–9 is singular and refers to Joshua). Typically, God interweaves promises and exhortations. The promise "I will be with you" sounds routine but is not to be skipped over. It is the promise God made to Isaac (Genesis 26:3) and repeated to Moses when announcing his implausible commission (Exodus 3:12). It is a promise God will reiterate to Israel in **exile** and will repeat to Mary when giving her an implausible commission, and it is the promise Jesus reiterates when sending off his disciples to disciple the world. In modern English "I will be with you" is inclined to suggest that we will have a sense that God is with us, but in the Bible it suggests something objective, not merely subjective. It means God will make sure things work out. Here God spells out the promise's implications. Joshua will succeed in the task set before him. This is what can enable him to be strong and stand firm.

The exhortations also relate to that possibility. The key to successful leadership is sticking close to the teaching Moses has bequeathed to him. One might have expected God to say that he is to keep this teaching in his mind; God actually says he is to keep it in his mouth. In other words, he is to "recite" it. The word God uses is one that denotes meditation, but not a meditation that goes on simply inside Joshua's head. When children are first learning to read, they often read out loud; only later do they learn to read silently. When Jews read Scripture, they mouth the words. This may seem less sophisticated, but it means that reading involves not only the mind but the body and thus potentially the whole person. It may then have a better chance of influencing the whole person's life. Joshua's having Moses' teaching on his lips in this way does not relate to his teaching it to the people. It is rather the foundation of his own life as Moses' disciple and God's disciple. The Psalms begin with a blessing on the person who recites God's teaching in this way and declare that such a person will find that his or her life goes well (Psalm 1). Joshua is being reminded that the key to his success as a leader is his simply being a committed disciple. By implication, God thereby also puts that principle before later leaders who read this story. A king such as Josiah in whose time a teaching scroll like Deuteronomy came to light is challenged to take this same exhortation seriously as key to his exercising his kingship.

The nine-and-a-half clans cannot avoid crossing the river, and the two and a half must do so with them even though they will then come back to settle east of the Jordan. Once the entire people is settled in the land, it will never have the one-ness it has here. The story in Judges will illustrate the point; none of the events it relates involves the whole people. Geography alone rules that out. But Israel remains one people, and the moment of entering the country west of the Jordan, the country originally designated the promised land, is a moment when this should be symbolized. One part of the body cannot be indifferent to the fate of the whole. Individual Israelite clans cannot behave as if the destiny of other clans is no concern of theirs; individual Christian congregations, denominations, or national churches cannot behave as if the destiny of other congregations or denominations, or of the church in another nation, is no concern of theirs.

Although the promised land lies west of the Jordan, God also speaks of its dimensions as extending to the Euphrates, as Solomon's empire did. The Old Testament has various ways of describing the extent of the promised land, couched in terms of the varying political situations of different contexts. It is not a concept with fixed boundaries. That might help one in thinking about modern Middle Eastern political questions.

JOSHUA 2:1–24

Meanwhile, in the Whorehouse

[1]From Acacias, Joshua son of Nun sent two men to investigate quietly: "Go and look at the country, and at Jericho." They went, and came to the house of a woman who was a prostitute, called Rahab, and slept there. [2]The king of Jericho was told, "Now. Some men came here this evening, Israelites, to investigate the country." [3]So the king of Jericho sent to Rahab: "Produce the

men who came to you, who have come to your house, because they have come to investigate the whole country." ⁴The woman had taken the two men and hidden them. So she said, "Yes, the men came to me. I didn't know where they came from. ⁵The gate was about to be shut at dark and the men went out. I don't know where the men went. Pursue after them quickly, because you can overtake them." ⁶So whereas she had taken them up to the roof and hidden them among the stalks of flax that she had on the roof, laid out, ⁷the [king's] men pursued them on the road towards the Jordan, to the fords, and the gate was shut after the men pursuing them went out.

⁸Before those men went to sleep, she went up to them on the roof. ⁹She said to the men, "I acknowledge that Yahweh has given you the country, and that a terror of you has fallen on us and that all the people who live in the country have dissolved in fear before you, ¹⁰because we have heard how Yahweh dried up the waters of the Reed Sea in front of you when you came out of Egypt and how you acted to the two Amorite kings across the Jordan, Sihon and Og, whom you devoted. ¹¹When we heard, our resolve melted. There was no spirit left in anyone on account of you, because Yahweh your God is God in the heavens above and on the earth beneath. ¹²So now, will you promise me by Yahweh, because I have shown commitment to you, that you will also show commitment to my father's household? Give me a true sign ¹³that you will let my father and mother live, and my brothers and sisters, and everyone who belongs to them, and that you will save our lives from death." ¹⁴The men said to her, "Our lives in place of you, to the death, if you do not tell about our business here. When Yahweh gives us the country, we will show commitment and truthfulness to you."

¹⁵So she let them down by a rope through the window, because her house was in the wall of the fortification and she was living in the fortification. ¹⁶She said to them, "Go into the mountains so the pursuers do not come upon you, so you can hide there for three days until the pursuers come back. After, you can go on your way."

[In verses 17–24 the men go on to tell Rahab to hang a red rope in her window so the Israelites know where she and her family are when they come to take the city. After hiding as she says, they return to the camp and report the terror of the local people, an indication that Yahweh has given the country to them.]

In this commentary, Joshua 2 is the only chapter for which I will not attempt to provide an opening story in accordance with the usual format of The Old Testament for Everyone series. How could I compete with this actual story about the adventure of two nice Jewish boys in the Jericho whorehouse (the same dynamic applies to the story in Genesis 29 about Jacob waking up and finding he has married the wrong girl) as a result of being sent off on an expedition by Joshua?

What on earth does Joshua think he is doing? Why does he need a couple of spies to check things out in Jericho? It isn't as if his army is going to attack it. All Israel is going to do is undertake a religious procession, blow their horns, and watch the city's walls fall down. It is going to be rather like the **Reed Sea** event. So why the reconnoiter? The question is given added point by the contrast with the previous ill-fated spy story in Numbers 13–14. There, it was God who commissioned the expedition, not Moses, though God's reasons for doing so are not clear, and one wonders whether it is a kind of test; certainly this is how it turned out. Further, Moses himself later speaks of the venture as the people's idea (Deuteronomy 1:22). So Joshua's initiative raises questions.

Jericho is a stunning oasis in a barren landscape, a thousand feet below sea level, too hot in the summer but pleasant in the winter. It is surrounded by barren wilderness, but Jericho itself possesses abundant water; it was described a couple of pages ago in the Old Testament as a city of palm trees (Deuteronomy 34:3). Apparently it was a bit like a Wild West town, with the saloon doubling as lodging house for people passing through Jericho as they traveled north-south along the Jordan Valley or east-west between **Canaan** and Moab (Elimelek and Naomi will later come this way, and Naomi will return this way with Ruth), and with the manageress doubling as madam. Canaanite cities often have double walls with living space in between, and Rahab evidently lives in such a setting. The boys have no option but to stay here, and the sheriff knows where to look for strangers in town.

Canaan comprises a collection of city-states, each with its "king" (or sheriff or mayor, you could say), and each controlling the area around it. They are independent of one another, but in Joshua's day they are under Egyptian control. Evidently the sheriff knows all about the Israelites hovering on the other side of the Jordan. Rahab's declaration that the city is paralyzed by the prospect of the Israelites storming across the river any day might be an exaggeration, but the sheriff knows he cannot ignore them, and he has deputies keeping an eye open for suspicious-looking strangers, one of whom will be on permanent stakeout duty across the street from Rahab's establishment. Rahab shares the sheriff's assessment of the situation but reacts to it differently.

The difference may reflect her relationship with her city. It is said that men have ambivalent feelings about women who make their sexual favors available; they both utilize them and disapprove of them. Economic factors are commonly what drive women into the sex trade; perhaps Rahab was a widow. Evidently she has family to be concerned for, but perhaps they had a hard time making ends meet, and this was the way she learned to survive without being dependent on them. A woman like Rahab will be a marginal figure in the society, part of it but not really part of it. So maybe it is easier for her to respond differently to what people are saying about the Israelites, as it will be possible for a woman such as Mary of Magdala to respond to Jesus in a way that most of the male pillars of the society cannot. Like the midwives in Exodus 1 or other women in Israel's story, she does not feel obliged to tell the male authority figures the truth when there is nothing truthful about the way they are behaving.

When the king hears about an event like the catastrophe at the Reed Sea or about the fate of the kings across the Jordan (see Deuteronomy 2–3), he determines to double his efforts to resist the invaders. Rahab is open to making different inferences. Rahab the Canaanite reacts the same way as Jethro the Midianite when hearing about the miracle at the Reed Sea (Exodus 19). Lots of other non-Israelite men and women accompanied Israel out of Egypt and joined them in journeying to Sinai and onward to the promised land; Jethro and Rahab give such people faces and names. They remind us that from the beginning Israel is not an ethnically exclusive people. Anyone who is prepared to recognize what **Yahweh** is doing is

13

free to join Yahweh's people. Rahab resembles Ruth in the way relationships of mutual **commitment** between her and these members of Israel are her route into recognizing who Yahweh is: not merely Israel's tribal god but "God in the heavens above and on the earth beneath."

The **Torah** had given no indication that Yahweh would make any exceptions when driving the Canaanites out of the country or that Israel was to make any exceptions when **devoting** the Canaanites, but the two men take for granted that there is no reason to drive out or devote anyone who submits to Yahweh. Like Jonah's declaration that all Nineveh is to be destroyed, whenever God threatens destruction the threat always presupposes "unless you repent." Rahab models the sensible way to respond to God's threats of punishment. Along with Ruth, she will appear in Jesus' genealogy in Matthew 1.

JOSHUA 3:1–17

On Getting Your Feet Wet

¹Joshua started early in the morning. They moved on from Acacias and came to the Jordan, he and all the Israelites, but stopped there before crossing over. ²After three days the officials passed through the camp ³and commanded the people, "When you see the chest of the covenant of Yahweh your God, with the Levitical priests carrying it, you yourselves are to move on from your places and follow it ⁴(yet there is to be a distance between you and it, some two thousand cubits by measure—do not go near it), so you may know the way to go, because you have not passed this way previously." ⁵Joshua said to the people, "Sanctify yourselves, because tomorrow Yahweh will do wonders in your midst." ⁶Joshua said to the priests, "Take up the covenant chest and go through to the front of the people." So they took up the covenant chest and went to the front of the people.

⁷Yahweh said to Joshua, "This day I will begin to make you great in the eyes of all Israel so that they may acknowledge that I am with you as I was with Moses. ⁸You yourself are to command the priests carrying the covenant chest, 'When you come to the edge of the water of the Jordan, stand in the Jordan.'"

⁹Joshua said to the Israelites, "Come here and listen to the words of Yahweh your God." ¹⁰Joshua said, "By this you will acknowledge that the living God is in your midst and that he will totally dispossess before you the Canaanites, the Hittites, the Hivites, the Perizzites, the Girgashites, the Amorites, and the Jebusites. ¹¹Now. The chest of the covenant of the Lord of all the earth is passing into the Jordan in front of you. ¹²So now get yourselves twelve men from the Israelite clans, one man for each clan. ¹³When the soles of the feet of the priests carrying the chest of Yahweh, Lord of all the earth, rest in the water of the Jordan, the water of the Jordan will break off upstream and stand as a single heap." ¹⁴So the people moved on from their tents to cross over the Jordan, with the priests carrying the covenant chest in front of the people. ¹⁵When the people carrying the chest came to the Jordan and the feet of the priests carrying the chest dipped into the edge of the water (the Jordan overflows all its banks the whole period of harvest), ¹⁶the water in the Jordan stood upstream. It rose as a single heap a great way off at Adam, a city near Zarethan. Going down to the Steppe Sea (the Dead Sea), it completely subsided.

So the people crossed over near Jericho. ¹⁷The priests carrying the chest of Yahweh's covenant stood steady on dry ground in the midst of the Jordan while all Israel was crossing on dry ground until the entire nation had finished crossing over the Jordan.

It's a nice image, "getting your feet wet." I think its background lies in this story. Often you can't achieve something or experience something or learn something without making a commitment that may seem risky. It would be nicer to have proof that things will be okay before you make the commitment, but life does not work that way. If you give in to commitment anxiety, you live without danger, but also without life. Ever since we first saw people hang gliding in the French Alps, my very short list of things I wanted to do before I die included "Go hang gliding." Eventually with a friend I drove into the foothills of the mountains northeast of where I live to an airstrip where we left our car to be driven along the steep and narrow unfenced track up the side of a mountain to its flatish top (I remember reflecting that I was more likely to die by the van careering off this track than by hang gliding). I got strapped in behind an experienced glider, and we ran to the edge of a cliff and jumped off. To realize your ambitions, at some point you have to jump off, or jump in.

When the Israelites came out of Egypt, Psalm 114 recalls, "the sea saw and fled, the Jordan turned back." You could infer from the psalm that the Israelites' crossing the **Reed Sea** and crossing the Jordan were two events that happened right together. Actually they were separated by a generation, and they happened to two different generations of the people, but they do belong together. They are the near-beginning and the near-end of a story. Crossing the Reed Sea follows on leaving Egypt; crossing the Jordan means entering **Canaan**. The people cross the Reed Sea in connection with God's putting the Egyptians in their place; they cross the Jordan in connection with God's putting the Canaanites in their place. The Egyptians forfeited the right to hold onto the Israelites by the attitude they took to them and their God. The Canaanites have done nothing wrong by the Israelites, at least not until the Israelites were on their doorstep (see the stories in Numbers 20–21), and there is a sense in which they cannot be blamed for taking action then. The Canaanites and the Israelites are not natural enemies and have not been at enmity. But the Canaanites have forfeited the right to hold onto their land by the waywardness and the faithlessness of their lives, their social order, and their religion—for instance, the practice of sacrificing their children to their gods (Genesis 15:16; Deuteronomy 9:4; 12:31). The moment of judgment has come for them as it came for the Egyptians.

The list of the seven nations is a traditional one. *Canaanites* is a general term for the peoples of the land; *Amorites* can have similar reference but here likely denotes the people east of the Jordan whom the Israelites have already defeated. The Hittites mentioned here will be the people around Hebron mentioned in connection with Abraham. The Hivites will play an important role in chapter 9. The Jebusites are the people living in Jerusalem, who are therefore important in light of the future importance of Jerusalem. *Girgashites* is just a name, as is *Perizzites*, though etymologically that implies "villagers," so it might not be an ethnic group but more a sociological one.

Joshua 3 tells its story in such a way as to show how it pairs with the Reed Sea story. Once again God is doing "wonders." Once again waters stand up in a "heap," and the people pass through on "dry ground." As the Reed Sea **deliverance** once led to the people's coming to trust in Moses, so these wonders will magnify the people's new leader in their eyes. Joshua 3 also tells its story to show how it pairs with the broader exodus-Sinai story. In preparation for God's appearing at Sinai, the Israelites spend three days sanctifying themselves. The preparations here will be similar to those at Sinai: they will keep away from anything that would make them taboo and unable to come near God at all (things such as death and sex and moral wrongdoing, because these are all alien to God's own being). They need to stay holy in those ways if they are to see God act. God's instructions at Sinai often warn about coming too close to the actual presence of the transcendent, awesome God, as subjects properly hesitate before going too close to a king. The people are to stay close in the sense that they are committed to following closely, but they are to keep in mind that this is the transcendent, awesome God. At the same time, the story has moved on since they were at the Reed Sea. Now they have the **covenant chest** to take with them. It is a more concrete symbol than the column of cloud and fire, which no longer appears.

The apparent reference to the Israelites crossing at harvest time is confusing. It would naturally make one think of high summer or fall, but chapter 5 locates the crossing at Passover time, in the spring, which makes more sense. It is in the spring that the river is at its fullest after the winter rains; the further you get into summer, the shallower the river's flow. Perhaps the reference has in mind the beginning of the long harvest season that starts at Passover and runs through to the fall. The crossing is a momentous event, yet even at Passover the river would be quite passable. Crossing it did not require a miracle. Like the Reed Sea deliverance (which was necessary only because of the weird route God made Israel take), the Jordan miracle is an extravagance on God's part. Like the Reed Sea miracle, it is a sign of **Yahweh**'s power and commitment that is designed to embolden the Israelites for all that is to follow. Like the Reed Sea miracle, it is open to being "explained" as a natural event (a fortuitous earthquake upriver), though that either destroys the point of the story or makes even more miraculous the way it happened at precisely this moment.

JOSHUA 4:1–5:1

Looking Forward and Backward

[1]When the entire nation had finished crossing over the Jordan, Yahweh said to Joshua, [2]"Get yourself twelve men from the people, one from each clan, [3]and command them, 'Carry yourselves twelve stones from here, from the midst of the Jordan, from the place where the priests' feet stood steady. Take them across with you and put them at the place where you stay for the night.'" [4]So Joshua summoned twelve men whom he appointed from the Israelites, one man for each clan. [5]Joshua said to them, "Cross over in front of the chest of Yahweh your God, into the midst of the Jordan, and lift up for yourselves, each man, a stone onto his shoulder, in accordance with the number of the Israelite clans, [6]so this may be a sign in your midst. When your children ask in the future, 'What are these stones to you?' [7]you are to say to them, 'The Jordan waters subsided before Yahweh's covenant chest; when it passed through the Jordan, the Jordan waters subsided.' These stones will be a memorial for the Israelites in perpetuity." [8]The Israelites did this as Joshua commanded. They carried twelve stones from the midst of the Jordan, as Yahweh spoke to Joshua, in accordance with the number of the Israelite clans, and took them across with them to the place where they would stay, and put them there. [9]The twelve stones Joshua set up (in the midst of the Jordan at the place where the feet of the priests carrying the covenant chest had stood) have been there until this day. [10]The priests carrying the covenant chest were standing in the midst of the Jordan until everything was finished that Yahweh had commanded Joshua to tell the people, in accordance with everything Moses commanded Joshua. The people speedily crossed over, [11]and when all the people had finished crossing over, Yahweh's chest and the priests crossed over to the head of the people. [12]The Reubenites, Gadites, and the half-clan of Manasseh crossed over organized into companies in front of the Israelites, as Moses had told them. [13]Some forty thousand

18

men equipped for a campaign crossed over before Yahweh to the Jericho steppes for battle. ¹⁴That day Yahweh made Joshua great in the eyes of all Israel. They revered him as they revered Moses, all the days of his life.

¹⁵Yahweh said to Joshua, ¹⁶"Command the priests carrying the declaration chest to come up out of the Jordan." ¹⁷So Joshua commanded the priests, "Come up out of the Jordan," ¹⁸and when the priests carrying Yahweh's covenant chest came up out of the midst of the Jordan and the soles of the priests' feet lifted out onto the dry ground, the Jordan waters returned to their place and went over all their banks as previously. ¹⁹When the people came up from the Jordan on the tenth day of the first month, they camped at Gilgal, on the eastern border of Jericho. ²⁰Those twelve stones that they had taken from the Jordan, Joshua set up at Gilgal. ²¹He said to the Israelites, "When your children ask their parents in the future, 'What are these stones?' ²²tell your children, 'On dry land Israel crossed over the Jordan here,' ²³because Yahweh your God dried up the Jordan waters in front of you until you crossed, as Yahweh your God did to the Reed Sea, which he dried up in front of us until we crossed, ²⁴so that all the peoples of the earth might acknowledge how powerful is Yahweh's hand, so that you might revere Yahweh your God all your days." ⁵:¹And when all the Amorite kings across the Jordan on its western side and all the Canaanite kings near the [Mediterranean] sea heard how Yahweh had dried up the Jordan waters in front of the Israelites until they had crossed, their resolve melted and there was no longer any spirit left in them because of the Israelites.

Yesterday I was comparing notes with a woman who lost her father the same month I lost my wife. She mentioned that her mother wasn't prepared to look forward, to imagine what the future would be like, and was only prepared to look backward, to remember what had been, whereas the woman herself was interested in looking forward, not looking backward. "I'm with your mother!" I said, to her slight consternation. The conversation helped me understand the question a therapist friend had asked me, about what new things I thought I might now do. It just seemed an odd question. I was more interested in looking to the past, in remembering, in recapturing the past (I have just put on the wall next to my desk some photos of Ann from the years before she was disabled). Now I realize that it was a natural question for some people, but not for me at the moment. Both anticipation and remembering are important. People like me who are inclined to remember are to be affirmed but also encouraged to anticipate; people who are inclined to live in the future are to be affirmed but they also need to be encouraged to reclaim the past.

For the sake of the generation entering **Canaan**, Joshua is full of anticipation regarding what is going to be; for the sake of coming generations, it emphasizes remembering. In Israel's later story, Gilgal is an important place of worship. With the age-old city of Jericho having lost importance, this place on the edge of its territory can become important for Israel as a place that commemorates their arrival in the country. Samuel leads Israel in confirming Saul's appointment as king there; twice in Saul's time it is a place of sacrifice (1 Samuel 11–15); Elijah and Elisha have a base there (2 Kings 1–4); and Hosea and Amos mention it as a place of sacrifice and pilgrimage. One can imagine Joshua's scenario being realized as Israelite families gather here for a festival and children point to the twelve stones and ask what they signify; and if they fail to do so because they are too busy running to the river to wade and swim, their fathers will tell them anyway over dinner.

The story now makes explicit the parallel between the Jordan crossing and the **Reed Sea** crossing and the broader exodus event. Like the Reed Sea crossing, this one is designed to demonstrate the power of **Yahweh** to the world as a whole, and the description of the **Amorite** and **Canaanite** kings dissolving in fear both confirms Rahab's description of them and indicates that Joshua's words are finding fulfillment. In turn, this recognition of Yahweh by other peoples is designed to win an obedient submission to Yahweh on Israel's part that will last all their days. As the Reed Sea event led to Israel's revering Moses, so this event did lead to Israel's revering Joshua. As the Israelites made their way from Egypt to the Reed Sea "organized into companies," so the Reubenites, Gadites, and the half-clan of Manasseh crossed over the Jordan "organized into companies" (the word comes only in these two contexts). As Israel walked through the Reed Sea "on dry land," so Israel walked through the Jordan "on dry land" (most of the occurrences of this expression come in one of these two connections). As the Reed Sea waters returned to their usual place once Israel had crossed, so did the Jordan waters. And the Israelites crossed the river and made their camp at Gilgal on the day that signified the beginning of the observance of Passover, with its broader commemoration of the exodus.

Israel developed no tradition of pilgrimage to the place where they were **delivered** at the Reed Sea (or to Sinai, whose location also therefore came to be uncertain). One reason might be that it was a long way. Locating the twelve stones at Gilgal and portraying the Jordan crossing as a repetition of the Reed Sea crossing meant that a pilgrimage to Gilgal could become a remembering of the Reed Sea deliverance as well as the people's arrival in Canaan. One can imagine how priests might reenact the event and bring it to life before the people. Maybe this explains part of the unevenness or jumpiness in the story—for instance, superficially it seems to speak of twelve stones set up in the middle of the river as well as twelve set up at Gilgal, though more likely both expressions refer to the same set. It is as much an account of an annual commemoration as of the event itself.

JOSHUA 5:2–15

Which Side Are You On? Neither

[2]At that time Yahweh said to Joshua, "Make yourself flint knives and circumcise the Israelites again, a second time." [3]So Joshua made himself flint knives and circumcised the Israelites at Foreskin Hill. [4]This is the reason why Joshua circumcised them. The entire people that came out of Egypt, the males, every one (the men in the army) had died in the wilderness on the way, after they came out of Egypt. [5]Whereas the entire people who came out had been circumcised, they had not circumcised the people born in the wilderness on the way, after they came out of Egypt. [6]Because for forty years the Israelites had gone about in the wilderness until the entire nation (the men in the army who came out of Egypt) were gone, the people who had not listened to Yahweh's voice and to whom Yahweh

had sworn not to let them see the land Yahweh had sworn to their ancestors to give us, a land flowing with milk and sweetness. [7]But he had raised up their sons in their place. It is these Joshua circumcised because they were uncircumcised, because they had not circumcised them on the way. [8]When they had finished circumcising the entire nation, they stayed where they were in the camp until they had recovered. [9]Yahweh said to Joshua, "Today I have rolled away the shaming of the Egyptians from you." That place has been called Gilgal ["Rolling"] until this day. [10]The Israelites camped at Gilgal and observed Passover on the fourteenth day of the month in the evening, in the Jericho steppes. [11]They ate of the produce of the country the day after Passover, flat bread and roasted grain that very day. [12]The manna stopped the day after they ate of the produce of the country. There was no longer any manna for the Israelites, but they ate of the yield of Canaan that year.

[13]When Joshua was at Jericho, he looked up and saw: there, a man standing opposite him, a drawn sword in his hand. Joshua went to him and said, "Are you for us or for our foes?" [14]He said, "No, because it is as commander of Yahweh's army I have now come." Joshua fell to the ground before him and prostrated himself, and said to him, "What is my lord going to tell his servant?" [15]The commander of Yahweh's army said to Joshua, "Take your shoes off your feet, because the place where you are standing is holy." Joshua did so.

We were discussing the book of Job in a class this week. I have abandoned giving a set lecture on the book because when students have read it as part of their preparatory homework, they come to class with many questions and issues they want to raise, and I let these form the agenda for the class. One student was concerned about the way Job as an individual seems to be just a pawn in the story and in God's dealings with the world. In our culture that seems obviously wrong, because it is the individual that counts, and we assume this is the biblical view. Ironically, someone quoted John 3:16 in this connection: "God so loved the world," as if John were saying, "God loved each individual." Actually John says God loved the *kosmos*, the world as a whole, the world as a system. Of course God does love each of us as individuals, but that isn't God's only priority. Indeed, this is one point God eventually makes to Job. Job as an individual is not the center of the world. There are other aspects to God's activity in the world than making sure that Job has a comfortable and intelligible life.

The commander of God's army makes a similar point in the delicious exchange with Joshua. His appearance to Joshua provides another parallel with Moses' story as it constitutes an equivalent to God's appearance at the burning bush, though it asserts authority over Joshua in a different way from the one that applied to Moses. Further, whereas it was immediately evident to Moses that he was confronted by something extraordinary, there is nothing obviously supernatural about the commander's appearance. He is just a warrior. So is he on Israel's side or on theirs? Joshua asks. The man refuses to accept that way of framing the question. Joshua has to take more seriously that he and his army are part of a bigger picture.

That closing part of the chapter leads straight into the story of the fall of Jericho. God's command to Moses to remove his shoes because he stands on holy ground led into God's declaration of intent to **deliver** Israel from Egypt and into the commission to go to Pharaoh to bid him let Israel go. The commander's parallel command to Joshua leads into God's declaration of intent to give Jericho into his power and leads into the commission to process around the city, in effect to bid it surrender to Israel.

The account of the circumcision and Passover completes the transition from the wilderness to the people's arrival in the promised land. There are yet further parallels with the exodus. There, the Israelites celebrated the Passover before God had actually done anything to bring them out of Egypt; it was an enactment they undertook by faith and as an expression of conviction about what God was going to do. Here, the Israelites celebrate Passover on the set day and eat flat bread in accordance with its pattern. They are thus eating the produce of the promised land. Their action is in keeping with the fact that they have arrived in the promised land and will no longer need the special provision associated with the wilderness. Yet it is an outrageous act of faith and hope. They have crossed the Jordan and entered the land, but in a way they are only

23

like some immigrants from Mexico who have crept across the U.S. border. Their problems are only beginning. The Israelites are behaving as if their occupation of the land is accomplished when actually they have not yet faced any of the current inhabitants of the land.

Perhaps this further highlights the importance of the mass circumcision that precedes the celebration of Passover. You cannot celebrate Passover if you are not circumcised. It is the sign of God's commitment to the people in **covenant** and the sign of the people's responsive commitment in covenant. It is astonishing to discover that no one has been circumcised since the people left Egypt. None of them has received the sign of the covenant! The passage perhaps implies that the failure to circumcise their sons is another sign of the wilderness generation's waywardness. So now it is as if circumcision were instituted a second time, and their now receiving the covenant sign means they are definitively reestablished as the covenant people to whom God is about the fulfill the second half of that specific commitment declared in Egypt. Stage one was bringing them out from the land where they served the Egyptian government; stage two is taking them into the land where they will serve God. Maybe the "reproach of the Egyptians" links with this. It had looked for all the world as if God was either incapable of bringing Israel to its new land or had simply abandoned Israel, and Moses has more than once specifically imagined the Egyptians saying so (e.g., Deuteronomy 9:28). The people's arrival in the land and this reestablishment of the covenant sign removes the basis for any such taunt. God makes the point by a characteristic paronomasia. The name Gilgal would remind people of the Hebrew word for "rolling away," *galal*. The mass circumcision at Gilgal is as if God has rolled away any suggestion of having abandoning the people.

The sudden "us" in verse 6 draws attention to the fact that reading Joshua does not mean merely reading a piece of objective history. This is a story written for people to listen to, people who identify with the Israelites involved in the events. For some Israelite readers, this would be the story of how God fulfilled promises to "us" in giving "us" the land we enjoy. For other

Israelite readers, it would be the story of how God fulfilled these promises regarding a land that "we," however, no longer enjoy because we have been thrown out of it as the **Canaanites** were and for the same reasons. But maybe that might not be the end of the story. Maybe God's having mercy on the children of the wilderness generation is a pattern that could be repeated for the **exile** generation. . . .

JOSHUA 6:1–21

Come Blow Your Horn

¹Now Jericho was closed from inside and from outside in the face of the Israelites. No one was coming out and no one was going in. ²But Yahweh said to Joshua, "See, I have given Jericho and its king [and] its fighting men into your hand. ³All the warriors are to go around the city, circling the city once. You are to do this for six days, ⁴while seven priests carry seven rams' horns in front of the chest. On the seventh day you are to go around the city seven times, while the priests blow on the horns. ⁵At the sounding of the ram's horn, when you hear the noise of the horn, all the company are to give a great shout, and the city's wall will fall flat and the company will go up, each person straight ahead."

⁶So Joshua son of Nun summoned the priests and said to them, "You carry the covenant chest while seven priests carry seven rams' horns in front of Yahweh's chest." ⁷He said to the company, "Pass on, go around the city, while the people equipped for a campaign pass on in front of Yahweh's chest." ⁸When Joshua had told the people, the seven priests carrying the seven rams' horns passed on in front of Yahweh and blew the horns, with Yahweh's covenant chest following them, ⁹and the people equipped for a campaign going in front of the priests who blew the horns, and the rear guard continuing to follow the chest, with the horns blowing. ¹⁰Joshua commanded the company, "You will not shout, you will not make your voice heard, no word will come out of your mouth, until the time I say to you, 'Shout!' and you will shout." ¹¹So he had Yahweh's chest go around the city, circling it once; then they came to the camp and spent the night in the camp. ¹²Joshua got up

early the next morning and the priests took up Yahweh's chest, [13]while the seven priests carrying seven rams' horns in front of Yahweh's chest went on and blew the horns, with the people equipped for a campaign going in front of them and the rear guard continuing to follow Yahweh's chest, and with the horns blowing. [14]They went around the city once on the second day and returned to the camp. So they did for six days.

[15]On the seventh day they started early, at sunrise, and went around the city according to this routine, seven times; only on that day did they go around the city seven times. [16]The seventh time, the priests blew on the horns, and Joshua said to the company, "Shout, because Yahweh has given you the city. [17]The city is to be an object devoted to Yahweh, it and everything in it, except that Rahab the prostitute is to stay alive, she and everyone with her in the house, because she hid the aides we sent. [18]Only you—be careful of what is to be devoted in case you become something that is to be devoted. If you take anything from what is to be devoted, you will make the Israelite camp into something that is to be devoted. You will bring trouble on it. [19]All the silver and gold and the objects of bronze and iron are holy to Yahweh. They are to go into Yahweh's treasury."

[20]So the company shouted when they blew on the horns. When the company heard the sound of the horn, the company gave a great shout, the wall fell flat, and the company went up into the city, each person straight ahead, and captured the city. [21]They devoted everything in the city, man and woman, young and old, ox and sheep and donkey, with the edge of the sword.

In New Orleans over the weekend for a meeting (I have such a hard job) I talked with Tom Wright, author of The New Testament for Everyone series, and with staff from the publishers. I remarked that the most demanding aspect of this project is having a story to begin each chapter, and someone asked if I would be able to incorporate a reference to New Orleans. This turns out to be easy, because I also spent time there listening to trumpeters blowing their horns. In Preservation Hall I listened to a band playing with the authentic traditional jazz configuration, its front line comprising clarinet, trumpet, and trombone, as it was before the saxophone was imported from dance bands.

In the open air on Bourbon Street was a band with an older feature, a tuba instead of a bass. This music started off as marching music; you can't march and play the bass at the same time.

Here is Joshua with the original marching band, blowing literal horns (made from ram's horns and made for noise, not melody), not metal trumpets (they appear in Israel only later). "Joshua fit the battle of Jericho" goes a song I didn't hear one of these bands play, but Joshua didn't fight. There was no battle at Jericho. If anyone fought at Jericho, as at the **Reed Sea**, it was not the Israelites but God. The Israelites simply process, blow horns, and shout loudly. While there is indeed a procession by a marching band, the essential involvement of the priests makes it more like the procession around the parish bounds that churches sometimes do. The presence of the **covenant chest** signifies God's presence. When the Israelites made their ill-fated attempt to conquer **Canaan** under their own steam, there was a link between their failure and their not taking the chest with them (Numbers 14:44). Yet on a later occasion they took it with them on another ill-fated expedition, and this didn't work (1 Samuel 4). If the project is God's, the chest as the symbol of their covenant relationship with God will be an effective sign of God's presence.

Then they **devoted** the things and the people there. Devoting things means giving them over to God. This sometimes implies giving them over for God's service, but it sometimes implies executing them, and both significances apply in this story. The plunder from Jericho is to be put in the sanctuary treasury; the living things are executed. We noted in the introduction how this commonly raises questions for Christians and Jews in the context of modernity, and we suggested some considerations to take into account in thinking about these questions. We will come back to them in connection with Joshua 10:22–27.

There is another related issue. Like other ancient cities, Jericho comprises a huge mound made of the remains of a sequence of cities that accumulated over the centuries, like the layers of a cake. Each time fire or war destroys a city, its people stamp down the remains and build again on top of them. So we discover the history of a city by digging down into these layers and seeking to interpret its remains. When you visit Jericho, you stand on top of the remains of the mound and look down into excavated areas that are (paradoxically) much older than the place where you are standing.

Before going to New Orleans, I planned to begin this chapter with a story from a time I once visited Jericho, where the ancient city stands alongside the modern city. A tour guide there humorously but also somewhat seriously assured his party that if they climbed down into the hole and looked by the walls there, they might find Joshua's trumpet. The walls to which he was pointing are actually a thousand years older than Joshua's day. There are no remains from Jericho that belong to Joshua's day. It seems that no one lived in Jericho at that time. That suggests that the story of his conquest of Jericho is just a story, a suggestion that might both cause us anxiety and offer us relief. I'm not sure it deserves to do either. It doesn't let us off the hook of the questions about the story's morality. It is this actual story that God was happy to have in his book, and it is this actual story that people read; not many of them read the archaeological reports. God apparently liked the story with its account of how the Canaanites deserved judgment and how God used Joshua in bringing it about.

If it is a more-or-less fictional story, at some stage some of the Israelites must have known. So why did they tell it? One answer is that it vividly symbolizes the fact that God gave Israel its land. Israel did not gain control of the land by its own efforts. All it did was process around, blow horns, and shout. And because it is true that God gave Israel the land and that Israel did not gain the land by its own efforts, it doesn't matter so much how factual is this vivid, concrete story that illustrates that truth. Admittedly we might then want to know how we can be sure that God gave Israel its land if it is not on the basis of the factual truth of this story. We then have to remind ourselves that even if the fall of Jericho happened, this wouldn't constitute proof that God gave Israel the land. That involves a step of faith. In reality, accepting that God gave Israel the land is part of a bigger step of faith involved in following the broader story of the Old and New Testaments.

JOSHUA 6:22–7:15

Who Are the Real Canaanites?

²²But to the two men who had investigated the country Joshua said, "Go into the prostitute's house and bring out from there the woman and all who belong to her, as you promised her." ²³So the young men who had done the investigating went and brought out Rahab, her father and mother, her brothers, and all who belonged to her. They brought out her whole family, and put them outside the Israelite camp. ²⁴So they burned down the city and everything in it, except they put the silver and gold and the objects of bronze and iron in the treasury of Yahweh's house, ²⁵but Joshua let Rahab the prostitute live, with her father's household and all who belonged to her. She has lived in the midst of Israel until this day, because she hid the aides Joshua sent to investigate Jericho.

²⁶At that time Joshua swore, "Cursed before Yahweh be the man who undertakes to build this city of Jericho. At the cost of his firstborn may he found it and at the cost of his youngest may he set up its gates." ²⁷Yahweh was with Joshua, and his fame spread through all the country. ⁷:¹But the Israelites broke faith in connection with devoting things when Achan son of Carmi son of Zabdi son of Zerah of the clan of Judah took some of the things that were to be devoted, and Yahweh's anger flared against the Israelites.

²Joshua sent men from Jericho to Ai, which is by Beth-aven (east of Bethel), saying to them, "Go up and investigate the country." So the men went up and investigated Ai ³and came back to Joshua and said to him, "The whole company should not go up. Some two or three thousand men should go up and strike down Ai. You should not tire the whole company there, because they are a small community." ⁴So some three thousand of the company went up, but they took flight before the men of Ai. ⁵The men of Ai struck down some thirty-six of them and pursued them [from] in front of the gate as far as the quarries and struck them down on the slope. The people's resolve melted and turned to water, ⁶and Joshua tore his clothes and fell on his face to the ground in front of Yahweh's chest until evening, he and the Israelite elders, and put dirt on their heads. ⁷Joshua said, "Oh, Lord Yahweh, why did you bring this people

across the Jordan at all in order to give us into the hand of the Amorites to destroy us? If only we had been content to live across the Jordan. ⁸As for me, Lord, what am I to say after Israel has turned its back in the face of its enemies? ⁹The Canaanites and all the inhabitants of the country will hear and turn against us and cut off our name from the earth, and what will you do about your great name?"

¹⁰Yahweh said to Joshua, "Get yourself up. Why are you falling on your face there? ¹¹Israel has done wrong. Yes, they have contravened my covenant that I commanded them. Yes, they have taken some of the things that were to be devoted. Yes, they have stolen things. Yes, they have acted deceitfully. Yes, they have put the things in their bags. ¹²The Israelites will not be able to stand before their enemies. They will turn their back before their enemies, because they have become something to be devoted. I will not be with you again unless you destroy from your midst the thing that is to be devoted. ¹³Get up, sanctify the people. Say, 'Sanctify yourselves for tomorrow, because Yahweh, the God of Israel, has said this: "There is something to be devoted in your midst, Israel. You cannot stand before your enemies until you have removed what is to be devoted from your midst." ¹⁴In the morning you are to come forward by your clans. The clan that Yahweh takes is to come forward by kin groups. The kin group that Yahweh takes is to come forward by households. The household that Yahweh takes is to come forward man by man. ¹⁵The one who is taken in the net is to burn in fire, he and all that belongs to him, because he transgressed Yahweh's covenant and because he committed an outrage in Israel.'"

I have tried being confrontational with God, but it doesn't work very well because God is capable of being confrontational back (as Job found). Once when I was fretting over my wife's illness, I said to God, "I don't really trust you with Ann"; and I sensed God replying, "Would you trust you with Ann if you were me?" (to which the answer was "No"). Another time I told God, "I don't think much of the way you deal with Ann"; and I sensed God saying back, "The way I treat Ann is between Ann and me; I'm not answerable to you." It was a tough response, but a strangely helpful one. If you talk straight, you may get a straight response, but that's better than not talking straight and thus not getting a response that tells you what God thinks and that makes you think about things a different way.

Joshua assumes it is okay to be confrontational with God; he also finds God being confrontational back. His argument overlaps with Moses' argument when God threatened to abandon Israel; God's name will be discredited by such action. But Moses knew Israel was in the wrong. In a sense you can't blame Joshua for not knowing, but he may be at fault for simply assuming that the problem lies in God. Or maybe that is often how things work in a relationship. I can easily assume that I am in the right and the other person is in the wrong, but when I come out with what I assume, I discover that the other person has another way of looking at the situation, one that makes me eat my words. Maybe in theory I could have worked this out or been less confrontational; but what's important is that the matter gets sorted out. There is a time for protest and a time for self-examination, but you may discover that the self-examination comes only by way of treating the conflict as a time for protest.

In Joshua 6 and 7 Rahab and Achan are juxtaposed, a **Canaanite** who doesn't behave like a Canaanite and an Israelite who doesn't behave like an Israelite. Indeed, Rahab is an extreme version of a Canaanite, as she embodies the inclination to sexual immorality that Israel associates with Canaanites, while Achan comes from the heart of Israel, from the clan that produces David. Israel knew that the distinction between Israel and Canaan was an ethnic one, but also that this was true only at surface level. The **Torah** sees Israel as an open community. People from other ethnic groups come to commit themselves to the God of Israel (they get converted, if you like), and they become effectively members of Israel. Sometimes that happens because they are refugees, migrants, or resident aliens who come to live in an Israelite community and choose to join it in a proper sense rather than staying there simply as foreigners. Sometimes they are people like Moses' father-in-law or Rahab who hear what God has done for Israel and know they must respond.

Since before New Testament times, Judaism has often been a missionary religion, and for varying reasons many people have come to join the Jewish people. Very many Jews alive today are

31

not physically descended from Jacob and his sons. This does not make them any less members of Israel. Adoption makes you a real member of a family. Admittedly, things seem a little different with Rahab. Like people in the Old Testament story such as Ruth "the Moabite" and Uriah "the Hittite," people always knew Rahab's ethnic background, and one function of her story is to explain how this particular Canaanite family came to be part of Israel "until this day," the day of the people telling the story. The story reminded people that for all the talk of destroying or **devoting** the Canaanites, God was never against the Canaanites as such. Canaanites could always come to believe in **Yahweh** and commit themselves to membership of Israel.

Conversely, just because you are physically an Israelite doesn't make you exempt from being devoted in that fatal sense. Both ways, commitment trumps ethnicity. Both ways, too, God doesn't deal with people in isolation from their families. What a savior Rahab was! Through her involvement in the sex trade she saved her family from poverty or servitude, then saved the Israelite spies, then saved her family through becoming committed to Yahweh. Likewise Achan brings the wrong kind of "devotion" on his family through his breaking faith with Yahweh. Individuals can dissociate themselves from their families; Lot's wife did so, and Ruth did so. But the story reminds individualistic cultures that we are not just isolated individuals. Having faith and breaking faith is inclined to hold the family together.

JOSHUA 7:16–26

Coveting Can Kill

[16]Early next morning Joshua got Israel to come forward by its clans, and the clan of Judah was taken. [17]He got the kin group of Judah to come forward, and took the kin group of Zerah. He got the kin group of the Zerahites to come forward man by man, and Zabdi was taken. [18]He got his household to come forward man by man, and Achan son of Carmi son of Zabdi son of Zerah of the clan of Judah was taken. [19]Joshua said to Achan, "My son, will you give honor to Yahweh, the God of

Israel and make confession to him? Will you tell me what you have done? Do not hide it from me." [20]Achan replied to Joshua, "It's true. I am the one who has done wrong against Yahweh, the God of Israel. This is what I did. [21]I saw in the spoil a fine coat from Shinar, and two hundred silver shekels, and a bar of gold weighing fifty shekels. I fancied them and took them. There: they are buried in the ground inside my tent, with the silver underneath." [22]Joshua sent aides and they hurried to the tent, and there: it was buried in his tent, with the silver underneath. [23]They took them from inside the tent and brought them to Joshua and all the Israelites, and they laid them out before Yahweh. [24]Joshua took Achan son of Zerah, the silver, the coat, the bar of gold, and his sons, his daughters, his ox, his donkey, his flock, his tent, and everything he had, and with all Israel he brought them up to Trouble Valley. [25]Joshua said, "How you have brought trouble on us! Yahweh will bring trouble on you this day." So all Israel pelted him with stones. They burned them in fire and pelted them with stones, [26]and raised a great heap of stones over them until this day. And Yahweh turned from his angry burning. That is why that place has been called Trouble Valley, until this day.

Today (as I am writing this) is Black Friday, when the stores hope to get their books into the black as the year draws toward an end. People will have been lining up all night or will have got up at crazily early hours to get a plasma TV for a hundred dollars. Last year an employee at a Walmart was trampled to death when the store doors opened. Yes, coveting can kill, or at least cause heartache and distress within the family. When I was nine, my parents kept a mom-and-pop store, and I used to steal from the till. Eventually my mother caught me and made me confess to my father. I acted contrite, but what I actually felt was remorse for getting found out, and I didn't immediately stop; I was simply more restrained and more careful (I did stop soon afterward).

Like us, the Old Testament assumes that individuals are responsible for their own lives, and specifically for their own wrongdoing. Parents are not to be put to death for their children, nor children for their parents; a person is to be put to death for his or her own wrongdoing (Deuteronomy 24:16).

This principle underlies all the Old Testament laws, as it underlies our laws. Yet we ourselves know that life is more complicated than this. When a court sends a mother or father to prison, it imposes a punishment on the children as well as the parent, because human beings are bound up in the web of life together. If I live as someone who thinks that acquiring "stuff" is very important, it will have a bad effect on my children in various ways. The way we are made as human beings means that the sins of the parents are visited on the children, though (according to God's calculations in the Ten Commandments) they are visited nowhere near as extensively as the way the positive aspects to parents' lives have consequences for the children. The Achan story assumes that the destiny of families is bound up together.

Maybe Achan's family was party to or complicit in his appropriating the plunder, but the story is not concerned to say so; its focus lies elsewhere. If what happens to Achan's family seems unfair to us and we want to get God or the Bible off the hook, we could ask whether Joshua shows some limitations in his way of looking at things. He did so in his assumption that the reversal at Ai was to be protested rather than taken as indicating that the people might be at fault. We have noted the oddness of his sending men to reconnoiter Jericho, which led to their ending up in the whorehouse. We will shortly read of his letting himself be conned through not consulting God about the Hivites' advances. In the Rahab story good comes out of the action, and arguably that also happens with the Hivites. Here, too, God accepts Joshua's action; it causes God's anger to subside. God's involvement with us often involves compromising with us as we are rather than insisting on taking no action until we get things absolutely right (and thus waiting forever). So maybe God was not so enthusiastic about the way Joshua treated Achan's family.

Perhaps God's compromising with us in this way is involved in the very idea of **devoting** enemies, which began in Numbers 21 as Moses' idea, not God's, though it was an idea God went along with, as God does here. Thus one significance of the Achan story is that the idea of devoting things is not one Israel applies only to other peoples. It applies to Israel itself.

It is the converse of the fact that a **Canaanite** like Rahab and her family can escape being devoted and killed. Israel has consecrated Jericho to God and has to give it to God. Joshua had pointed out that appropriating any of its stuff would mean that the consecration and the requirement of "devotion" would be contagious. Again, this at least involved Joshua in dotting the i's and crossing the t's of what Moses says in Deuteronomy, but it does place a strong disincentive to plundering, and for that matter to making war at all for the sake of what a nation can get out of it. You cannot gain from war. What you might take as your own belongs to God.

Joshua's action might also seem unfair to Achan himself. The Old Testament usually assumes that a person who acknowledges wrongdoing and repents finds forgiveness and is spared, though this does not always work. It does not apply to Saul, or to David; God does spare David from the execution that might appropriately follow his having Uriah killed, but God lets his baby die and lets the rest of his life unravel. Here, that contagion has come to affect Achan, his family, his animals, and their home, and it is for this reason that Achan's confession does not lead to his finding forgiveness and being spared. Perhaps in all three cases the confession and repentance are insufficiently serious, and there is more remorse than repentance in their stance. I rather think that a bigger factor is that, as usual, one should be grateful for being an ordinary person living in ordinary times. For leaders and for people living in crucial times, the stakes are high, and this fact catches Achan as it will catch Saul and David. But their fate also reminds us that for ordinary people living in ordinary times there are wrongdoings whose consequences you can't undo. A promiscuous man who gets AIDS and infects his wife, then gets converted, probably does not get healed through his turning around; neither does his wife. A woman who takes drugs while pregnant and then repents probably still gives birth to a baby who is an addict.

Achan's horrifying story incidentally provides us with a picture of how interrelationships worked in Israel as the people as a whole divide into clans (tribes as they are usually called), kin groups, and households. The story actually speaks of six levels of relationship—Achan, Carmi, Zabdi, Zerah, **Judah**, and

Israel as a whole. According to Genesis, Jacob/Israel was father of Judah, and Judah was father of Zerah. Zabdi is apparently the current head of this kin group. Maybe Carmi has died (as he is mentioned only as Achan's father), and Achan is thus the head of a household within the kin group, maybe as a man in middle age. The household is the smallest unit in Israel, headed up by its senior male. Within Achan's household would be his sons and their wives, and possibly some unmarried sons and daughters. The children belonging to his sons and their wives would also be part of the household, though none are mentioned in his case. So it is more like an extended family in Western thinking. Achan's own brothers, who were also the sons of Carmi, would be heads of similar households within the kin group. It would be within the kin group as a whole that the head of the household looked for wives for his sons, and they would then join his household; conversely, when his daughters married, they would join their husband's household, within the kin group. The household's size would mean they did not all live in the same physical house (or tent, at this stage), and excavations of Israelite villages reveal that houses were located in clusters (which would mean that people within a household could get away from one another!).

JOSHUA 8:1–21

The Importance of a Game Plan

[1]Yahweh said to Joshua, "Don't be afraid. Don't be dismayed. Take the entire fighting force with you. Set off and go up to Ai. See, I have given into your hand the king of Ai, his city, his people, and his country. [2]You are to treat Ai and its king as you treated Jericho and its king, only its plunder and its cattle you may treat as spoil for yourselves. Set yourself an ambush for the city, behind it." [3]So Joshua and all the fighting force set off to go up to Ai. Joshua chose thirty thousand men, strong fighters, and sent them by night. [4]He commanded them, "See, you are going to set an ambush for the city, behind the city. Don't be very far from the city, and all of you be alert. [5]I and all the people that are with me will draw near the city, and when they

come out to engage us like they did the first time, we will flee before them. ⁶They will come out after us until we have drawn them away from the city, because they will say, 'They are fleeing before us as they did the first time.' When we flee before them, ⁷you yourselves will get up out of your ambush and seize the city. Yahweh your God will give it into your hand. ⁸When you have taken the city, set the city on fire. You are to do as Yahweh said. See, I have commanded you."

⁹So Joshua sent them and they went to the ambush and settled down between Bethel and Ai, west of Ai. Joshua spent the night in the midst of the people. ¹⁰Early in the morning Joshua mustered the company, and he and the Israelite elders went up ahead of the company to Ai. ¹¹All the fighting force that was with him went up. They drew near and arrived in front of the city and camped north of Ai. There was a dip between them and Ai. ¹²He took five thousand men and set them as an ambush between Bethel and Ai, west of the city. ¹³So they put in place the fighting force as a whole that was north of the city, and the ambush west of the city, and Joshua went that night into the midst of the valley.

¹⁴When the king of Ai saw this, early in the morning the men of the city quickly went out to engage Israel in battle, he and all his company, at the set place facing the Steppe. He didn't know there was an ambush for him behind the city. ¹⁵Joshua and all Israel let themselves be beaten before them and fled in the direction of the wilderness. ¹⁶The entire company in Ai called to one another to pursue them. So they pursued Joshua and tore out of the city. ¹⁷Not a man was left in Ai or Bethel who did not go out after Israel. They left the city open and pursued Israel. ¹⁸Yahweh said to Joshua, "Hold out the javelin in your hand toward Ai, because I shall give it into your hand." So Joshua held out the javelin in his hand toward the city, ¹⁹while the ambush quickly got up out of its place. They ran when he held out his hand, entered the city, and took it. Quickly they set the city on fire, ²⁰and the men of Ai turned back and looked: there, the smoke from the city went up to the heavens and there was no scope for flight, this way or that, when the people fleeing to the wilderness turned into being the pursuers ²¹as Joshua and all Israel saw that the ambush had taken the city and that the smoke from the city was going up. So they turned back and struck down the men of Ai.

Three weeks ago I went to my first American football game. It was also my first experience of tailgating in the warm sunshine and of eating breakfast burritos, which (accompanied by mimosas) were perhaps the highlight of the day. I was interested to compare the game with rugby football, which I played as a teenager; for instance, in rugby you can kick forward but not pass forward, but in American football it is the opposite. The football game was as long as a rugby or soccer game except that it was actually three times as long because it continually stopped and started. In the stops and starts (I was told) a key role is fulfilled by the plays that the coach has devised and the team has rehearsed. There is a little of this in soccer, and in rugby the three-quarters (roughly equivalent to quarterbacks) may look as if they are running one way but then switch by means of a scissors movement. But tricks or plays are much more important in American football, as are strategies for the different parts of the game as a whole. (I wonder if that is why coaches are paid so much.)

At Jericho and at Ai God gave Joshua game plans, quite different plans for the two places, yet both expressing how it was not by military power that Israel was going to take **Canaan**. At Jericho the Israelite army had no role at all. God made the city walls collapse. In contrast, the Ai plan involved no divine intervention. If you had been there and things happened as the story relates them, at Jericho you would have been wondering what made Jericho's walls fall, and you would be feeling sorry for its people. At Ai you would be admiring Joshua's stratagem and feeling a bit sorry for its people because they were so gullible. Sometimes God acts by miracles, and sometimes God acts through human means.

You would also be admiring the Israelites' stamina. As they enter the country from across the Jordan, they would need to proceed by climbing up into the heart of the mountain spine of Canaan via Ai and Bethel, which is close by (the modern main road from Jericho to Jerusalem was not a main route in those days). I have gone up that road, and I don't recommend it for people of nervous disposition. You climb steep mountain slopes from a thousand feet below sea level to three thousand feet above sea level. Then, if you had been with Joshua, you would have been expected to fight a battle.

How did God give Joshua the idea for the stratagem he was to implement? I imagine Joshua going to the meeting tent as Moses did when he needed guidance from God, though to judge from the beginning of this chapter, that wasn't where Joshua began in the conversation; at least, it wasn't where God started. The Achan story has been profoundly discouraging. By implication, Joshua's whole way of looking at the expedition had been wrong when he sent off men to reconnoiter and then used ordinary military calculations to work out how to take the city (three thousand men will do it).

God knows Joshua needs encouragement. The Ai story shows that if you sort things out with God, you can have a new start. This motif recurs throughout the Old Testament and runs into the New. Israel making the gold calf at Sinai; the sons of Aaron offering alien fire in the sanctuary; the Israelites at Kadesh unable to believe they can enter Canaan (and then trying to do so when God has forbidden it); Judas betraying Jesus, and Peter denying that he knows him; Ananias and Sapphira dying because they falsified their pledges: things are always going wrong, but God never allows this to be the end of the story. So God begins by encouraging Joshua to pick himself up, dust himself off, and start all over again, not because he has the resources to do so but because God is still committed to him. In paradoxical witness to this point, it is not a calculated number of people that go up to take the city. The whole people is taking possession of the country, and the whole people is involved in the action, with the elders (not the military commanders) at the head of the procession. Indeed, now the Israelites are to be allowed to take the plunder! When Israel has got the point about everything being owed to God, it is possible to be more easygoing.

There in the meeting tent God ministers to Joshua, and there in the tent Joshua has an idea. He cannot believe it is a coincidence that the idea surfaces when he has come to seek God's guidance about what to do now. Or maybe he knows the idea comes from his brain (or perhaps it came from one of his commanders), and he consults God about whether the idea is a good one by means of the Urim and Thummim (these were some means of putting something to God, in response to which God could say yes or no), and God says, "Yes."

39

It is even clearer than is the case with Jericho that in Joshua's day no one lived in Ai. The name gives the game away: "Ai" means "ruin." It has been a ruin for a thousand years in Joshua's day. First Kings 16:34 confirms that Jericho was a ruin for centuries after Joshua's day, as Joshua said it should be. So one can imagine Israelites going down to Gilgal to celebrate the way God gave them the country and passing these ruins and making them the subject of stories that expressed in vivid terms the fact that God gave them the country. There is no evidence that this is how the stories came into existence, but it makes sense of the data.

JOSHUA 8:22–35

It's Over Even When It's Not Over

²²Now these [Israelites] came out of the city to engage them, and in relation to Israel [the people from Ai] were in the middle, some [Israelites] on the one side and some on the other, so they struck them down so that they did not let anyone remain as survivor or escapee. ²³The king of Ai they took alive and brought him to Joshua. ²⁴When Israel had completed slaughtering all the inhabitants of Ai in the open country, in the wilderness where they had pursued them, and all of them had fallen to the edge of the sword until they were finished, all Israel went back to Ai and struck it down with the edge of the sword. ²⁵All those who fell that day, men and women, were two thousand, the entire population of Ai. ²⁶Joshua did not draw back his hand with which he held out his javelin until he had devoted all the inhabitants of Ai. ²⁷Only the cattle and the plunder in that city did Israel take as spoil for themselves, in accordance with Yahweh's word that he commanded Joshua. ²⁸Joshua burned Ai and made it a permanent ruin, a desolation until this day. ²⁹The king of Ai he impaled on a tree until evening. At sunset Joshua commanded, and they took down his corpse from the tree, threw it at the entrance of the city gate, and erected over it a great heap of stones, until this day.

³⁰Then Joshua built an altar for Yahweh the God of Israel on Mount Ebal ³¹as Moses, Yahweh's servant commanded the Israelites, as it is written in the scroll of the teaching of Moses— an altar of whole stones on which no one had wielded iron.

They offered up on it burnt offerings to Yahweh and sacrificed fellowship offerings. [32]He wrote there on the stones a copy of the teaching of Moses that he had written, in the presence of the Israelites. [33]All Israel, the elders, officials, and rulers, were standing on each side of the chest, facing the Levitical priests who carried Yahweh's covenant chest, alien and native alike, half of them facing Mount Gerizim and half of them facing Mount Ebal as Moses, Yahweh's servant, had commanded beforehand, to bless the people of Israel. [34]After this, he read out all the words of the teaching, the blessing and the curse, in accordance with all that is written in the scroll of teaching. [35]There was not a word of all that Moses commanded that Joshua did not read out in front of the congregation of Israel, with the women and young people and the aliens who went in their midst.

My Bible study group last week got depressed about the state of the church and the world, not so much because of how things are in this particular place at this particular time but because of how things continue to be in the world in general, two thousand years after Jesus. Scandals and shortcomings in the church and the continuing waywardness of the world make it tempting to think that Jesus' coming made very little difference. To be truthful, I was the person who was lugubrious. Many of the Bible study group are people in their twenties, bright-eyed and bushy-tailed, and maybe I need to learn from them how to see the glass as half full not half empty. In truth, I have no doubt that Jesus' coming was the decisive event in world history that guarantees the fulfillment of God's purpose for the world, even though that fulfillment seems so far away.

On Mount Gerizim and Mount Ebal, Joshua makes a similar assumption. Narrated somewhat later in the book, this celebration would seem less remarkable. Here it is extraordinary. Israel has crossed the Jordan and climbed onto the mountain ridge, but that is only a beginning. What would the people of Shechem have made of the Israelites' actions at this moment? When Israel has occupied much more of the country, God will observe in Joshua's old age that "there is very much of the country still to take possession of" (Joshua 13:1). Yet here Joshua behaves as if it's over. It resembles the football game I described

41

in connection with Joshua's having a game plan; long before it was officially over, it was already over for the local team, whose fans were streaming out of the stadium to get a jump start on the traffic. Maybe "then" in verse 30 should not be taken too literally, and the ceremony took place "later," when the country's occupation was further advanced. The book's placing the event here is then even more significant in suggesting that Israel's initial victories did guarantee the fulfillment of God's intentions for them.

The ceremony also places a challenge before them. They have been given the country in fulfillment of God's word to them; they have to be committed to living by God's word to them. Making a copy of Moses' teaching symbolizes their commitment to doing so. Because the **covenant chest** contains the stone tablets inscribed with the basic covenant requirements, to stand on either side of the covenant chest for the reading of the covenant blessings and curses adds to the symbolizing of this commitment. The story emphasizes the involvement of the whole people even more than it had emphasized them in connection with winning those initial victories at Jericho and Ai. The ceremony embraces both men and women, young and old, native-born Israelites and aliens who have chosen to associate themselves with Israel and become part of **Yahweh**'s people. Your sex, age, or ethnic background makes no difference. All have benefited from what God has done; all must accept the obligations that follow.

Deuteronomy 27 records the instruction from Moses that Joshua is here fulfilling. The two mountains rise on either side of a broad valley in which stands the city of Shechem, the modern city of Nablus, at the heart of the northern part of the West Bank. It is where Genesis locates Abraham's arrival in **Canaan**, where God first appears to him and promises the country to his offspring, and where Abraham builds an **altar**; he then moves on to camp between Bethel and Ai. So Joshua and the Israelites are repeating Abraham's journey, in the necessarily reverse order as they come from the opposite direction. They are also repeating Abraham's action, with similar significance, when they build an altar that signifies Yahweh's presence in this country and Yahweh's claim on it. For Abraham and for Joshua, their initial arrival in the country and their putting their mark on a little bit of it is a kind of guarantee that God's promise will be fulfilled with regard to the whole of it. Yes, the glass is half full.

Burnt offerings and fellowship offerings are the two regular kinds of sacrifice. Each evening and morning the people of Israel offer burnt offerings in the sanctuary, suggesting their giving of themselves and all that they have to God, their giving to God the day that has passed or the day that is about to begin, and their seeking God's blessing for it. Fellowship offerings do not follow such a routine, because people sacrifice those when they have particular reason to be grateful to God for doing something for them or answering a prayer, or they do so as "freewill offerings," voluntary offerings when they simply want to express their love for God. Here their fellowship offerings will reflect their appreciation for the symbolic completion of their occupying the country, the fulfillment of God's promise to them.

Notwithstanding their freedom to take plunder from Ai, the end of the account of the victory over the city likewise emphasizes the complete nature of the obedience that Israel must offer God. Once again Joshua fulfills a role like Moses (in Exodus 17) as he holds up his hand, holding a javelin in a way that suggests directing the forces of heaven; this is more than a mere earthly battle. Israel is God's agent in bringing God's judgment, and it wields God's power in doing so. The execution of the king is a judicial act, undertaken in the way prescribed by Deuteronomy 21:22–23. His impaling demonstrates toward the heavens that judgment has been exacted. Taking down his body recognizes that even execution is a horrible thing; a Jewish interpretation notes that even a man who deserves to be executed is a man made in God's image.

We may again note that this is not the way God usually expected Israel to relate to other nations. There were horrifying special aspects to the story of Israel's beginnings. We may be glad that God does not act in judgment on us the way God acted in judgment on the Canaanites, but it is also appropriate for us to be a little scared about the way we as modern nations deserve God's judgment to fall in this way, not least in light of the way Jesus speaks about God judging the nations when they are separated into sheep and goats.

JOSHUA 9:1–21

How to Get Taken In

[1]When all the kings across the Jordan, in the mountains, in the foothills, and along the entire coast of the Mediterranean Sea to near Lebanon (the Hittites, the Amorites, the Canaanites, the Perizzites, the Hivites, and the Jebusites) heard, [2]they gathered together to fight with Joshua and with Israel with one accord. [3]But the inhabitants of Gibeon heard what Joshua had done to Jericho and Ai, [4]and they for their part acted with cunning. They went like envoys and took worn-out sacks for their donkeys and worn-out wineskins, cracked and mended, [5]with worn-out, patched shoes on their feet, and worn-out clothes on themselves; all the bread they had as their provisions was dry and hard. [6]They went to Joshua in the camp at Gilgal and said to him and to the Israelites, "We have come from a country a long way away, so now, make a treaty with us."

[7]The Israelites said to the Hivites, "Maybe you are going to live in our midst. How can we seal a treaty with you?" [8]They said to Joshua, "We will be your servants." Joshua said to them, "Who are you? Where do you come from?" [9]They said to him, "Your servants have come from a country a very long way away by reason of the name of Yahweh your God, because we have heard the report about him, about all he did in Egypt, [10]and all he did to the two Amorite kings the other side of the Jordan, King Sihon of Heshbon and King Og of Bashan, in Ashtaroth. [11]Our elders and all the inhabitants of our country said to us, 'Take provisions with you for the journey and go to meet them and say to them, "We will be your servants, so now, seal a treaty with us."' [12]This is our bread: we brought it hot as our provision from our houses on the day we left to come to you, but now—here, it is dry and hard. [13]These are the wineskins that we filled new—here, they are cracked. These are our clothes and our shoes: they are worn-out from the very long journey."

[14]So the people took some of their provisions and did not consult Yahweh. [15]Joshua made peace with them and sealed a treaty with them to let them live, and the community leaders gave them their oath. [16]Three days after they sealed the treaty with them, they heard that they came from nearby, that they were living among them. [17]So the Israelites set out and came to their cities on the third day. Their cities were Gibeon, Kephi-

44

rah, Wells, and Forest Town. [18]The Israelites did not strike them down because the community leaders had given them their oath by Yahweh the God of Israel. The whole community complained at the leaders, [19]but all the leaders said to the whole community, "We ourselves gave them an oath by Yahweh the God of Israel. We cannot now touch them. [20]We will do this to them. We will let them live, and there will not be wrath against us because of the oath we swore to them." [21]So the leaders said to them, "They will live," and they became woodcutters and water carriers for the whole community, as the leaders declared to them.

I have known people who seem to consult God about every detail of their lives, from what to have for dinner to what courses to take next quarter, what college to attend, where to buy a house, or whom to marry. To be honest, I consulted God about the last one myself, but I suspect that usually God is inclined to reply, "Don't ask me; *you* are going to have to live with her." God is passionately interested in those details of our lives as I am passionately interested in those details of my sons' lives, but that doesn't mean I want to decide on the answers for them. Because God is a loving Father, I assume he takes the same attitude. God wants us to make decisions for our lives. But there are occasions when it would be wise to consult God, as there are occasions when a son might be wise to consult his mother or father (I don't remember my sons ever doing so, but if they read this, they will doubtless e-mail me to say, "What about x and y and z?"). So it becomes a judgment call to perceive when one of those occasions comes. (Of course God sometimes offers us unsolicited advice—at least, God does so to me; and I am sure my sons will tell me I have done so. But that's another story.)

"Mum, if we were supposed to kill all those **Canaanites**, how come there are all those people from Gibeon and Forest Town and Whatnot working in the temple?" Children's questions can be embarrassing. "Umm, well, that Joshua guy, he was a great guy, but. . . . He was always a brave guy. You know we could have been in the promised land nearly half a century sooner if Joshua had had his way. He was one of the only two people who came to investigate the country who reckoned God could make it possible for us to take possession of it, but the others won [the story is in Numbers 13–14]. He was always like that. And he was capable of being very wise on Sundays, Tuesdays, and Thursdays, but he wasn't so clever on Mondays, Wednesdays, and Fridays. He was really committed to God, but somehow he sometimes seemed not to see the implications of this commitment. That's what lies behind those Hivites (they are a subset of the Canaanites) still being around."

In a way it's a funny story. If Joshua was rather gullible, the Hivites were rather clever. So the story is both funny and serious, like some movies and TV programs. Yes, Joshua was stupid, but the Old Testament sees this as a moral and religious fault and not just as a possibly endearing quirk. Wisdom is tied up with reverence for God and faithfulness to other people. Joshua acted not only without thinking but without asking what God thought. The story in Joshua has implied that this has been a problem with Joshua on earlier occasions, in connection with the reconnoitering of Jericho and with the first time the people tried to take Ai and then with his assumption that God was at fault when that failed. This is the first time that the story is explicit about the problem. Joshua could surely have seen that there was something fishy about these Hivites' story and could have asked God what to do instead of just sampling their stale bread and believing their rather vague story (they never make specific where it is that they allegedly come from). He knows consulting God is the kind of thing Moses used to do; he was in charge of the tent where Moses went to ask God things. Ignoring that possibility, he makes peace and makes a treaty. They are two powerful words. **Peace** or *well-being* is one of the key words for describing Israel's relationship with God. *Treaty* is the word that also refers to a **covenant** between God and Israel. These words have no business getting applied to relationships with people like the Hivites (as Deuteronomy 7 and 20 make explicit).

The story shows a recognition that a leader has to be especially perceptive about when to consult God. Joshua was the senior pastor who could carry the leadership team with him and then find the congregation as a whole complaining in the way they did against Moses, with the difference being that here they are in the right, even if they joined in the sampling. It's pretty humiliating for Joshua.

JOSHUA 9:22–10:11

How to Swallow Your Pride

²²So Joshua summoned them and spoke to them: "Why did you deceive us in saying, 'We live a very long way away from you,' when you are living among us? ²³So now you are cursed. None of you will stop being a servant, woodcutters and water carriers for the house of my God." ²⁴They replied to Joshua, "Because your servants have been repeatedly told that Yahweh your God had commanded Moses his servant to give you the entire country and destroy the country's inhabitants before you. We were very fearful for our lives because of you. So we did this thing, ²⁵and now, here we are, in your hands. Do according to what is good and proper in your eyes to do to us." ²⁶He did so to them: he rescued them from the hands of the Israelites, and they did not slaughter them. ²⁷That day Joshua made them woodcutters and water carriers for the community and for Yahweh's altar until this day, at the site he would choose.

¹⁰:¹King Adoni-zedek of Jerusalem heard that Joshua had taken Ai and devoted it, doing to Ai and its king as he did to Jericho and its king, and that the inhabitants of Gibeon had come to peace terms with Israel and were among them. ²They were very fearful, because Gibeon was a big city, like one of the royal cities, because it was bigger than Ai, and all its men were warriors. ³So King Adoni-zedek of Jerusalem sent to King Hoham of Hebron, King Piram of Jarmuth, King Japhia of Lachish, and King Debir of Eglon, saying, ⁴"Come up to me and help me, and we will strike down Gibeon, because it has come to peace terms with Joshua and the Israelites." ⁵So the five Amorite kings, the king of Jerusalem, the king of Hebron, the king of Jarmuth, the king of Lachish, the king of Eglon, and all their armies joined together, came up, encamped against Gibeon, and fought against it. ⁶The people of Gibeon sent to Joshua in the camp at Gilgal, saying, "Don't hold back your hand from your servants, come up to us quickly, deliver us, help us, because all the kings of the Amorites who live in the mountains have gathered together against us." ⁷So Joshua and

the entire fighting force went up from Gilgal, his company and all the fighting men. [8]Yahweh said to Joshua, "Don't be afraid of them, because I have given them into your hand. Not one of them will stand against you." [9]Joshua came upon them by surprise; he had marched all night from Gilgal. [10]Yahweh threw them into confusion before Israel; he struck them down in a great rout at Gibeon and pursued them in the direction of the Beth-horon ascent and struck them down as far as Azekah and Makkedah. [11]While they were fleeing from Israel on the Beth-horon descent, Yahweh threw big stones from the heavens as far as Azekah. More died through the hailstones than the Israelites slaughtered with the sword.

In the church where I was a young assistant pastor, I shared a house with an older man called Charles who in U.S.-speak would be called the janitor but in Brit-speak was called the caretaker. I don't remember how he had been appointed, but it was common for someone to get such a job by an ordinary job-hiring process; it wasn't required that he or she be a churchgoer. The same was true about the janitors/caretakers at the church we belonged to just before we came to the United States. Apparently the theory was that they didn't need "spiritual" qualifications for this kind of work. The same applied to the organist at a church we belonged to in between these two—more surprisingly, because you might have thought that involvement in leading music was more of a "spiritual" business. In all these cases, I felt a bit uneasy about the arrangement. But in two out of the three, I watched the people concerned become more involved in church life as time went by.

"But Mum, you didn't explain how those Hivites came to be working in the temple every day." As well as asking embarrassing questions, children may notice when our answers are incomplete. The five Hivite cities are all within five or ten miles north or west of Jerusalem. This is of no great significance in Joshua's day. There is no thought in anybody's mind (except perhaps God's) that Jerusalem will ever be of political or religious significance. It's just an obscure little town in the mountains, off the main road. If anywhere looks destined to be the capital city for Israel (if Israel should ever need such a thing), it's Shechem, where they had their blessing-and-cursing ceremony. Everything will change once David has his bright idea and Jerusalem becomes Israel's capital and David turns it into the central sanctuary, where the **covenant chest** is. The sanctuary will need considerable support staff, all the more when the temple is built at "the site **Yahweh** will choose." That is where the local people come in. Keeping the sacrificial system going requires a lot of wood for burning the sacrifices and a lot of water for various aspects of the ritual. The local people become the labor force.

Genesis 9 describes Noah as invoking a curse on **Canaan** that will mean his always being the lowest of servants to his brothers, and Joshua is bringing that curse up-to-date. Translations often refer to Canaan and/or the Hivites as slaves, but that word gives a misleading impression; they are simply a labor force. While the story does not comment on whether it was Joshua's business to curse the Hivites for making a fool of him (as Genesis did not comment on whether it was Noah's business to curse Canaan because his dad made a fool of Noah), there is no suggestion that being servants means ill-treatment or oppression, and it's preferable to being dead.

The Hivites are like Rahab and her family, who were due to die as part of God's judgment on the Canaanite peoples as a whole. Rahab knew how to react when she heard about what Yahweh had been doing with the Israelites, and she became part of the Israelite community without losing the awareness that ethnically she was a foreigner. The average Canaanite king reacted by seeking to resist what Yahweh was doing and seeking to put an end to these uppity Israelites, and he paid for this with his life. The Hivites fell somewhere in between. They too had heard what Yahweh had been doing with the Israelites, but they hadn't responded either with Rahab's straightness or with the other kings' hostility. So they ended up in a support role in the temple. We don't get told whether they ever came to identify with Israel's commitment to Yahweh in the way Rahab did, and Moses' Midianite father-in-law Jethro did, and Ruth did, but at least they had the chance to do so.

There is another aspect of this process that the stories of Jethro, Rahab, Ruth, and the Hivites have in common. In each case, the possibility of their becoming committed to Yahweh was intrinsically tied up with their relationships with Israel or with individual Israelites. I have a friend who married someone who was an agnostic but became a Christian through the marriage. I have another friend who married an agnostic, and he has stayed an agnostic. It is easy to make a case for Christians not marrying agnostics. Yet it is typical of God not simply to abandon someone because he or she fails to keep the rules. By no means does the personal relationship guarantee that someone will come to commit himself or herself. But it opens up the possibility.

"You see, son, when you have promised something, you have to keep your word, even if the other people deceived you, and even if you should never have let yourself be deceived. Who knows, God may bring good out of it." Joshua had to swallow his pride.

JOSHUA 10:12–27

No Compromise

[12]Then Joshua spoke to Yahweh, on the day Yahweh gave up the Amorites before Israel, and said in the presence of Israel, "Sun stand still at Gibeon, moon at the Aijalon Valley!" [13]The sun stood still, the moon stopped, until the nation took redress from its foes (is this not written in the Jashar Scroll?). The sun stood in the midst of the heavens. It did not hurry to set for a whole day. [14]There has been no day like it before or since, when Yahweh listened to a man's voice, because Yahweh fought for Israel.

[15]Joshua and all Israel with him went back to Gilgal, [16]and these five kings fled and hid in a cave at Makkedah. [17]Joshua was told, "Five kings have been found hiding in a cave at Makkedah." [18]So Joshua said, "Roll big stones to the cave mouth and appoint men over it to keep guard over them. [19]But you, do not stop, pursue your enemies and attack them from the rear. Don't let them get to their cities, because Yahweh your God has given them into your hand." [20]When Joshua and the Israelites had finished striking them down in a very great rout until they were finished, though some survivors escaped from them and got to their fortified cities, [21]the entire company went back to

the camp to Joshua at Makkedah in safety. No one opened his mouth to the Israelites. ²²Joshua said, "Open the cave mouth and bring these five kings out of the cave to me." ²³They did this: they brought these five kings out of the cave to him, the king of Jerusalem, the king of Hebron, the king of Jarmuth, the king of Lachish, the king of Eglon. ²⁴When they brought these kings to Joshua, Joshua summoned all the Israelites and said to the army officers who went with him, "Come forward and put your feet on the necks of these kings." They came forward and put their feet on their necks. ²⁵Joshua said to them, "Don't be afraid. Don't be dismayed. Be strong. Stand firm, because Yahweh will act like this to all your enemies with whom you are fighting." ²⁶After this Joshua struck them down. He killed them and impaled them on five trees. They were impaled on the trees until evening. ²⁷At the time of sunset Joshua gave command and they took them down from the trees and threw them into the cave where they had hidden and put big stones on the cave mouth until this very day.

Six months ago, a doctor who performed late-term abortions was shot dead in church in Kansas, and at his funeral people from another Kansas church carried posters declaring, "God Sent the Killer." Their declarations affirmed that the doctor's own work was an expression of God's wrath on a sinful nation but that the murder was then also a further expression of God's wrath. Their proclamations involve looking at current events in light of Old Testament passages such as this story of Joshua "exacting redress" of the **Canaanites** for their waywardness.

There is a sense in which the easiest way to respond to such arguments is simply to say that Joshua was wrong, that he misunderstood God, and that the New Testament then shows us a more excellent way. This can make us feel better, but it raises further problems and doesn't really get us anywhere, because the people who use Scripture in this way view Scripture as the inspired and authoritative word of God, and they aren't open to the claim that Joshua was simply wrong (and on that, I agree with them). They can correctly comment that the New Testament shows no indication of unease about Joshua's action. I have noted in the introduction that Joshua is one of the New

Testament's great heroes (see Hebrews 11). The saintly Stephen, about to be martyred and to pray for his killers' forgiveness in the same way as Jesus did, nevertheless rejoices in the way the Israelites with Joshua dispossessed the nations that God drove out before their ancestors (see Acts 7). For us as modern people, there is a disjunction between praying for your enemies' forgiveness and rejoicing in the Joshua story; for Stephen there was not.

To describe us as modern people in this connection is not to imply that we think more clearly than they did; rather the opposite. They could see something that we might not. They did not jump from "Joshua did this as God's agent" to "therefore God also sends people to do this today." There was something unique about what God achieved through Joshua. It is noticeable that the story here unusually describes the kings as **Amorites**. That was the term God used when explaining to Abraham that it would be a long time before it was proper to give his descendants the country; the Amorites' waywardness did not yet justify God's doing so. Now it does. But only once did God give the Israelites the land and take up the waywardness of the land's occupants in order to do so, as well as commission Israel to be the means of exacting the divine redress. Never again in the Old Testament did God act this way, and it looks as if Stephen knew that. I don't suppose this argument would convince the people carrying the poster in Kansas, but at least it works with their presupposition that the Bible is inspired and authoritative and it has some coherence in the way it views the Old Testament and New Testament.

We will be helped in understanding this actual story by some awareness of geography. The heartland of the country where Israel eventually lived was the mountain range running for a hundred miles north-south, with Jerusalem and Bethel-Ai near the center. It approximately corresponds to the area known in the twentieth and early twenty-first century as the West Bank, if we ignore the crucial wedge in the center of that area running from Tel Aviv to Jerusalem. To the west those mountains slope down toward the Mediterranean; to the east they tumble more steeply to the river Jordan. At this moment the Israelites are encamped at Gilgal by the Jordan. They have made their presence felt on the top of the mountain ridge in different ways at Ai and at Shechem, the big city slightly farther north and slightly farther south on the ridge in connection with Gibeon and the cities of the Hivites. The five kings come from yet farther south and west. Jerusalem is just south of Gibeon. Hebron is some way farther south on the ridge, dominating its southern half as Shechem dominates its northern half. Jarmuth, Lachish, Eglon, Azekah, and Makkedah are on the opposite, western side of the ridge from Gilgal and Jericho, in the lower hills between the southern part of the ridge and the sea. Beth-horon is on the route down from Gibeon toward the coast. (Some of these places appear on the map at the beginning of this volume.)

We could think of these kings as more like a combination of sheriffs, mayors (though unelected), and pastors. It was reasonable for the king of Jerusalem to panic about Joshua's gaining a bridgehead among his immediate neighbors, the people in Gibeon and related cities, and the other kings will know that they are next in the firing line. They can behave like the Gibeonites or like Rahab, or they can fight. They choose to fight, and they pay the penalty, because "**Yahweh** fought for Israel." As an account of how God gave Israel its land, maybe we are to read it as more like an inspired Western than like an inspired report in the main evening news on network TV. God can speak through either form. But we will have to be careful that we are not once again slanting our reading as a result of our hang-ups as modern people.

The same issues are raised by the account of the sun standing still (and the supernatural hailstorm that preceded it). No doubt God could have altered the way the solar system worked in order to facilitate Joshua's expedition, but I can't see it as very likely, and I am more inclined to reckon that both Joshua and the storyteller are speaking poetically about daylight that seemed to last much longer than one would have expected (the Jashar Scroll, of which we know nothing apart from what this passage says, was apparently a collection of celebratory songs). That again reflects my hang-ups as a modern person. In neither case does our assumption about how literally the story speaks make a significant difference to the story's point. Yet I suspect that once again our reading of it requires a different set of assumptions from the ones we bring to the evening news or to a history book, a set more like the ones for reading imaginative literature or watching movies. God likes all these forms of communication and expression and inspires examples of them all.

JOSHUA 10:28–43

Welcome to the Wild Wild West

[28]That day Joshua took Makkedah and struck it down, it and its king, with the edge of the sword. He devoted them, along with every person there. He did not let any survivor remain. So he dealt with the king of Makkedah as he had dealt with the king of Jericho. [29]Joshua and all Israel with him passed on from Makkedah to Libnah and fought against Libnah. [30]Yahweh gave it, too, into Israel's hand, it and its king, and [Joshua] struck it down with the edge of the sword, along with every person there. He did not let any survivor remain. So he dealt with its king as he had dealt with the king of Jericho. [31]Joshua and all Israel with him passed on from Libnah to Lachish, camped against it, and fought against it. [32]Yahweh gave Lachish into Israel's hand. [Joshua] took it on the second day and struck it down with the edge of the sword, along with everyone there, just as he had done to Libnah. [33]Then King Horam of Gezer came up to help Lachish, and Joshua struck him down with his people until he did not let any survivor remain for him. [34]Joshua and all Israel with him passed on from Lachish to Eglon, camped against it, and fought against it. [35]That day they took it and struck it down with the edge of the sword. Every person who was there he devoted that day, just as he had done to Lachish. [36]Joshua and all Israel with him went up from Eglon to Hebron and fought against it. [37]They took it and struck it down with the edge of the sword, with its king and all its cities and every person there. He did not let any survivor remain, just as he had done to Eglon. He devoted it and every person in it. [38]Joshua and all Israel with him went back to Debir and fought against it. [39]He took it and its king and all its cities. They struck them down with the edge of the sword and devoted everyone in it. He did not let any survivor

54

remain. As he had done to Hebron, so he did to Debir and its king, as he had done to Libnah and its king. ⁴⁰So Joshua struck down the whole country: the mountains, the Negev, the foothills, and the slopes, with all their kings. He did not let any survivor remain. Anything that breathed he devoted, as Yahweh the God of Israel had commanded. ⁴¹Joshua struck them down from Kadesh-barnea to Gaza, all the country of Goshen, as far as Gibeon. ⁴²All these kings and their countries Joshua took at a single stroke, because Yahweh the God of Israel fought for Israel. ⁴³Then Joshua and all Israel with him went back to the camp at Gilgal.

"Are you serious?" someone said to me on Thursday as we sat in a jazz club talking about interpreting the Bible and I made a statement she thought was outrageous (I think I had commented on the disastrous results of interpreting the Bible in light of the creeds). "Everything I say is serious," I said, "even the funny things. Especially the funny things." Yet quite often I may exaggerate. I have told myself a million times not to exaggerate. It's called hyperbole: exaggeration in order to emphasize, to make a point more clearly and more forcefully.

"Joshua struck down the whole country." It sounds as if he had completed the conquest of **Canaan**, though the context immediately makes clearer that "the whole country" doesn't mean that. It does mean the whole of the area south of Gibeon, roughly the bottom half of the mountain heartland, the bottom third of the promised land as a whole (which also includes the part to the far north; the next chapter will come to that). The towns mentioned in chapter 10 pretty much cover the key places in this part of the country.

The broader context of Joshua will make something else clear. It will tell us, for instance, how Caleb got Debir captured on behalf of **Judah** (Joshua 15:15–19), how Judah couldn't dispossess the Jebusites who lived in Jerusalem (Joshua 15:63), how **Ephraim** didn't dispossess the Canaanites who lived in Gezer, though eventually they became a conscript labor force like the Gibeonites (Joshua 16:10), and how Judah attacked the Canaanites who lived in Hebron (Judges 1:10). All this is weird because Joshua 10 gives the impression that there should be no one left in Debir, Gezer, or Hebron; and talk of Joshua conquering the whole southland turns out to have a rather significant exception if it doesn't include Jerusalem.

Historically, one consideration to keep in mind is that presumably the hapless inhabitants of these cities didn't simply wait within them for Joshua to come and slaughter them. Cities under attack don't do that. As the Old Testament observes elsewhere, when a city is under attack, its people run to the hills. They sit out the siege and the battle and the departure of the attackers, then come back home and start their lives over again when the attackers have gone. That helps to explain the way some cities and peoples have to be attacked, defeated, and annihilated on several occasions, like a monster in a sci-fi movie that you think you have destroyed but that has a mysterious power to keep regenerating.

Yet the story doesn't draw attention to such facts. It lets the oversimplified, hyperbolic story stand. Why would it do that? The popularity of the Western or its more recent equivalent, the video game, helps us see some aspects of the answer. Entertainment will come into it; the Joshua story was written for people to enjoy, to make them smile and shout. Yet its inclusion in Scripture suggests that Israel saw more in it than that. With the Western and the sci-fi movie and the videogame, another factor is the way they often portray the victory of good over evil. The Joshua story expresses the truth that God is committed to putting down evil in the world. The kind of evil that Israel saw in the **Canaanites**, such as their willingness to sacrifice their children, is not one that God allows to go on forever. Wicked peoples get their comeuppance.

Admittedly this portrayal stereotypes people. Traditional Westerns picture Native Americans typically as "bad Injuns," which helps European Americans justify taking their land and critique their attempts to hold onto it; we blame the victim. The Israelites stereotype the Canaanites. At the same time, the Old Testament is quite happy to let that stereotyping deconstruct. So Rahab was the "good Injun" and Achan was the "bad cowboy," and when Israel goes in for practices such as sacrificing children, God treats it the same way as God treated the Canaanites. In other words, these stories function as warnings. Later Israel cannot afford simply to identify with Joshua's

Israel. It needs to see the fate of the Canaanites as potentially and actually its own fate.

The way the story itself speaks suggests that the hyperbole has at least two other functions. One is to glorify God for the way promises were fulfilled. There is a real sense in which no exaggeration is involved. The whole land did come to belong to Israel. The story simply compresses the process whereby this happened. There were later centuries when Israel could look proudly over this land that it had taken from the Canaanites, and the story then reminds Israel who gave it this country. When I had my first interview with my seminary principal on arriving as a student with a good degree from my undergraduate college, one of the first things he said was "Ah, what hast thou that thou didst not receive?" He was quoting from 1 Corinthians 4 in the King James Bible; that is how I still remember it. Israel needs to remember that it did not get hold of the country by its own achievement. God gave it.

There were other centuries (more of them, actually) when Israel had lost control of most of this land and it was under the sovereignty of an empire like that of the **Assyrians** or of other local peoples such as the Edomites. There would then be a certain poignancy or sadness about recalling how they once controlled the whole land. In reminding them that God gave them the country, it also reminds them that God had taken it away precisely because they had become too much like the Canaanites. But God could give it back to them.

JOSHUA 11:1–15
Welcome to the Wild Wild North

¹When King Jabin of Hazor heard, he sent to King Jobab of Madon, the king of Shimron, the king of Achshaph, ²and the northern kings in the mountains, the steppe south of Kinnereth, the foothills, Naphoth Dor on the west, ³the Canaanites on the east and on the west, the Amorites, Hittites, Perizzites, and Jebusites in the mountains, and the Hivites at the foot of Hermon in the country of Mizpah. ⁴These came out, all their armies with them, a numerous company, like the sand on the seashore in number, with very many horses and chariots. ⁵All

these kings joined forces; they came and camped at Merom Waters to fight with Israel. [6]Yahweh said to Joshua, "Don't be afraid of them, because tomorrow at this very time I am going to give them up slain before Israel, all of them. You are to hamstring their horses and burn up their chariots." [7]So Joshua and all his fighting force with him came upon them at the Merom Waters by surprise. They fell on them, [8]and Yahweh gave them into Israel's hand. They struck them down and pursued them as far as Great Sidon and Misrephoth Waters, and as far as the Mispeh Valley on the east, and struck them down. He did not let any survivor remain. [9]Joshua dealt with them just as Yahweh said to him: he hamstrung the horses and burnt up the chariots. [10]Joshua then went back and took Hazor and struck down its king with the sword, because Hazor was formerly head of all these kingdoms. [11]They struck down with the edge of the sword every person there, devoting them. Nothing that breathed was left. And he burned up Hazor.

[12]All these royal cities and their kings Joshua took. He struck them down with the edge of the sword, and devoted them as Moses, Yahweh's servant, had commanded. [13]Yet all the cities that are standing on their mounds Israel did not burn, except that Joshua burnt Hazor alone. [14]All the plunder in these cities and the cattle the Israelites took as spoil for themselves. Yet all the people they struck down with the edge of the sword until they had annihilated them. They did not leave anything that breathed. [15]As Yahweh had commanded his servant Moses, so Moses had commanded Joshua, and so Joshua did. He did not omit anything of all that Yahweh had commanded Moses.

As you drive north from Lake Galilee on the road that leads from Jerusalem or from the Mediterranean, you can fork right and cross the Bridge of the Daughters of Jacob toward Damascus along the route that Abraham would have taken when he first came to **Canaan** and the route Saul was taking when he got knocked over by Jesus. Alternatively you can continue north toward Caesarea Philippi and the Lebanese border (it is bewildering how chronologies and stories crisscross). If you do the latter, you can immediately drive over a hump that is actually the edge of the huge city of Hazor, a tell going back into pre-Israelite times. One can see how, standing at this key junction dominating the routes going in different directions, it came to be the head of the kingdoms in the area.

I have a great DVD called *Biblical Archaeology from the Ground Down* that includes sequences concerning the archaeological investigation of Hazor and an interview with the lead archaeologist, Amnon Ben-Tor, a slight, mustached, winsome, and funny professor from the Hebrew University of Jerusalem. The upper city of Hazor (the downtown, if you like) got destroyed and incinerated in a huge fire in the thirteenth century, the time when the Israelites were arriving in Canaan. "So who set it on fire?" Ben-Tor asks with a smile, and goes on to speculate. Was it the Canaanites themselves, or the Egyptians? Why would either of these intentionally destroy and mutilate Canaanite and Egyptian statues? Was it the **Philistines**? We have no evidence of their presence here in this period. Why not assume that it was Joshua and the Israelites, as the story says? Ben-Tor goes on to laugh over the fact that his willingness to see Joshua's activity here means he gets called "Orthodox" (a kind of Jewish equivalent to being called "fundamentalist").

The story of Joshua's victory at Hazor is another divinely inspired cowboy story, full of hyperbole, but it's not just a fictional story. The natural way to read the archaeological evidence is as implying that the Israelites indeed won a spectacular victory here. This points to an irony. We have noted that Joshua did not destroy Jericho and Ai; in his time, there were no towns there to destroy. The story of Hazor is much less well-known, but it's much more historically plausible and a much more impressive miracle. Hazor was indeed "the head of all these kingdoms," a huge city, and thus now a monumental tell.

Admittedly, it remains unwise to sell one's soul to archaeology. There are unresolved questions about the history of Hazor, and theories about its history may change. There have been past versions of the way archaeology "proves the Bible right" that got overturned, and this then gives the impression that archaeology "proves the Bible wrong." Another contributor to that DVD points out that in any case archaeology can never prove the really important element in the Bible story, what it has to say about God. In this sense, it is the Bible story that matters.

There are two other noteworthy aspects of the story to which archaeology doesn't speak. One is that God didn't tell Joshua to kill all the people in Hazor, though Joshua did so. What God told Joshua to do was hamstring the horses and burn up the chariots—that is, destroy the military hardware, the equivalent of the tanks and fighter planes. Then the country can have "rest from war." That fits with the emphasis elsewhere (not least in the Jericho story) that it isn't military hardware that decides the outcome of wars. If God is involved, all you may need to do is blow your trumpets. If God is not involved, all the horses and chariots in the world may not win your victory. As Isaiah 31 puts it when **Judah** is tempted to rely on an alliance with Egypt and is trying to import horses and chariots from there, "the Egyptians are human beings, not God, and their horses are flesh, not spirit."

The other noteworthy aspect of the story is that it keeps emphasizing that Israel was able to gain control of the country because Joshua kept doing exactly what God said. We have noted that the story also makes clear that this, too, is an exaggeration. In reality, the good guys in a Western were actually people with flaws, and the Bible has more in common with film noir, in which the good guys always have flaws. But in connection with Israel's getting hold of the country, the story thinks its statement about Joshua is near enough true and of key importance. It invites Israel into the typical Old Testament combination of hope and obedience. The story is not an invitation to military action like Joshua's; we have noted that the Old Testament does not speak of anyone after Joshua's day being expected to slaughter the Canaanites. Obedience takes different forms in different contexts. What God said to Moses and what Moses said to Joshua are not what is being said in later contexts. But the principle that you do what God says and then live in hope is a principle that abides.

Excuse me, if it's a cowboy story, why is it in the Bible? Why is it more important than other cowboy stories? One response to that question is to note that it is part of the bigger story, which is the most important story in the world. Like the British and other nations, people in the United States are inclined to regard themselves as God's special people. They aren't. There is only one special people, and that is Israel, the people from whom Jesus was born. This cowboy story is special because it's part of Israel's story. In effect, the speech/sermon of Stephen in Acts 7 and the list of heroes in Hebrews 11 make that point. Joshua is part of the story that leads to Jesus. No Joshua, no Jesus. Indeed, rather neatly Joshua is Jesus' real name (compare the way messianic Jews call him Yeshua); "Jesus" is a grecized form of the name. Conversely, in the Greek translation of the book of Joshua that many people in New Testament times would have used, Joshua's name is Jesus.

JOSHUA 11:16–12:24
Why Were They So Stupid?

¹⁶So Joshua took all this country: the mountains, the entire Negev, the entire country of Goshen, the foothills, the Steppe, the mountain country of Israel and its foothills, ¹⁷from Mount Halak which goes up to Seir and as far as Baal-gad in the Lebanon Vale beneath Mount Hermon. He captured all their kings, struck them down, and killed them. ¹⁸For a long period Joshua made war with all these kings. ¹⁹There was no city that made peace with the Israelites except the Hivites living in Gibeon. All of it they took in battle, ²⁰because it issued from Yahweh to stiffen their resolve to engage in battle with Israel so that [Joshua] might devote them without there being any grace for them, rather so that he might annihilate them as Yahweh commanded Moses. ²¹At that time Joshua went and cut down the Anakim from the mountains, from Hebron, Debir, and Anab and all the mountains of Judah and all the mountains of Israel, with their cities. Joshua devoted them. ²²None of the Anakim were left in the country of the Israelites. Only in Gaza, Gath, and Ashdod did they remain. ²³So Joshua took the entire country, just as Yahweh spoke to Moses, and Joshua gave it to Israel as its own, as shares for the clans; so the country had rest from war.

[Joshua 12:1–24 gives a summary of the areas east of the Jordan that Israel took possession of, and a list of the thirty-one kings of cities west of the Jordan whom Israel defeated.]

The night before last I ate dinner early, drank a glass or two of wine, didn't eat dessert, and then had a cup of coffee later.

This pattern works if I want to sleep well, so I try to stick to it. Last night I ate late, and the server at the restaurant told me the chocolate soufflé was rather good, so I ate it. It wasn't so wonderful, but I may have come to that opinion because I was already full; I had already ignored another resolve by eating some of the fries that came with the burger. When the server told me about them, I could have said, "Hold the fries," but I failed to do so. And I didn't sleep (I will have a nap in a minute). The server had softened my resolve to eat sensibly, or perhaps he stiffened my inclination to be self-indulgent.

God hardened the heart of the **Canaanite** kings, the Joshua story comments; that's a more literal translation. I have translated the phrase "stiffened the resolve" because in English the heart is inclined to suggest especially the emotions, whereas in the Bible it suggests the inner being more generally, and if it has a more precise focus, it is the will. The heart suggests the formulating of attitudes and the making of decisions. As we put it, these kings had to "make up their minds" what they were going to do about the Israelites. In the event, they behaved stupidly, like me in my small ways. Instead of recognizing the implications of what they had heard about the Israelites, like Rahab and the Hivites, they tried to stop them.

Why were they so stupid? The Bible doesn't always attribute people's stupidity to God's closing their minds, but sometimes it does so. God speaks of it in Isaiah 6, and Jesus takes up God's words in explaining that his reason for telling parables is to hinder people from understanding what he says (Mark 4). Jesus likewise assumes, as this story does, that people can reach a point where there is not any grace for them, only weeping and gnashing of teeth. In each case, closing their minds is God's act of judgment, as was the case when God hardened Pharaoh's heart or stiffened his resolve. In each case, people have reached the point where God says, "That's it," and deals with them by encouraging them to continue in their moral stupidity. The way the Old Testament tells its story, God's hardening people's hearts doesn't mean doing some weird manipulation of their synapses that makes them do something they don't want to do so that they then find themselves acting in a certain way and saying to themselves, "I don't know why I am doing this; it's not like me." It's not that Pharaoh and the Canaanite kings were previously nice people who suddenly started behaving out of character. They were slave drivers and child killers. God's action, if you like, was a bit the way God gives people up to their own instincts, as Romans 1–2 describes it.

Neither thus does the Joshua story merely imply that it doesn't distinguish very sharply between God's doing something deliberately and God's being behind everything that happens in the world. God is indeed in some sense wholly sovereign in the world and thus has to accept responsibility for things that happen even if they weren't the direct divine intention. That would mean that when you look back at events and see (for instance) the way the Canaanites put a noose around their own necks, in some sense God must have intended it, especially if you assume that God must have known ahead of time how they would behave.

Maybe that way of looking at how things work out in the world makes sense, but there is no suggestion that it is the story's framework for looking at events. It does not see the Canaanites as acting out of character, but neither does it see God as uninvolved in what they do. My assumption is that God's involvement and human responsibility work together in a similar way to the relationship between parents and children, teachers and students, or masters and servants; this fits with other aspects of the way God's relationship with us works. As teacher I dangle in front of my students ideas and incentives to get them to act in a certain way (such as, if they turn in their papers early, I will give them feedback so they can resubmit them if they wish). But they decide whether to do so.

My picture for understanding God and the Canaanites involves seeing the relationship as a kind of negative version of that process. Imagine that one of my students has been turning in assignments late, and I think he or she should really fail the course (that has happened); and suppose someone encourages him to go to an important rock concert on the evening of a class, which can also imperil passing the class (that, too, has happened). God's hardening the Canaanites' resolve involves God's dangling ideas in front of them a little like that, with their deciding to follow where they lead. God encouraged them to reckon that the risk of losing to the Israelites was worth taking. They agreed to follow that encouragement. They don't have to do so; indeed, when Isaiah tells people that God is set on blinding their minds, I think he rather hopes to shake them to their senses so that his warning does not come true. That is regularly how the prophets operate. Even stimuli that can put people down are also stimuli that can pull them up in a good way. Only afterwards will you know which way God's words through a prophet work—whether they lead to softening or hardening. God failed to bring the Canaanites to their senses, and God is okay with that because God is okay (which does not mean enthusiastic) about bringing judgment on people if they cannot be turned around.

JOSHUA 13:1–14:15

The Country That Remains to Be Possessed Is Very Great

[1]Now Joshua was old, advanced in years. Yahweh said to him, "You yourself have become old, advanced in years, whereas the country that remains to be possessed is very great. [2]This is the country that remains. All the region of the Philistines and all [that of] the Geshurites, [3]from the Shihor close to Egypt as far as the territory of Ekron to the north counts as belonging to the Canaanites (the five lords of the Philistines, the people of Gaza, Ashdod, Ashkelon, Gath, and Ekron); the Avvim [4]on the south; all the Canaanite country, Mearah belonging to the Sidonians as far as Aphek (as far as the Amorite territory); [5]the country of the Gebalites and the whole of Lebanon on the east from Baal-gad beneath Mount Hermon as far as Lebo-hamath; [6]all the inhabitants of the mountains from Lebanon as far as Misrephoth Waters, all the Sidonians. I myself will dispossess them from before the Israelites. Just allocate it by lot to Israel as its own, as I commanded you. [7]So now divide this country as their own to the nine clans and the half-clan of Manasseh.

[The rest of chapter 13 records the allocation of the land east of the Jordan to Reuben, Gad, and the other half of Manasseh, though it notes that Israel did not dispossess the Geshurites and the Maacathites, who continue to live among the Israelites, and that no allocation was made to Levi because its allocation came

from the people's offerings. Chapter 14 then introduces Joshua's
allocation of the land west of the Jordan to the rest of the clans.]

[14:6]The Judahites came to see Joshua at Gilgal. Caleb the son of Jephunneh the Kenizzite said to him, "You yourself know how Yahweh spoke to Moses the man of God concerning you and me, at Kadesh-barnea. [7]I was forty years old when Moses, Yahweh's servant, sent me from Kadesh-barnea to investigate the country, and I brought him back an account that was in accordance with how things were in my mind. [8]My brothers who went up with me made the people's resolve melt, but I myself wholly followed Yahweh my God. [9]That day, Moses promised, 'The country on which your foot trod will be a possession for you and your descendants in perpetuity, because you wholly followed Yahweh my God.' [10]So now, right: Yahweh has kept me alive, as he declared, for forty-five years since Yahweh made this declaration to Moses when Israel was going through the wilderness. So now, here I am today, eighty-five years old. [11]I am still as strong today as I was on the day Moses sent me. As my strength was then, so is my strength now, for battle and for going out and coming in. [12]So now, give me these mountains that Yahweh spoke of that day, because you heard that day that Anakites are there, and big fortified cities. Perhaps Yahweh will be with me and I will take possession of them as Yahweh spoke." [13]So Joshua blessed him and gave Hebron to Caleb the son of Jephunneh as his own. [14]Therefore Hebron came to belong to Caleb son of Jephunneh the Kenizzite as his own, until this day, because he followed after Yahweh the God of Israel. ([15]Hebron's name formerly was Arba's Town; he was the big man among the Anakites.) And the country had rest from war.

At my wife's memorial service in England this past summer, I saw one of my cousins whom I had not seen for over a decade, and this week I had a Christmas card from her. She wrote, "Various members of the family have asked me whether you would ever return to the U.K. to live," and expressed the hope that we would all see more of one another (which I think we will). "I'm fishing, aren't I?" she concluded. So in the note I sent with some of my Christmas cards I said, "A number of people have wondered whether I will go back to England. It's said that you shouldn't make decisions of that kind for a year after losing someone; but anyway, at the moment I feel I have not run out of vocation or energy or marbles, and as long as I have those, I shall carry on teaching and going to Malibu for lunch on Saturday or Sunday." There are a lot of things I still want to do in the United States before I retire.

So I identify a bit with Caleb. In more literal terms, eighty-five maybe implies something more like fifty-plus, so he was younger than I am, but then the project he wants to bring to completion involves physical strength; to finish The Old Testament for Everyone series I just need to continue sitting at this desk rather than slumping over, but I will ride my bike to seminary in a moment if it stops raining on the assumption that I do need to keep a bit more active than just sitting.

Students sometimes come to talk to me about what they want to do with their lives, about how to set goals and then reach them, and they are then bemused when I tell them (mostly truly) that I have never had any aims in life; I am where I am by total accident. That's the trouble with being British. Caleb is more like someone born in the United States. He was that way when he was "forty" (let's imagine him literally being in his late twenties, like some of my students). He and Joshua were among the young men commissioned to discover what the promised land was like. The other ten were gloomy, British guys who saw only the problems. Conquering this country was going to be impossible; the **Canaanites** were big fellers. Caleb and Joshua believed in the motto "Yes, we can!" It was not simply that they had different ethnic genes, though Caleb did (we will come back to that). "I wholly followed **Yahweh** my God," he says. It is an odd expression in Hebrew: more literally "I filled up after Yahweh my God." In the detailed account in Numbers 13–14, Joshua and Caleb declare, "If Yahweh is pleased with us, he will bring us into this country and give it to us. . . . Only, you must not rebel against Yahweh. . . . Yahweh is with us. Don't be afraid of them." Caleb combines confidence and diffidence. Here, too, he says "perhaps." He doesn't want to be presumptuous. But he knows God can make it possible.

God promised that Caleb and Joshua would not fail to enter the promised land, unlike the people who didn't believe it was possible, and now he wants to cash his check. When the scouts had reconnoitered the country a generation ago, they had entered it from the south and thus via Hebron, and it was there that they saw the big guys who frightened the pants off most of them. Caleb knows Israel will face the same challenge in the same area, and he is itching to have a go at those guys. He wants to be given the biggest challenge there is. He has not run out of vocation or energy or marbles. (Well, maybe his enthusiasm for fighting big guys makes you wonder about the marbles, but that's a Brit speaking again.)

His request also illustrates how it is indeed the case at the end of Joshua's life that "the country that remains to be possessed is very great," notwithstanding earlier comments about how "Joshua took the entire country" (Joshua 11:23). In principle Joshua has done so, having won some spectacular victories in different parts of the country. But Caleb's request is just one of the notes in Joshua that indicates how much there is still to do.

JOSHUA 15:1–17:11

Living as Women in a Man's World

[Joshua 15:1–12 specifies the boundaries of Judah.]

15:13To Caleb son of Jephunneh [Joshua] gave the town of Arba, the father of Anak (that is, Hebron) as a share in the midst of Judah, in accordance with Yahweh's word to Joshua. 14Caleb dispossessed from there the three Anakites, Sheshai, Ahiman, and Talmai, the descendants of Anak. 15He went up from there against the inhabitants of Debir; the name of Debir was formerly Scroll Town. 16Caleb said, "Whoever strikes down Scroll Town and takes it: I will give him Achsah my daughter as wife." 17Othniel the Kenizzite, a relative of Caleb, took it, and he gave him Achsah his daughter as wife. 18When she arrived, she urged him to ask her father for some land. She got off her donkey and Caleb said to her, "What is it?" 19She said, "Give me a present, because you have given me land in the Negev, so give me springs of water." So he gave her the upper and lower springs.

[The chapter goes on to list the towns in Judah's territory but finally notes that the Judahites could not dispossess the Jebusites from Jerusalem and that they live with the Judahites there "until

67

this day." Joshua 16:1–17:2 then describes the allocations of Ephraim and begins to describe the allocation of the half of Manasseh who live west of the Jordan.]

[17:3]Now Zelophehad son of Hepher son of Gilead son of Machir son of Manasseh had no sons, but only daughters. These are the names of his daughters: Mahlah, Noah, Milcah, and Tirzah. [4]They came to see the priest Eleazar, Joshua son of Nun, and the leaders, saying, "Yahweh himself commanded Moses to give us a possession among our male relatives." So he gave them a possession among their father's male relatives in accordance with Yahweh's word. [5]Manasseh's shares fell as ten, apart from the land of Gilead and Bashan across the Jordan, [6]because Manasseh's daughters received a possession among his sons, while the land of Gilead belonged to the remaining descendants of Manasseh. [7]Manasseh's boundary ran from Asher to Michmethah, opposite Shechem. The boundary goes right, to the inhabitants of En-tappuach ([8]the region of Tappuach belonged to Manasseh, but Tappuach on the boundary of Manasseh belonged to the Ephraimites). [9]The boundary descends to the Kanah Wash. South of the wash, these cities belong to Ephraim, in the midst of Manasseh's cities, with Manasseh's boundary north of the wash and its outlet at the sea. [10]To the south belongs to Ephraim, to the north to Manasseh, with the sea as its boundary. It reaches Asher on the north and Issachar on the east, [11]but within Issachar and Asher, to Manasseh belong Beth-shean and its dependencies, Ibleam and its dependencies, the inhabitants of Dor and its dependencies, the inhabitants of En-dor and its dependencies, the inhabitants of Taanach and its dependencies, and the inhabitants of Megiddo and its dependencies (the third is Napheth).

I was talking to a student who was disillusioned with her denomination because of its attitude toward women's ministry. Women had played a key ministerial role in the movement that issued in the denomination, but the denomination had been taken over by men and no longer allowed women to minister with the authority and freedom that they had at the beginning. A further sadness was that the student appreciated so many of the distinctive emphases of the movement and the denomination; if she totally abandoned it and joined another denomination, she would lose touch with those. Women do exercise leadership in her denomination, but they have to do so in subtle ways that avoid disturbing the modus vivendi that developed there. One can see the same story repeated in the early church, where women originally had an authority to minister that later disappeared, and one can see it in Israel in the person of someone such as Moses' big sister. Women have to develop strategies for living in a male-dominated world without going under.

Achsah does so. Her father treats her as a prize to the man who will take Debir or Kiriath Sepher, "Scroll Town" (maybe it was where records were kept). This seems scandalous in the modern West, though it may express only an extreme version of some attitudes about marriage that appear in most human cultures. In the modern West we assume that marriage is essentially a personal relationship in which people find their soul mates and that the decision about whom to marry is their business alone, but this is simply one of our cultural assumptions. These don't seem to generate a society characterized by stable marriage or stable families, and there is evidence to suggest that other cultural assumptions may work just as well.

Maybe Achsah will have had the chance to look at the husband her father proposes and say, "Not on your life"; certainly other Old Testament stories imply that a woman could do that. What we do learn about Achsah certainly makes that plausible. She doesn't look like someone you could push around. When she moves in with Othniel, she hatches a plan with him to lean on Caleb for some (more) land; we know from chapter 14 that Caleb is no wimp even if he is eighty-five, and it looks as if she has her father's genes. When she comes back home and alights off her donkey with a determined look on her face, Caleb can see there is trouble brewing. It looks as if the story is compressed; it first speaks of land, which would perhaps be the dowry Achsah brings with her into the marriage but which remains legally hers. It then presupposes this gift of land and raises the question of water. Debir is land in the south, south of Hebron where Caleb himself had his share, and it is therefore very dry. It is country that is becoming desert-like. Achsah manipulates the men in her life in order to ensure she gets a better deal than the one they originally propose. She is an astute businesswoman like Abigail and the woman in Proverbs 31.

Achsah, her father, and her husband are all Kenizzites, people who trace their ancestry back to Kenaz, a descendant of Esau (see Genesis 36). Esau was the man God did not choose in choosing Jacob (Israel) instead. Indeed, God bracketed the Kenizzites with people such as the Hittites and **Canaanites**, whose land would be given to Abraham's descendants (Genesis 15:19). By a nice irony, Caleb's name is similar to the Hebrew word for "dog," *celeb*. You don't give holy things or give the children's food to Gentile dogs, Jesus says (Matthew 7:6; 15:26). But even the dogs can eat the scraps from under the table. Caleb was the ultimate faithful dog, and he ate more than crumbs. With Joshua, this man who was not a born Israelite had much confidence that **Yahweh** could give the people the land. As Rahab contrasts with Achan, Caleb contrasts with nearly all the Israelites. He reminds Israel again that being born an Israelite does nothing for you unless you are committed to Yahweh and that not being born an Israelite doesn't exclude you from being Israelite by adoption.

Zelophehad's daughters had taken on Moses head-on in a community context in the way Achsah took on her father in a family context; perhaps they knew Moses would be able to see the ghost of his big sister looking over their shoulder. They now take on Eleazar. Numbers 27 tells of how their father died without fathering any sons, which by the usual rules meant his land would go to his brothers. "That's not fair," they said. God and Moses saw they had a case and made a new rule: daughters have priority over brothers in this situation. The men did come back next day and say, "Err . . . this new rule is going to screw up the whole land allocation system if they inherit the land and then marry into another clan." That led to an amendment to the rule: the daughters can marry anyone they like as long as he comes from their own clan (which is what would likely happen anyway, there being no online dating service to put them in touch with nice boys in a clan far away). It was still a victory, but it meant some compromise with the system. The daughters don't then retire to their tents and take up knitting, satisfied with their moral victory (not that there is anything wrong with knitting; my favorite feminist is a big knitter). They come and knock on Eleazar's door (he was party to the original negotiations) to say, "Where's our land, then?"

JOSHUA 17:12–19:21

Roots; or, Home Is Where Your Share Is

¹²The Manassites could not take possession of these cities; the Canaanites were determined to stay in this region. ¹³When the Israelites became strong, they put the Canaanites to conscript labor; they did not actually dispossess them.

¹⁴The Josephites spoke with Joshua: "Why have you given me as a possession one allotment, one allocation, when I am a big people that Yahweh has blessed so much?" ¹⁵Joshua said to them, "If you are a big people, get yourselves up into the forest and clear it there in the country of the Perizzites and the Rephaim, if the mountains of Ephraim are too narrow for you." ¹⁶The Josephites said, "The mountains are not enough for us, and there is iron chariotry among all the Canaanites who live in the area of the plain, in Beth-shean and its dependencies and the Jezreel Plain." ¹⁷But Joshua said to the household of Joseph, to Ephraim and Manasseh: "You are a big people. You have great strength. You will not have one allotment, ¹⁸because the mountains will be yours, because they are forest but you will clear them and its farthest limits will be yours, because you will dispossess the Canaanites, because they have iron chariotry, because they are strong."

¹⁸:¹The entire Israelite community assembled at Shiloh and set up the meeting tent there. While the country was subdued before them, ²there remained seven clans among the Israelites who had not been allocated their possession. ³Joshua said to the Israelites, "How long are you going to show yourselves slack about going to take possession of the country that Yahweh the God of your ancestors has given you? ⁴Provide yourselves three men per clan and I will send them to set about going through the country and laying it out with a view to their possession of it. Then they are to come to me ⁵and divide it into seven shares. Judah is to stay by its territory in the south and the household of Joseph are to stay by their territory in the north. ⁶You yourselves are to lay out the country as seven shares and bring it to

71

me here so I can cast lots for you here before Yahweh our God. [7]Because there is no share for the Levites in your midst, because Yahweh's priesthood is their possession, and Gad and Reuben and the half-clan of Manasseh have received their possession across the Jordan to the east, which Yahweh's servant Moses gave them."

[The rest of chapters 18–19 tells of the implementing of this plan and records the areas to be taken by the remaining seven clans, Benjamin, Simeon, Zebulun, Issachar, Asher, Naphthali, and Dan.]

Waiting for the jazz to start last night, I was reading a book about the opening chapters of Matthew's Gospel (other people who are on their own stare at their iPhones). It noted how the list of names occupying the bulk of the first chapter is a compressed narrative; it summarizes the entire Old Testament story from Abraham to David and from David to the **exile** and from the exile to Jesus' birth, to convey how Israel's story leads to Jesus' story and how Jesus' story issues from Israel's story. There are other ways of reading Israel's story; believing in Jesus is what makes you read it that way. But there are no other ways of understanding Jesus. You have to read the story that lies behind him. I once met someone who came to faith in Christ through reading these opening verses of Matthew. Most Christians would think this weird; we skip over them, not realizing their key significance for understanding him. This person was herself Jewish. For Gentiles it was just a list of names, but these verses enabled her to see that Jesus could be her Messiah.

The Old Testament incorporates lots of lists of names that by this means tell people who they are by reminding them of their history. The distinctive feature of Joshua 13–19 is that it is dominated by lists of place names. Why would they be in the Bible? What would they do for people who read them?

One function they fulfill is that they put flesh on the bones of the statement that God fulfilled the promise to give Israel the land. Truth often lies in the details. God did not merely give Israel the land of **Canaan**. God gave Israel Ophrah and Ziklag and Shunem and Aphek and all the other scores of places listed in chapters 18 and 19 and elsewhere in this section of the book.

God lies in the particulars. They make God's fulfilling promises concrete, and they do so especially in contexts when they don't look like the truth. Whenever Joshua was written, it is unlikely to have been in a time when Israel occupied all the land that Joshua here allocates to the clans. As the story itself notes, in Joshua's day they had not actually occupied all the land. The two Joseph clans protest the fact that the allocations are just theoretical lines on the map. Notwithstanding those stories about great victories over the Canaanites, the lines on the map ignore the reality of continuing Canaanite power. David's day was the time when the map became more than theory, but three centuries after that, these Joseph clans had been overwhelmed by the **Assyrians**, and a century or two later the **Judahites** lost control of their land to the **Babylonians**. The story of Joshua's allocation of the land dares its readers to believe that God still intends it to belong to them and will bring this about. God did that in part in bringing the Judahites back from **exile,** and did so more spectacularly in the way the Jewish people gained control of the entire country during the Second Temple period, the period after the exile, albeit they then came under the domination of Rome.

The detail would also mean that individual clans, kin groups, and households could find themselves in these allocations. Like Christians, Jews don't read from these sections of Joshua very much during services, but they use some of them, so one can imagine children nudging their parents when the lesson mentions Sukkoth or Kedemoth or Lake Galilee because it is where they live. They are part of the story of God's giving the country to Israel. Each family lives where it lives because God's promises were fulfilled.

There are other more tricky contexts in which one can imagine these lists being important. Suppose two clans and thus two particular families get into a dispute about which of them a particular segment of the country belongs to. The boundary lists ought to enable the clans to resolve disputes. Then the story about the two Joseph clans illustrates how it would give the clans a challenge. That story presupposes they had three kinds of land within their share, and they might not be the only clans of which this was true. The main areas where the Israelites originally settled were mountainous though quite capable of supporting a population of farmers. They were pretty much unoccupied in Joshua's day, so it would be quite practicable for the clans to settle there, and archaeological investigations indicate that many new village settlements came into being in this period (this doesn't prove they were Israelite settlements, but it nicely fits the biblical story). But the more valuable areas of the country were in the valleys and plains, and naturally this is where the Canaanite cities were; the Joseph clans point out that they are going to need quite some dislodging, despite the list of fine victories the story has given us. The third area is the region in the mountains that was covered by trees. Go and cut the trees down, then, says Joshua, who is quite prepared to be tough. The encounter between Joshua and the two clans reflects yet another aspect to the intricate story of the way Israel came into possession of Canaan. There was divine provision, all right, but it was not all miracle. The story involved circumstantial factors and the making of allowance for human factors and the need for some pure hard work.

JOSHUA 20:1–21:43

Everything Came True

[1]Yahweh spoke to Joshua: [2]"Speak to the Israelites: 'Provide for yourselves the asylum cities that I spoke to you about through Moses, [3]for a homicide who strikes a person down by accident, without realizing, to flee there. They will be an asylum for you from the blood restorer. [4][The homicide] will flee to one of these cities and stand at the entrance to the city gate and state his case in the hearing of that city's elders. They will admit him into their city and give him a place and he will live with them. [5]If the blood restorer pursues him they will not surrender the homicide into his power because he struck his neighbor down without realizing and he was not his enemy in previous days. [6]He will live in that city until he stands before the community for a decision, until the death of the great priest who is there in those days. Then the homicide may return and come to his city and his home, to the city from which he fled.'" [7]So they sanctified Kedesh in Galilee in the mountains of Naphthali and

Shechem in the mountains of Ephraim and Arba's City (that is, Hebron) in the mountains of Judah. ⁸Across the Jordan, east of Jericho, they provided Beser in the wilderness, on the plateau, from the clan of Reuben, Ramoth in Gilead from the clan of Gad, and Golan in Bashan from the clan of Manasseh. ⁹These were the designated cities for all the Israelites and for the alien residing in their midst to flee there, anyone who struck a person down by accident, and he would not die by the hand of the blood restorer, until he stood before the community.

²¹:¹The heads of the families of the Levites came to see Eleazar the priest, Joshua the son of Nun, and the heads of the families of the Israelite clans. ²They spoke to them at Shiloh in the country of Canaan: "Yahweh himself commanded by means of Moses to give us cities to live in, with their pasturelands for our livestock." ³So the Israelites gave the Levites part of their allotments in accordance with Yahweh's word.

[There follows a list of the cities spread through the country that were given to the Levites.]

⁴¹Yahweh gave Israel the entire country that he promised to give their ancestors. They took possession of it and lived in it. ⁴²Yahweh gave them rest on all sides in accordance with everything he had promised to their ancestors. Not one man of all their enemies stood against them; all their enemies Yahweh gave into their hand. ⁴³No word fell, of every good word that God had spoken to the household of Israel. Everything came about.

Less than three weeks ago I received one of those standard e-mails from a student: she did not think she would be able to finish her coursework by the deadline. Except that it was not the standard e-mail. She had been told that she had a brain tumor, and she was to have brain surgery the day before the end of the term. I got her to tell the story in the last class, and we prayed for her. Five days ago she had the surgery, and the doctors found not a tumor but an abscess. She is in a lot of pain, and it will take time to recover fully, but she will do so. Her mother commented before the surgery that there were so many people praying for her that the tumor didn't have a chance, but I guess in her heart of hearts she knew that life doesn't work like that, probably not for most people who have tumors diagnosed. Yet we seize on an occasion when the tumor turns out not to have a chance and take it as giving us a clue to the true nature of reality and of life, an indication of where life really is going and how it will ultimately turn out. Theologically, the fact that Jesus rose from the dead is more significant than the fact that nobody else has yet done so.

The last paragraph in Joshua 21 indicates that the Old Testament sees things in an analogous way. It makes clear that the Israelites are by no means in complete possession of **Canaan**. It also tells a sequence of stories about victories the Israelites won, and it takes these as more significant indications of the real truth about Israel's occupation of the land than the mere fact that there is much of the land still to be occupied. Though it continues coolly to acknowledge that fact, it nevertheless coolly allocates the unoccupied land.

One might draw an analogy with an aspect of the way prophets speak. They say, "God has restored Jerusalem" when it is still in ruins (and for that matter they say, "The end has come upon my people Israel" when it is doing fine, thank you). Because God has determined these events; they are in effect actual even though they are—well, not actual. God has determined to give Israel the whole land and has given a foretaste of that reality in the victories it has won, so God's giving the whole land can be spoken of as actual. In a while it will be actually actual (and it became so). Faith gives substance to things that are literally still hopes (Hebrews 11). But it doesn't do so because you are whistling in the wind. It does so because you have some firstfruits of the fulfillment, and can therefore trust God for the completion.

The asylum cities were Israel's way of ensuring that someone did not get treated as a murderer when he or she did not deserve it. In principle, in Israel when someone did something wrong or when there was a conflict in the community, the matter was handled locally. The family and the village elders were key to the process, and there were no professional police or lawyers or jails or fines. With regard to murder, the victim's family had the right to procure the execution of the murderer; it was the responsibility of someone in the family designated the "blood **restorer**." It may well be that with murder, as with other offenses, usually the concern was not with punishment but with compensation in some form—for instance, who would take responsibility for a family if someone murdered its head? But one can imagine that the way blood cries out from the ground means that families sometimes simply want "justice," and that this is especially so in the grieved and angry aftermath of a violent death. One danger is then that the wrong person gets executed, as happens in modern societies that practice the death penalty. The main point of the asylum cities was to prevent that. A person who had accidentally killed someone could take refuge in one of them so there was time for feelings to cool and for the community to investigate what had happened. The rules in the **Torah** about this come in Numbers 35. Maybe the point of the reference to the senior priest's death is that it in some way compensates for the death that occurred, which was a blot on the community even if it happened by accident.

The Levites were allocated no land because the people's tithes and other offerings would provide for them, but they needed places to live and pasturage for their flocks, so they are allocated cities to live in and land around them as pasturage. Although the Old Testament places most emphasis on the Levites' role as assistant ministers in the central sanctuary, the sanctuary would not need the whole clan all the time, and it would be odd if they lived all over the country if their work was entirely focused on the sanctuary. The chapter perhaps presupposes two or three other roles that the Old Testament sometimes mentions. Their official task as the Torah prescribes it also involved teaching the whole community, and it would be logical if they were therefore spread throughout the country. Indeed, there were sanctuaries spread through the entire country, and the Levites were responsible for the ministry at these sanctuaries. The asylum cities were also Levitical cities, implying they had a role in connection with asylum arrangements; they were the nearest thing Israel had to lawyers and police. They function on behalf of the central government to maintain some oversight over the way life is administered, decisions are taken, and justice is administered.

JOSHUA 22:1–34

The Universal and the Local

[Verses 1–8 relate Joshua's sending off the clans who are going to live east of the Jordan.]

⁹So the Reubenites, Gadites, and the half-clan of Manasseh went back from being with the Israelites at Shiloh in the country of Canaan to go the country of Gilead, to the country of their holding, which they had acquired by Yahweh's word through Moses, ¹⁰and came to the region of the Jordan in the country of Canaan. The Reubenites, Gadites, and the half-clan of Manasseh built an altar there at the Jordan, an altar big in appearance. ¹¹The Israelites heard, "Now. The Reubenites, the Gadites, and the half-clan of Manasseh have built an altar near Canaan, in the region of the Jordan, across from the Israelites."

¹²So the Israelites heard, and the whole community of the Israelites gathered at Shiloh to go out to war against them. ¹³The Israelites sent the priest Phinehas the son of Eleazar to the Reubenites, Gadites, and the half-clan of Manasseh in the country of Gilead, ¹⁴and ten leaders with him, one leader for each ancestral household (for all the clans of Israel). Each was the head of an ancestral household in the divisions of Israel. ¹⁵They came to the Reubenites, Gadites, and the half-clan of Manasseh in the country of Gilead and spoke with them: ¹⁶"The whole community of Israel has said this: 'What is this breaking of faith that you have committed against the God of Israel in turning away today from Yahweh, in building yourselves an altar, rebelling today against Yahweh? ¹⁷Was the waywardness at Peor a small thing to us, from which we have not cleansed ourselves this day, and which brought an epidemic on Yahweh's community, ¹⁸and you yourselves will turn away from Yahweh today? If you rebel against Yahweh, tomorrow he will be wrathful with the whole community of Israel. ¹⁹Yet if the country of your holding is taboo, cross over into the country of Yahweh's holding where Yahweh's dwelling is and hold land among us. Do not rebel against Yahweh and do not rebel against us by building yourselves an altar other than the altar of Yahweh our God. ²⁰When Achan son of Zerah broke faith in connection with "devoting," didn't wrath come on the whole community? He was not the only one who perished for his waywardness.'"

²¹The Reubenites, Gadites, and the half-clan of Manasseh spoke to the leaders of the divisions of Israel: ²²"The God of Gods, Yahweh, the God of Gods, Yahweh, he knows, and Israel—they will know: if it was in rebellion or in breaking faith against Yahweh, do not deliver us today, ²³[if it was] for building ourselves an altar to turn away from Yahweh. Or if it was for offering up a burnt offering or a grain offering on it, or for sacrificing fellowship offerings on it, Yahweh—he may require it of us. ²⁴Really we did it out of anxiety about this: we said, 'Tomorrow your children may say to our children, "What do you and Yahweh the God of Israel have in common? ²⁵Yahweh has made the Jordan a boundary between us and you, Reubenites and Gadites. You have no share in Yahweh."' Your children would stop our children from revering Yahweh. ²⁶So we said, 'Do let's act for ourselves by building an altar, not for burnt offering or sacrifice ²⁷but it will be a witness between us and you and coming generations.'"

[The closing verses report how the deputation is satisfied and reports back to the rest of the clans.]

Like a number of denominations, the Anglican/Episcopal church to which I belong is in a mess because different parts of the world and different groups in the same parts of the world hold conflicting views about the real nature of Christian faith and discipleship. The fracas focuses on same-sex marriage but involves other issues, such as women's ministry, and questions that lie behind those issues, such as the authority of Scripture, the authority of the church's tradition, the way we relate to the cultures we belong to, and the way one might expect different parts of the church to come to shared decisions about such questions. One aspect of this fracas that distresses me is the aggressive way Christian leaders speak to one another about the issues. They don't sound like people speaking the truth in love. Admittedly some of my colleagues might laugh at my saying this, because they are aghast or offended from time to time at the straight and aggressive way I can speak when we are discussing some issue.

One intriguing feature of the story of the eastern clans and their **altar** is the straight, aggressive, nonbourgeois way Joshua speaks. In the Bible, politeness is not a virtue (last Sunday's Gospel reading in our church had John the Baptist calling people a nest of snakes). Indeed, here in Joshua 22 it's not just a matter of speaking but of action. The western clans hear that the eastern clans have built an altar, and they muster for war. Excuse me? Fortunately Joshua combined preparations for war with diplomacy; while the western clans started preparing to force the eastern clans into line, Joshua sent the senior priest and some heavies to read the riot act to the eastern clans and make them an offer they could not refuse. It's the Wild West again, and it worked.

My troubled denomination is the Anglican *Communion*, a worldwide fellowship. Different parts of that communion have felt they had to act in ways that impaired the fellowship because of how they felt Christian faith had to be expressed in their context, or for the sake of safeguarding the integrity of the Christian faith or of the denomination as a whole. For Israel, too, there is a tension between the whole and the parts. When the eastern clans have joined with their brothers and sisters in invading **Canaan** so that they also have their place to live, Joshua sends them off to settle east of the Jordan as they wish, with God's blessing and a share in the plunder the people as a whole have collected. Their home is actually not such a long way from the central sanctuary, not as far away as where the northern clans live. Nevertheless it is a long way psychologically and even theologically, in country that does not strictly belong to the promised land. Yet God had been willing to adapt to the clans' desires when this area fell into Israel's lap because of its inhabitants' stupidity and because these clans spotted how fine the land was. The question is, how can they express their oneness with the other clans yet also be at home where they are?

The Jewish people has always lived with this question. To one degree or another, most of the clans would live with it, as most were located some distance from the central sanctuary. In later Old Testament times the Jewish community in Egypt built a sanctuary on the Nile; we have correspondence between them and the Jerusalem community that reflects the tension between their maintaining an expression of faith in their own context and their having a common faith and observance with the Jerusalem community.

When the eastern clans built themselves an altar near the Jordan, Joshua blew a fuse because they seemed to have made a unilateral declaration of independence from the western clans. It was equivalent to dividing up Christ or dividing up the body of Christ (Paul speaks in similar terms about dividing an individual congregation in 1 Corinthians 1:10–13; 12:12–14). God's purpose for Israel depended on its being one people. Having one central sanctuary and one central place of sacrifice was a symbol and expression of that. Thus Joshua piles up really serious expressions to describe the eastern clans' action. They have broken faith, turned away from **Yahweh**, rebelled against Yahweh, committed waywardness, endangered their relationship with God, and endangered that of the whole people. It's as bad as the sin at Beth-peor or the action of Achan.

You might think Joshua is over the top. Ironically (the eastern clans protest), the point about the altar they built was to honor the importance of the central altar as the place for sacrifice, not to deny it. They weren't going to sacrifice on the altar they made. In a way it was like having a photo of the "proper" altar, something to remind them of it, a "witness" to it, and even more a witness to the western clans that the eastern clans kept the actual altar in mind. So the argument got resolved, and everyone could live happily ever after.

JOSHUA 23:1–16

The Peril of Other People's Faiths

[1]A long time later, after Yahweh had given Israel rest from all their enemies around them, and when Joshua was old, advanced in years, [2]Joshua summoned all Israel, its elders, its leaders, its rulers, and its officials, and said to them, [3]"I am old, advanced in years. You have seen everything Yahweh your God did to all these nations on your account, because Yahweh your God is the one who has fought for you. [4]See, I have allotted to you these remaining nations as a possession for your clans, from the Jordan (yes, all the nations I cut off) and the Mediterranean Sea in the west. [5]Yahweh your God—he will push them back on

your account and dispossess them before you so that you may take possession of their country as Yahweh your God declared to you. [6]You are to be very firm about taking care to do everything written in Moses' teaching scroll, without turning from it to the right or left [7]and without going among these nations (these that remain with you), invoking or swearing by the name of their gods or serving them or bowing down to them. [8]Rather, you are to attach yourselves to Yahweh your God, as you have done until this day.

[9]"Yahweh has dispossessed great and powerful nations before you. Not one man stood against you until this day. [10]One man of you pursues a thousand, because Yahweh your God—he has fought for you, as he declared to you. [11]You are to take great care for yourselves to dedicate yourselves to Yahweh your God, [12]because if you do turn and attach yourselves to what is left of these nations (these that remain with you) and intermarry with them and have sex with them and they with you, [13]recognize clearly that Yahweh your God will not continue to dispossess these nations before you. To you they will become a trap and a snare, a whip on your sides and thorns in your eyes, until you perish from upon this good soil that Yahweh our God gave us.

[14]"So. I am now going the way of all the earth. You are to acknowledge with all your soul and all your being that not one thing has failed of all the good things that Yahweh your God declared to you. Everything has come about for you. Not one of the words has failed. [15]As every good word that Yahweh your God spoke to you has come about for you, so Yahweh will cause every bad word to come about for you until he eliminates you from this good soil that Yahweh your God has given you. [16]When you contravene the covenant of Yahweh your God that he commanded you and go and serve other gods and bow down to them, Yahweh's anger will burn against you and you will perish quickly from this good country that he has given you."

In the aftermath of 9/11, the U.S. State Department financed visits to universities and seminaries in the United States by Muslim scholars from abroad as part of efforts to foster mutual understanding between "the Muslim World" and "the Christian World." An amusing effect for me during one of these visits was to discover that the foreign Muslims and I, as a foreign Christian, had a conviction in common: that religion and state are much more interwoven in the United States (where they are constitutionally separate) than they are in Europe (in countries where they are constitutionally linked). This observation generated a storm of protest from U.S. members of the relevant discussion. Not long after this event, I took part in a symposium on Muslim banking in our city; Muslim banking operates in a way that seeks to work within the terms of the Koran's ban on lending for interest; Jews and Christians usually ignore the equivalent Old Testament law.

Such involvement with people from other faiths can thus be an illuminating experience. It contrasts sharply with the attitude to people of other faiths that Joshua commends, so that Joshua has important insights to offer us. In practice, the Israelites learned from people of other faiths in both positive and negative ways. Coming up against the faith of people such as the **Canaanites** and the **Babylonians** helped the Israelites articulate the real nature of faith in **Yahweh**. It also led them into error. Sometimes they came consciously to serve gods other than Yahweh, but it's easy to see when someone has done that. More subtly, they came to attribute to Yahweh characteristics of a Canaanite god that were in conflict with God's real nature.

Both these ways of being influenced by the Canaanites lie in the background of Joshua's warning about avoiding contact with them. The people who wrote and read the book of Joshua were not just talking theory or indulging in unwarranted, narrow-minded religious or ethnic prejudice. They were people who knew the way Israel had let itself be led astray and had paid the price for it (we will soon be reading about it in the book of Judges). The Canaanites were a technologically, politically, religiously, and theologically sophisticated and advanced people. The Israelites were none of those. The main way they had won victories over the Canaanites was through God's doing something extraordinary, not through their own capacities. They needed to take account of how easy it is to be influenced by sophisticated people. As Joshua puts it, such people become a trap and a snare, both in the sense that they lead them astray and in the sense that they cause them trouble and pain.

Intermarriage with the Canaanites would be a surefire way of getting into a mess. Even if an Israelite who married a

Canaanite was able to maintain commitment to Yahweh, the life of the family was compromised by the commitment of the husband or wife to serving other gods. It would change the way you deal with problems, the way you pray, and the way you understand religious commitments. It would compromise the sense in which you could teach your children about what God had done for Israel and about its implications. Of course the book of Joshua has made clear that if a Canaanite makes a commitment to Yahweh, like Rahab, that's quite different; there is then no problem about intermarriage. Joshua is talking about the average Canaanite who sticks by his or her original commitment. The principle is not an ethnic one but a religious one. Yet at the same time, in traditional societies these two principles are harder to keep separate than they are in the secularized West.

The principle concerns "attaching yourselves" to Yahweh. Joshua uses the verb that appears in Genesis 2 for a man attaching himself or cleaving or sticking to his wife, and he links attaching oneself or cleaving or sticking to Yahweh with avoiding intermarriage. The verb is not merely referring to the sexual act but to the way marriage means a commitment of the whole person and the forming of a new family. It reorients your whole life. So does attaching yourself to another god.

To put it another way, it's about **covenant**. The Old Testament has not yet directly spoken of marriage as a covenant, though its picture of the commitment involved in marriage implies a similar understanding. Marriage involves making a commitment to one another before God. How is that possible when one person makes this commitment in the name of the real God and the other does so in the name of a deity whose nature is misconceived, one who is in reality much less than what that person thinks? Another point about covenant emerges here. Ideally in Western marriage the covenant involves two people on equal terms, but it is not of the essence of covenant for the two parties to be on equal terms, and our ideal Western understanding of marriage does not provide a good analogue for the relationship between us and God. That is an unequal relationship. God is the senior party. As Joshua puts it, the covenant is something that God "commanded." The essence of covenant is not mutuality but a solemn commitment that you cannot get out of without betraying yourself.

Once again Joshua wildly exaggerates the extent to which God's promises have been fulfilled, but the readers would know that he only anticipates a fulfillment that God will see to and by their day has seen to. God did fulfill those promises. So the readers need to be wary about the way God's warnings can also find fulfillment, as they also did.

JOSHUA 24:1–33

"You Can't Serve Yahweh." "Yes We Can!"

¹Joshua assembled all the clans of Israel at Shechem and summoned Israel's elders, leaders, rulers, and officials, and they presented themselves before God.

[Joshua reminds them of their story, of God's taking Abraham from Mesopotamia, dealing with the Egyptians, bringing the Israelites through the wilderness, and dispossessing the Canaanites.]

¹⁴[Joshua said,] "So now, revere Yahweh and serve him wholly and truthfully. Put away the gods your ancestors served beyond the River [Euphrates] and in Egypt, and serve Yahweh. ¹⁵If it is bad in your eyes to serve Yahweh, choose for yourselves today whom you will serve, whether the gods your ancestors served beyond the River or the gods of the Amorites whose country you are living in. I and my household, we will serve Yahweh." ¹⁶The people replied, "Far be it from us to abandon Yahweh to serve other gods, ¹⁷because Yahweh our God—he is the one who brought us and our parents up from Egypt, from a household of serfs, and who did before our eyes these great signs, and took care of us the entire way we went and among all the peoples through whose midst we passed; ¹⁸and Yahweh drove out all the peoples (the Amorites) living in the country from before us. We too will serve Yahweh, because he is our God."

¹⁹But Joshua said to the people, "You can't serve Yahweh, because he is a holy God. He is a passionate God. He will not carry your rebellions and wrongdoings. ²⁰If you abandon Yahweh and serve foreign gods, he will turn and bring trouble on you and make an end of you, after having been good to you." ²¹The people said to Joshua, "No, Yahweh is the one we will

85

serve." ²²Joshua said to the people, "You are witnesses against yourselves that you yourselves have chosen for yourselves Yahweh, to serve him." They said, "We are witnesses." ²³"So now put away the foreign gods that are among you and direct your spirits to Yahweh the God of Israel." ²⁴The people said to Joshua, "Yahweh our God we will serve. To his voice we will listen."

²⁵On that day Joshua sealed a covenant for the people and laid down for them an authoritative law, at Shechem. ²⁶Joshua wrote these things in a scroll of God's teaching. He got a big stone and set it up there under the oak that was in Yahweh's sanctuary. ²⁷Joshua said to all the people, "Now. This stone—it will be a witness against us, because it—it heard all Yahweh's words that he spoke with us. It will be a witness against us so that you do not act deceitfully toward your God." ²⁸And Joshua sent the people off each to their possession.

[The book closes by recording the death of Joshua and of the priest Eleazar, and also the burial of Joseph's bones at Shechem.]

I often get students to talk about whether they like the God of the Old Testament, and I usually get one of three responses. There are people who have no hesitation about saying they do, and they refer to God's love, mercy, and faithfulness, which the story indeed illustrates, but they seem to have sidestepped the tougher aspects of the way the Old Testament speaks. Then there are people who are deeply troubled by its references to God's wrath and are inclined to contrast the Old Testament God of wrath with the New Testament God of love, as if the New Testament God was not wrathful. And there are people who try to hold together the two sets of data. (There are also people who avoid the question by saying that they love God, which is rather a different issue.)

That third stance is surely the one Joshua would approve. He has spoken much of God's reliability in fulfilling promises; indeed, he has much exaggerated the extent to which the promises have been fulfilled in his day. Here he talks tough, in more than one sense. First, God is "holy." It's the only time God is described thus in Joshua. The other times the word *holy* appears it refers to the ground where Joshua stands and to the plunder the people find in Jericho, and that helps to show how describing someone or something as holy in the Old Testament does not so much make a point about morality or righteousness as about being different, special, extraordinary. The Old Testament knows God is righteous and so on; it just doesn't use the word *holy* in this connection. Reminding people that God is holy reminds them that God is someone you can't mess with. When you know that God is loving, faithful, and merciful, as the Israelites did, you need to remember this other fact about God as well. Joshua underscores that point by adding that God is passionate. The word is often translated *jealous*, which is an aspect of passion, but the Hebrew word has this broader meaning. God feels things really strongly. That's another reason you can't mess with God, especially if you belong to God's people. It's hard for God to dismiss our unfaithfulness with a shrug of the shoulders. God can hardly "carry" our rebellions and wrongdoing in those circumstances. This may seem an odd statement, because carrying our rebellions and wrongdoing was part of God's self-description at Sinai in Exodus 34. God does do that, but parents can reach a point with their (grown-up) children, and teachers can reach a point with their (grown-up) students, when they must say "That's it!" and God is also like that. Joshua needs the people to recognize those dynamics to a relationship with God. Paradoxically, there is a sense in which it's safer not to make a commitment to God at all. If you make the commitment, the stakes are higher if you don't keep it. So Joshua talks tough about the people as well as about God. His referring to their putting away foreign gods is a surprise. Surely we should have heard about their possessing foreign gods somewhat earlier? In Joshua's own context, it may carry an interesting implication. The scene is Shechem, where Israel erected the **altar** and made the commitment in chapter 8. What was odd is that they had not fought the people of Shechem or attacked the city. So if we connect one or two dots into rather a big picture, maybe this is an occasion when such people made their commitment to **Yahweh**, the whole community doing what Rahab did. That would explain the toughness of Joshua's argument and their need to put away other gods, and it would fit in with other indications that the Israelites' becoming a settled and united people in **Canaan** was not just a matter of Israel killing off or chasing off its previous inhabitants.

Historically, that question will more likely have arisen much later than Joshua's day. The story will be telescoping events as it does in describing all God's promises as being fulfilled already. In later centuries, there will be an ongoing need that people who come to see themselves as belonging to Israel truly recognize what belonging to Israel implies. One thing joining Israel in this way implies is that Israel's story becomes their story. If I ever become a citizen of the United States, I will find that I was on the winning side in the Revolutionary War instead of on the losing side, which is where I am at the moment. (Admittedly British people don't think about it that much. I was hardly conscious that the United States had once been part of the British Empire and that we had lost it until I came to the United States and found that this history is very important.)

Of the hundreds of thousands of people who belonged to Israel in David's day or Isaiah's day, maybe only a small number were the physical descendants of people who had been in Egypt and come through the wilderness to the promised land, as only a small number of people in the United States are descendants of the people who brought about the birth of the nation. But the larger number were like people who had been adopted into a new family. They were just as much members of the family as people who were born into it. The story of the people who came from Egypt became their story, and they had to live with the implications and become the exodus people and the **covenant** people.

JUDGES 1:1–36

Real Life Is More Complicated

¹After Joshua's death, the Israelites asked of Yahweh, "Who is to go up for us against Canaan first, to do battle with them?" ²Yahweh said, "Judah is to go up. Yes. I have given the country into its hand." ³Judah said to its brother Simeon, "Go up with me into the territory that I am to possess in Canaan and I too will go with you into the territory that you are to possess." So Simeon went with them. ⁴Judah went up and Yahweh gave the Canaanites and Perizzites into their hand. They struck them

down at Bezek, ten thousand of them. ⁵They found Adoni-bezek at Bezek and did battle against him, and struck down the Canaanites and Perizzites. ⁶Adoni-bezek fled but they pursued him and captured him. They cut off his thumbs and big toes. ⁷Adoni-bezek said, "Seventy kings with thumbs and big toes cut off used to glean under my table. As I have done, so God has requited me." They brought him to Jerusalem, and he died there. ⁸The Judahites did battle against Jerusalem, took it, and struck it down with the edge of the sword, and the city they set on fire. ⁹After that, the Judahites went down and did battle against the Canaanites living in the mountains, the Negev, and the foothills.

[The chapter goes on to reprise victories at Hebron and elsewhere.]

²²Joseph's household, too, went up against Bethel, Yahweh being with them. ²³Joseph's household sent to investigate Bethel (previously the city's name was Luz). ²⁴The spies saw a man coming out of the city and said to him, "Will you show us the way into the city, and we will keep commitment with you." ²⁵He showed them the way into the city and they struck the city with the edge of the sword, but the man and all his family they let go. ²⁶The man went to the country of the Hittites and built a city, and called it Luz (that is its name until this day). ²⁷But Manasseh did not dispossess Beth-shean and its dependencies, Taanach and its dependencies, the inhabitants of Dor and its dependencies, the inhabitants of Ibleam and its dependencies, or the inhabitants of Megiddo and its dependencies. The Canaanites were determined to stay in this country. ²⁸When Israel became strong, they put the Canaanites to conscript labor. They did not dispossess them at all. ²⁹Nor did Ephraim dispossess the Canaanites living in Gezer. The Canaanites lived in their midst at Gezer.

[The chapter further describes how Zebulun, Asher, and Naphtali did not dispossess the inhabitants of cities in their areas, and how the Amorites drove Dan out of their area and held on to some territory.]

This week Barack Obama made what might be the most fateful decision of his young presidency in sending thirty thousand more soldiers into Afghanistan. By the time you read this commentary, we may know whether this produces the desired results. Not being the president, I have the luxury of not having to come to a conclusion about whether it is the right move, and many pundits have the luxury of being able to pontificate about how it could be the wrong move. In 1947 Winston Churchill described democracy as "the worst form of government except all those other forms that have been tried," and Obama's action may be the least worst action. In some ways it clashes with the ideals that people attributed to him in voting for him (and that do attach to him), but when you sit in the White House you have to be pragmatic as well as have ideals. This same week the Israeli prime minister, Benjamin Netanyahu, has also astonished people by declaring himself in favor of a two-state settlement arrangement in the Middle East and of a freeze on settlements. That, too, has been read as a leader discovering that being in charge imposes the necessity to be pragmatic. Indeed, today the news described President Obama as "taking what he could get" on some of his biggest priorities (health care and climate change), "at least for now" because he has not given up on his ideals.

God is like that. Skimming Joshua can give the impression that the Israelites occupied **Canaan** by means of a divinely enabled blitzkrieg that put them in control of the entire country and disposed of all the Canaanites in one go, but we have seen between the lines of Joshua many acknowledgments that in reality it was more complicated, and this beginning to the book of Judges (which reads more like a footnote to Joshua) puts that fact upfront, repeating some paragraphs from Joshua.

Among other things, Judges 1 indicates that the Israelites' occupation of Canaan was actually quite piecemeal. **Judah** and Simeon won this bit; the Joseph clans ("Joseph's household") won this bit. It uncovers a very human process. Did God really want the clans to cut off Adoni-Bezek's thumbs and big toes? Well, maybe the man himself saw it as better than being killed, and he recognized the poetic justice in the action (possibly the point about it when taken by him and taken against him would be to stop them and him engaging in war again). Did the Israelites have any business turning the Canaanites into a conscript labor force (this doesn't imply "forced labor") when the **Torah** spoke about **devoting** them or at least driving them out? Again, maybe the Canaanites saw themselves as fortunate that the Israelites didn't interpret Deuteronomy too literally (and maybe they were right in their interpretation). The chapter indicates that there was ebb and flow in the process whereby Israel gained control of Canaan. Judah captured Jerusalem and killed everyone there; but later we discover that the city is still occupied by the Jebusites, who had presumably made themselves scarce on that earlier occasion and then returned home after Judah was safely gone. Only in David's day does the city become Israelite. So the chapter indicates that the process reflected practicalities. There were things the Israelites could not do because the Canaanites were technologically more sophisticated. The Danites never did manage to occupy their area.

God was involved in a human process not unlike the one whereby any people comes to take over another people's territory; indeed, Amos 9 comments on the way God was involved in the **Philistines'** gaining their land in Canaan (!!) just as God was involved in the Israelites' gaining theirs. There is a troublesome side to this truth. We might like to think of God as involved in the world in a wholly peace-loving way, given that God's ultimate aim is presumably peace loving. Perhaps the problem is that if God insisted on that, it would mean not being involved in the world at all, or being involved only in supranatural ways. God gets God's hands dirty in being involved in the world in its messiness.

Yesterday a friend was describing a messy split that had occurred in her church; the deacons had sacked the pastor; he had started a new congregation down the street; and half the congregation and staff had gone to join him. My friend rather suspected that the deacons had done wrong by the pastor, though one might think that his subsequent action raised some questions, too. She wondered whether she should leave rather than continue her ministry to the youth in the church. I asked her whether she thought God had left the church. My hunch is that God doesn't do that very often. If God were involved with the church only when it does the right thing in the right way, God would never be involved with it at all.

JUDGES 2:1–3:4

The Power of Forgetting

[1]Yahweh's aide came up from Gilgal to Weepers and said, "I took you up from Egypt and brought you to the country I promised to your ancestors. I said, 'I will not annul my covenant with you ever. [2]You yourselves will not seal a covenant with the inhabitants of this country. You will tear down their altars.' You have not obeyed my voice: what is this that you have done? [3]So I have also said, 'I will not dispossess them from before you. To you they will be adversaries. Their gods will be a snare to you.'" [4]When Yahweh's aide spoke these words to all the Israelites, the people lifted up their voice and wept. [5]So they called that place Weepers, but they sacrificed there to Yahweh.

[6]When Joshua sent the people off, the Israelites went each to their own part to take possession of the country. [7]The people served Yahweh all the days of Joshua and all the days of the elders who lived on after Joshua, who had seen all Yahweh's great work that he did for Israel. [8]Joshua son of Nun, Yahweh's servant, died as a man of one hundred and ten years. [9]They buried him on his own territory at Timnath-heres in the mountains of Ephraim, north of Mount Ga'ash. [10]All that generation also joined their ancestors, and another generation arose after them that did not acknowledge Yahweh or the work he had done for Israel. [11]The Israelites did what was unacceptable in Yahweh's eyes. They served the Masters [12]and abandoned Yahweh, their ancestors' God, who had brought them out of Egypt. They followed other gods from among the gods of the peoples around them and bowed down to them, and aroused Yahweh's anger. [13]When they abandoned Yahweh and served the Master and the Ashtoreths, [14]Yahweh's anger flared against Israel and he gave them into the hand of people who plundered them. He surrendered them into the hand of their enemies all around. They could no longer stand against their enemies. [15]Wherever they went out, Yahweh's hand was against them to bring trouble, as Yahweh had said and as Yahweh had sworn to them. It was very hard for them. [16]But Yahweh raised up leaders and they delivered them from the hand of their plunderers.

[Judges 2:17–3:4 expands on how this became a pattern in Israel's life and how it links with Yahweh's not dispossessing the Canaanites, who served to test Israel's commitment to Yahweh.]

Last night I went to the first performance in Los Angeles of the musical version of *The Color Purple*, a fabulous concoction of music, dance, and drama vividly bringing to life the tough reality of many women's experience (and not just in the African American community) but ending with a note of encouragement and hope. Near the end, as in the novel, Celie prays to "dear God, dear stars, dear sky, dear peoples, dear everything, dear God." The words reminded me of some comments by Ross Douthat in *The New York Times* (December 20, 2009), describing James Cameron's also-recent blockbuster *Avatar* as "Cameron's long apologia for pantheism—a faith that equates God with Nature, and calls humanity into religious communion with the natural world." The article describes this faith as Hollywood's religion of choice, embodied in many other movies because it is a faith that people in the United States (both Christian and non-Christian) love. It helps to bring God closer to human experience in a way that avoids God's interfering with us in ways we might not like.

There are overlaps between **Canaanite** religion and such a faith, and thus there are overlaps between the attraction of Canaanite religion for Israelites and a nature faith's attraction for people in a Western cultural context. The Old Testament often refers to Canaanite deities as Baals, but *Baal* is an ordinary word for Lord or Master, so I refer to them as the **Masters**. Judges also mentions the Ashtoreths; there are various ways of spelling that word, and this may be an insulting Israelite way of spelling it, because it combines the consonants of the name, in the form that the Canaanites and other Middle Eastern people would use with the vowels of a Hebrew word for "shame." Maybe that's a coincidence, but the effect is that even naming this deity suggests it is something shameful. Ashtoreth or Astarte or Ishtar (various forms of the name) was a particular goddess, but like the word for Master the name came to be used as a general term, in this case for a goddess. So the Masters and the Ashtoreths denote Canaanite deities, male and female, in general.

The Canaanite gods and goddesses were involved in political events and war but also in the natural world and the cosmos. They stood behind the sequence of day and night, of rain and sun, of winter and summer, of seedtime and harvest, of life and death. That may have been their attraction to Israelites. In their experience as Exodus and Joshua relate it, **Yahweh** focuses on political events and war, on getting the people out of Egypt and into Canaan, and less on the natural world and the cosmos. Now that the Israelites are in Canaan, they need a deity who knows how to make the crops grow as well as how to make things happen on the political front. Further, as generations pass, they want to be able to keep in touch with their family members after they die and maybe learn from them. The Canaanites knew about making the crops grow and knew about making contact with family members after they died; or rather (they said), their gods did. One can see why they would be attractive to the Israelites. The lively nature of the dysfunctional family life of the Canaanite gods and goddesses, with their fighting and sex and drinking and procreating and dying and coming back to life, may also have intrigued the Israelites, even if they also professed to be appalled by it.

Involvement with the Canaanite gods characterizes Israel's life for many centuries, from when Israel comes into existence in Canaan on into the period after the **exile**. Judges portrays the period it covers as a series of stories of apostasy, divine chastisement, divine mercy, and restoration. With variations, the sequence keeps repeating itself. Part of the logic of the sequence is suggested by the expression for "what was unacceptable" and "trouble," which represent the same Hebrew word. People do what is bad; God therefore makes bad things happen to them. Judges will portray these events as involving "Israel"; although now that Israel is spread over Canaan, more literally they involve individual clans or combinations of clans in different parts of the country. The expression of God's mercy comes in raising up a **leader** to **deliver** the people.

If you are a bit mystified by the order of events at the end of Joshua and the beginning of Judges, this is a good sign; it indicates that you have been paying attention. Joshua died at the end of the book of Joshua, and Judges began with a reference to his having died, but some of the events in Judges 1 have already been described in the book of Joshua as happening in Joshua's lifetime, and early in Judges 2 he is alive again, then dying. This kind of jerkiness is common enough in the Bible; it's an indication that the scriptural writers were less anal than I am when I am grading student papers, and that God took their side in including material in his book. If you want to tidy things up in your mind, think of it like this. The book of Joshua anticipates some things that happened after Joshua's day because they were the fulfillment of the project he began. The opening words of Judges indicate that the book is basically about what happened "after Joshua's death," and the mission of Yahweh's **aide** sums up a key aspect of what things were like over subsequent decades and centuries. But chapter 2 then includes a recap so as to start the detail of the main story with Joshua's actual death, and it subsequently gives a more detailed summary of what things were like. The rest of the book will provide that series of illustrations of the pattern that runs through Israel's story from Joshua to Saul.

JUDGES 3:5–31

Unlikely Saviors

⁵When the Israelites settled among the Canaanites, Hittites, Amorites, Perizzites, Hivites, and Jebusites, ⁶they took their daughters for themselves as wives and gave their daughters to their sons, and served their gods. ⁷Thus the Israelites did what was unacceptable in Yahweh's eyes. They put Yahweh their God out of mind and served the Masters and the Asherahs. ⁸Yahweh's anger flared against Israel and he surrendered them into the hand of Cushan-rishathaim the king of Aram-naharaim. The Israelites served Cushan-rishathaim for eight years. ⁹But the Israelites cried out to Yahweh and Yahweh raised up Othniel the Kenizzite, Caleb's brother, who was younger than he, as a deliverer for the Israelites, so that he might deliver them. ¹⁰Yahweh's spirit came on him and he led Israel. He went out to do battle and Yahweh gave Cushan-rishathaim king of Aram into his hand. His hand was strong over Cushan-rishathaim, ¹¹and the country was quiet for forty years.

When Othniel the Kenizzite died, ¹²the Israelites again did what was unacceptable in Yahweh's eyes. Yahweh gave Eglon king of Moab power over Israel because they did what was unacceptable in Yahweh's eyes, [13]and he got the Ammonites and the Amalekites to join him, and went and struck down Israel and took possession of Palms City. [14]The Israelites served Eglon the king of Moab for eighteen years. [15]The Israelites cried out to Yahweh and Yahweh raised up for them a deliverer, Ehud son of Gera, a man restricted in the use of his right hand, a Benjaminite. The Israelites sent tribute by his hand to Eglon the king of Moab. [16]Ehud made himself a sword with two edges, eighteen inches in length. He girded it under his coat on his right side, [17]and presented the tribute to Eglon the king of Moab. Now Eglon was a very fat man. [18]When [Ehud] had finished presenting the tribute, he sent off the people who had been carrying the tribute [19]but himself returned from the carved stones near Gilgal and said, "I have a secret message for you, your majesty." The king said, "Silence," and all the people who stood in attendance on him went out from his presence. [20]When Ehud came to him, he was sitting in the cool upper room that he had, alone. Ehud said, "I have a word from God for you," and [Eglon] got up from his seat. [21]Ehud put out his left hand, took the sword from on his right side, and plunged it right into him.

[The rest of the chapter describes how Ehud escapes and leads the Ephraimites in reversing the domination of Moab over Ephraim, and briefly tells of how Shamgar son of Anat killed six hundred Philistines and thus also "delivered Israel."]

My father was a machine minder in a printing works, and my mother was a seamstress. I was the first person in my extended family to stay at school beyond the age of fourteen. I have more than thirty cousins; only one other has been to college. I am not the kind of person who ends up as an Old Testament professor in one of the biggest seminaries in the world, so I know from my own experience that God isn't bound by people's social background or accent or family history.

The stories about Israel's **deliverers** or **leaders** reflect that fact. After outlining the principle or pattern that runs through these stories, Judges now begins a series of concrete instances that embody the pattern.

First, God is not bound by eldest-ism. Even in the modern world, on the death of a monarch the eldest son succeeds to the throne, and Othniel's elder brother was the Caleb whom Joshua 14–15 showed to be a star, but that doesn't make God unwilling to use his little brother or make Othniel bashful about finding himself as God's agent, and it doesn't make Israelites hesitant to recognize Othniel's leadership. His emergence is God's response when the people **cry out**, even though they are paying the penalty for their waywardness. As a result of it they are under the domination of some people from the northeast of Israel in the area of modern Syria. The extraordinary nature of Othniel's achievement is an indication that God's dynamic and forceful **spirit** is at work. (*Asherahs* is likely here simply an alternative for *Ashtoreths* in 3:14 and refers to goddesses in general, as **Masters** refers to gods in general.)

Second, God is not bound by ableism. There were certain forms of service in which God did not allow someone who was handicapped to take part; the rules in Leviticus require that a priest should be a "complete" person. While there was some symbolism about wholeness in that, it did not mean God wasn't prepared to use someone who was handicapped. There was also some symbolism in this. Ehud couldn't use his right hand. It is thus ironical that he was a Benjaminite, because *Benjamin* means "son of the right hand." He couldn't even live up to his own clan's name. While the description might simply mean he was left-handed, the form of expression suggests a disability, but his inability to use his right hand becomes God's means of making him Israel's deliverer. More than any other chapter in Judges (maybe any other chapter in the Bible), the story of Ehud turns upside down our assumptions about what a holy book ought to be like; the story gets much more scatological in the verses that follow the ones that are translated above. One can imagine how Israelite teenagers loved hearing it. God uses a disabled man and uses a gruesome story about a disabled man.

Third, God is not bound by ethnocentrism; God makes Shamgar son of Anat a person who delivered Israel. The name Shamgar is not Israelite, and Anat is the name of a **Canaanite** deity, so it is not too adventurous to infer that Shamgar was a Canaanite. The unfortunate Canaanites were being pressed from the west by the **Philistines,** and Shamgar evidently won a victory over some of them. Now the Philistines became Israel's own rivals and oppressors, so any victory over the Philistines could be seen as a means of God's delivering Israel. Thus, presumably without realizing it, Shamgar was God's servant in this respect. While **Yahweh** forbade Israel from some forms of involvement with the Canaanites (specifically, from intermarrying with them) because of what this would do to their relationship with Yahweh, this did not stop Yahweh from using the Canaanites.

Each of these three incidents involves **Israel**, as will be the case with the rest of the incidents that Judges will describe, but the individual stories also indicate that this does not mean the whole people of Israel is directly involved. Each of the oppressing peoples is one that borders or invades Israel on a particular side, and each of the acts of deliverance thus involves just some of the clans, not all twelve. To speak of these incidents as involving Israel constitutes a reminder that the clans do belong together. When one suffers, all suffer; when one sins, the whole people is affected; when God delivers one clan, that is important for all the clans.

The stories also schematize the timing of the history. Their recurrent statements that people had rest or were oppressed "for forty years" (never thirty or fifty) is a sign of this; it means the peace or the oppression lasted for a long time, for ages, for a whole generation, rather than for just a year or two. These storytelling conventions also explain how adding up all the numbers in the book produces a total figure that we cannot fit between Joshua and Saul, if we assume that they follow on each other and are strictly chronological. The periods of oppression could have overlapped if they were directly affecting different parts of the country.

Our modern inclination is to explain events in the history of nations and of the church in empirical and natural cause-effect terms. We see the effect of economic and social factors in the way history unfolds. We do not instinctively bring God into the picture. The Old Testament likewise from time to time shows that it is aware that history works out in cause-effect terms and reflects the ambitions and needs of nations and individuals, but it does not confine itself to that level of explanation. While it does not offer a theological or ethical explanation of every event, it does of some. A book such as Judges thus invites us to look at history from this other perspective. We will not always be able to see religious or theological or ethical meaning in what happens in events, but we may sometimes be able to do so.

JUDGES 4:1–24

Three Strong Women and Three Feeble Men (I)

¹The Israelites continued to do what was unacceptable in Yahweh's eyes when Ehud had died. ²Yahweh surrendered them into the hand of Jabin, the Canaanite king who reigned in Hazor. The commander of his army was Sisera; he lived in Haroshet-of-the-nations. ³The Israelites cried out to Yahweh, because [Sisera] had nine hundred iron chariots and he had subjugated Israel by force for twenty years. ⁴Now Bee, a woman who was a prophetess, the wife of Torches, was leading Israel at that time. ⁵She would sit under Bee's Palm between Ramah and Bethel in the mountains of Ephraim, and the Israelites would come up to her for a decision.

⁶She sent and summoned Lightning son of Abinoam, from Kedesh in Napthali, and said to him, "Yahweh the God of Israel has definitely commanded: 'Go, lead to Mount Tabor, and take with you ten thousand men from Naphtali and Zebulun. ⁷I will lead Sisera, the commander of Jabin's army, to you, to the Kishon Wash, with his chariotry and his forces, and I will give them into your hand.'" ⁸Lightning said to her, "If you go with me, I will go, but if you do not go with me, I will not go." ⁹She said, "I will indeed go with you, only the glory will not be yours on the route that you are going, because it is into the hand of a woman that God will surrender Sisera." So Bee arose and went with Lightning to Kedesh, and ¹⁰Lightning issued a summons to Zebulun and Naphtali at Kedesh. Ten thousand men went up behind him, and Bee went with him.

¹¹Now Heber the Kenite had separated from Cain, from the descendants of Hobab, Moses' father-in-law, and pitched his tent by the oak at Saanannim, near Kedesh. ¹²Sisera was told, "Lightning son of Abinoam has gone up to Mount Tabor," ¹³and Sisera issued a summons to all his chariotry (nine hundred iron chariots) and all the company that was with him from Haroshet-of-the-nations to the Kishon Wash. ¹⁴Bee said to Lightning, "Up, because this is the day that Yahweh has given

99

Sisera into your hand. Yahweh has definitely gone out ahead of you." So Lightning went down from Mount Tabor, with the ten thousand men following him, [15]and Yahweh threw Sisera, his chariotry, and all the army into confusion at the edge of the sword before Lightning. Sisera got down from his chariot and fled on foot, [16]while Lighting pursued the chariotry and the army as far as Haroshet-of-the-nations. All Sisera's army fell to the sword. Not one was left.

[The chapter then tells how Sisera takes refuge with Heber, but Heber's wife Jael kills him.]

Men can have mixed feelings about strong women, though for me strong women are not as worrying as strong men. Before my wife became disabled, she was quite capable of standing up to me; in my head I can still hear her saying, "John!" as a rebuke. I wish she were still able to say it. She was usually right, or at least plausible. In the seminary where I was the principal, on a particular occasion one of my women colleagues came to see me during a financial crisis to make me face up to the need to make a tough decision, to make someone's post redundant and thus to fire the person. I half-knew that this was needed, but I was not facing it. For a woman, the downside to being tough may mean frightening men away; one or two great single women I have known have been tough people who had that effect on potential husbands.

Marriage customs in a traditional society make it harder for a tough woman to get left on the shelf; her father should still be able to marry her off. There may be some irony in the way Judges alludes to marriage in Bee's case. In Hebrew, her name is *Deborah*, but that is the Hebrew word for a bee, and there was a sting in Bee's words. The irony lies in the description of her as "the wife of Torches." Translations also traditionally treat this word, *Lappidoth*, as her husband's name, but it is an odd name, because it looks like a feminine word, so it may hint that Bee was "a fiery woman," which she was, rather than that her husband was; certainly he has no other place in the story. Maybe there wouldn't be much room for another powerful person in their marriage. Maybe Bee would have needed someone to look after the house while she went about being a prophetess and a **leader**. She is the first prophet(ess) since the time of Miriam and Moses.

Whereas institutional ministry in the Old Testament (notably that of priests) belongs to men, when God wants to break into the regular institutional arrangement, prophecy is one way God does so, and women are sometimes the people God then speaks through. Thus Bee can be a fourth example of an unlikely savior (following on the three in chapter 3), of God working against human expectations and categories. Perhaps the word order here suggests that it was because she was a prophetess that she was able to be a leader and a person to whom Israelites came for decisions (the word for *decision* is related to the word for *lead*). It looks as if people came from quite a distance, because her office was located in the middle of the country, whereas Hazor lies in the far north and the battle takes place in between, in the plain between the main mountain ridge and the mountains of Galilee.

Jael was also a tough woman, a little in the mode of Ehud. Her husband, too, is missing from the story, and that fact perhaps contributes to the death of Sisera. He had reason to think he would be safe in Heber's encampment because there was an alliance between Heber and Sisera's boss, but Heber and Jael were related to Moses. In the absence of Heber, Jael does not feel bound to give priority to politics over family, and she knows how to use her femininity on Sisera. She welcomes the exhausted warrior into her tent, feeds him, lulls him to sleep, then hammers a tent peg through his skull. The result is that the glory for Israel's victory goes to a woman rather than to Lightning. Again there is an irony about his name *Barak*. Whereas the name means Lightning, *Barak* does not live up to his name. He loses the glory in two senses as it goes first to Bee and then to Jael.

The third strong woman is Sisera's mother, of whom we shall hear in Judges 5.

If you have been reading Joshua and Judges sequentially, you will be surprised to find Jabin the king of Hazor putting in an appearance here, since Joshua has already killed Jabin, slaughtered the city's inhabitants, and burned the city (see Joshua 11). There are two ways of relating the two chapters. In reading Joshua, we have noted indications that the story there is compressed and that it anticipates the completion of Israelite control of **Canaan**, which happened only some time after Joshua's day. One can then see the stories in Judges as part of the continuation of that process. So Joshua's Israel did take Hazor and kill Jabin, but it did so after Joshua's own day. If that seems implausible, you could relate Judges 4 to another aspect of the Joshua story, which can also be read as implying that there were various Canaanite cities that Joshua attacked and took but that the Israelites did not then attempt to hold onto. The inhabitants of a city such as Hazor, who had fled rather than waiting for Joshua to annihilate them, could therefore subsequently return to reoccupy their city; and it would not be surprising if a later king had the same name as an earlier one.

We noted in the introduction and in the comment on Joshua 10:22–27 that sensitive Western readers are troubled by the violence of people such as Bee and Jael, but apparently God wasn't. Here, they are part of the way "God subdued King Jabin of Canaan before the Israelites" (verse 23). The New Testament includes this event among the achievements of the people who acted by faith in conquering kingdoms, becoming powerful in battle, and routing foreign armies, though with a final reverse irony it is Lightning whom it actually names (Hebrews 11:32–34).

JUDGES 5:1–31a

Three Strong Women and Three Feeble Men (II)

¹ Bee and Lightning the son of Abinoam sang that day:
² "At leaders taking the lead in Israel, at the people offering
    themselves freely: praise Yahweh!
³ Listen, kings! Give ear, sovereigns!
    I myself, I will sing for Yahweh, I will make music for
    the God of Israel.
⁴ Yahweh, when you came forth from Seir, when you
    marched from the region of Edom,
    Earth trembled, yes heavens poured,
    Yes, clouds poured water, ⁵mountains quaked,
    Before Yahweh the one of Sinai, before Yahweh the God
    of Israel."

[Verses 6-18 describe the crisis and pressure Israel was living with until Bee as "a mother in Israel" drove them to take action. The verses celebrate the way different clans came together, though they note that some held back.]

19 "Kings came then fought, kings of Canaan fought,
    At Taanach by Megiddo's waters; they took no plunder of silver.
20 From the heavens the stars fought, from their courses they fought with Sisera.
21 The Kishon Wash swept them away, the rushing wash, the Kishon Wash.
    (Go on with strength, my soul!)
22 Then horses' hooves pounded, with the galloping, the galloping of his mighty ones.
23 'Curse Meroz,' Yahweh's aide said, 'Utterly curse its inhabitants,
    Because they did not come when Yahweh was helping, when Yahweh was helping against the warriors.'
24 Most blessed of women be Jael, wife of Heber the Kenite, most blessed of tent women.
25 He asked for water, she gave milk; in a nobles' bowl she presented curds.
26 She put out her hand for the tent peg, her right hand for the workmen's hammer.
    She hammered Sisera, smashed his head, shattered and pierced his temple.
27 Between her feet he bowed down, he fell, he lay; between her feet he bowed down, he fell.
    Where he bowed down, there he fell, destroyed.
28 Through the window Sisera's mother peered, gazed through the lattice:
    'Why is his chariot taking a long time to come, why has the noise of his chariots delayed?'
29 The wisest of her ladies answer her; indeed she gives her reply to herself:
30 'They must have found and divided the spoil, a woman, two women, for each man.
    Spoil of dyed cloth for Sisera, spoil of dyed cloth embroidered, two embroidered cloths for the necks as spoil.'

103

> [31a] So may all your enemies perish, Yahweh, but may his
>   friends be like the sun coming out in strength."

The other Sunday we sang the hymn "Come Thou Fount of
Every Blessing," whose second verse begins, "Here I raise my
Ebenezer." I asked if anyone knew what this referred to, and
hardly anyone did. (The answer is in 1 Samuel 7.) I knew the
answer to that question, but on another recent Sunday we sang
the "Battle Hymn of the Republic," which includes lines such
as "in the beauty of the lilies Christ was born across the sea,"
and I have a harder time working out what that means, or in
holding in my head the combinations of imagery that it incorporates. This is the nature of poetry. It takes up imagery that
enlivens the poet and/or that will resonate with people reading
the poem and packs it together into a dense whole that requires
slow reading. The very power with which it speaks in its own
context makes it hard for the poem to have the same impact in
another context.

There are many aspects of Bee's poem that are hard to interpret, especially in the middle section, which I have summa-
rized above, and in part this reflects the simple fact that it is a
poem. Maybe aspects of it would have puzzled Israelite readers;
they would have had to work hard to understand it. Admittedly
the challenges it presents to a reader are different from those of
other Old Testament poems in the Prophets and the Psalms,
and this may reflect the fact that it is either a very old poem or
that it is deliberately written in an old-fashioned style. Either
way, for an Israelite it might be a bit like our reading Shake-
speare. But it is no coincidence that as a prophetess Bee speaks
in poetry, like Miriam and most of the later prophets. Prophecy
has to use human words to express profound divine truth, and
poetry is the natural form for expressing profound truths.

Bee's poem parallels the Psalms and the Latter Prophets in
that it comprises short sentences dividing into two (or three)
parts that correspond to one another or contrast with one
another in some way. It also uses a form that is characteristic of older poems in which the second half of a line partially
repeats the first before adding something new, almost like the
blues. The reason may be the same if poems were sometimes

composed orally: the repetition gives the poet time to compose the next words.

Like much of the praise in the Psalms, the praise poem is addressed to human beings (specifically, the world's kings) whom the poet challenges to join in recognizing the greatness of God that has been manifested in the events it celebrates. It knows that there is a sense in which God's "natural" abode is south of **Canaan** in Sinai, or rather that Sinai is a portal between earth and heaven, so this is the direction from which God comes to take action in Israel, traveling through Edomite territory.

The language of earth's trembling and heaven's pouring rain may indicate that Israel's victory involved rain clogging the enemies' chariots. The battle takes place in the plain between the mountains of **Ephraim** and the mountains of Galilee, near the big Canaanite cities of Megiddo and Taanach. The Kishon Wash or Wadi runs there; it is usually just a stream, but it could become more of a torrent after sudden rain. On the other hand, the talk of the stars also fighting reminds us not to be too prosaic in interpreting the poetic images.

The poem also gives distinctive testimony to the importance of the human beings' actions. This victory was not like that at the Red Sea or at Jericho, when people just watched God act. Paradoxically, despite the fact that the situation seems hopeless and there seemed no way the Israelites could do anything about their oppression, Bee had summoned them to take action, because God was going to give them an impossible victory. While God did so, the victory depended on the clans offering themselves and God working through and with them to do something supernaturally extraordinary. Thus the poem is scathing about clans that held back. Most of all, it lauds the achievement of Jael in doing away with the enemy general. That is how God's enemies deserve to be dealt with, Bee finally notes.

We don't know why Meroz comes in for distinctive critique, but in any case the curse on Meroz is present to offer a contrast to the blessing on Jael. We don't even know whether the people of Meroz were Israelites, but certainly Jael is a Kenite, not an Israelite. The contrast between Jael and the people who held back from responding to Bee's call parallels that in Joshua between Rahab the responsive Canaanite and Achan the wayward Israelite. Once more, being an Israelite does not guarantee blessing, and being a foreigner does not exclude you from blessing or from being God's servant.

The closing lines offer a further contrast. There in his home town is Sisera's mother, evidently an important person in her own right with her body of servants. They are looking forward to the return of the victorious general, imagining their men raping the women who belong to their victims and plundering their possessions, bringing some nice things back for their women at home. They are due for disappointment.

JUDGES 5:31b–6:24

On the Unimportance of Spiritual Insight

[31b]So the country was quiet for forty years, [6:1]but the Israelites did what was unacceptable in Yahweh's eyes. So he gave them into the hand of Midian for seven years, [2]and the hand of Midian was strong over Israel for seven years. Because of Midian, the Israelites made themselves refuges in the mountains, caves and strongholds. [3]When Israel had sowed, Midian, Amalek, and the easterners would come up. They would come up against Israel [4]and camp against them, and destroy the country's produce until you come to Gaza. They would not leave anything alive in Israel, either sheep or ox or donkey, [5]because they and their livestock would come up with their tents, come like a locust swarm in quantity; there was no counting them or their camels. So they came to the country to destroy it, [6]and Israel became very low because of Midian, and the Israelites cried out to Yahweh. [7]When the Israelites cried out to Yahweh because of Midian, [8]Yahweh sent someone as a prophet to the Israelites. He said to them, "Yahweh the God of Israel has said this: 'I am the one who brought you up from Egypt, took you out of the household of serfs, [9]rescued you from the hand of Egypt and from the hand of all your oppressors; I drove them out from before you and gave you their country. [10]I said to you, "I am Yahweh your God. You will not revere the gods of the Amorites in whose country you are living." You did not listen to my voice.'"

[11]Then Yahweh's aide came and sat under the terebinth at Ophrah belonging to Joash the Abiezrite. His son Gideon was

beating out wheat in the winepress to keep it safe from Midian. [12]Yahweh's aide appeared to him and said to him, "Yahweh is with you, mighty warrior." [13]Gideon said to him, "Pardon me, my lord: if Yahweh is with us, why has all this happened to us? Where are all the wonders our ancestors related to us, saying, 'Yahweh did indeed bring us up from Egypt'? Yahweh has now abandoned us and given us into the hand of Midian." [14]Yahweh turned to him and said, "Go in this strength of yours and deliver Israel from the hand of Midian. I have indeed sent you." [15]He said to him, "Pardon me, my Lord: how can I deliver Israel? Why, my kin group is the weakest in Manasseh and I am the youngest in my father's household." [16]Yahweh said to him, "But I will be with you, and you will strike Midian down as if they were one man." [17]He said to him, "If I have found favor in your eyes, will you give me a sign that it is you speaking with me? [18]Will you not leave here until I come to you and bring out my offering and place it before you?" He said, "I will stay until you come back."

[In verses 19–24 Gideon presents a kid goat, flat bread, and broth on a rock, and the divine aide makes fire from the rock, and the fire consumes the offerings.]

I have just been talking to a couple I have not seen for a year or two, exchanging news about our children and their marriages and their families. This other couple has several daughters. The last of these was almost thirty, still unattached, and was sad and worried about that. To make it worse, she had committed herself to go and work in a refugee camp for three years, where it seemed unlikely she would meet someone. Her mother told her to make a list of the qualities she was looking for in the man of her dreams, to hold it before God, and to ask God to lead this man to her or lead her to this man. This seems to me a very dangerous piece of advice, though I am all in favor of asking God for impossible things as long as you recognize that God does not grant all our prayers. But the woman did make her list, and against all odds a fellow American came to work in the same camp. . . . Well, you can work out the end of the story. She e-mailed her mother and told her that he exactly fitted the list; they are about to marry, and they will no doubt live happily ever after. Let the credits roll. Let the audience mop their eyes and leave the theatre wishing this was true for them.

Gideon is a guy maybe more like most of us. He would certainly be initially hesitant to make his list. There he is, beating wheat inside the family winepress. This makes the story's later Israelite audience snigger. Everybody knows you beat out wheat in the most open place possible, preferably on top of a hill, so you can then hurl the beaten wheat into the air and let the wind carry away the chaff, and you are left with a nice stack of pure wheat. In contrast, a winepress is a small structure, built in some sheltered place, where you can tread the grapes and let the pure juice flow down into the collecting basin. Crush wheat in a winepress?!

This image shows how crushed and humiliated the Israelites themselves are, and there is a perfectly good reason, the usual one that runs through Judges. Instead of being able to spread out and occupy the whole land from their original base in the mountain heartland of **Canaan**, they have been driven back into the heights of the mountains to hide from raiding parties of peoples from the east and south, semisettled tent-dwelling people such as the Israelites' ancestors were. If you stood on a height and looked down on them, their black tents looked like a swarm of locusts spreading over a field, and they ate up everything like locusts, too. As usual you could explain this in economic and political terms; the Midianites were behaving no differently from the way the Israelites did when they had the chance, like (say) settlers in the Americas pushing back native peoples. But Judges knows that in this case there is another level of explanation. This has happened because (in its usual formula) the Israelites have behaved in a way that offends **Yahweh**.

It looks as if the Israelites don't realize that, and neither does Gideon. They **cry out** to God in the way they had done in Egypt when they didn't deserve the trouble they were in, and God speaks straight to them in return, apparently without sympathy, pointing out the way they deserve the mess they are in. It illustrates the free and straight way Israel and God can speak to each other. No words need to be minced on either side. One might then expect that God will wait for a spot of repentance before doing something, but that would suggest that the relationship between God and Israel is contractual.

Even though they deserve the mess they are in and have done no repenting, God initiates the process whereby they will be **delivered** from their oppressors. The pattern thus repeats the pattern in Exodus. God appears to Gideon as God appeared to Moses, to conscript him in connection with this deliverance, and Gideon shows as little enthusiasm and insight as Moses did, but it doesn't make any difference.

The divine **aide** greets Gideon in the winepress, where he is looking over his shoulder every five minutes to make sure the Midianites aren't about to arrive: "Yahweh is with you, mighty warrior!" The audience sniggers again. Gideon also looks rueful. Evidently he does not know about any prophetic message in which God had said, "You quite deserve the trouble you are in." As usual, God does not answer his "Why?" even by pointing this out, but leaps over that to the question behind Gideon's question. Gideon does not really want an answer to the question of theodicy. He wants some action. The good news is that he is about to get some. The bad news is that he is the means of God's deliverance being put into effect. At one level, his incredulous response is quite reasonable. He has shown no more leadership ability than anyone else in his obscure family. As was the case with Moses, God determines to use someone who is a failure, without obvious potential and without religious insight, because God's using someone does not depend on that person's leadership qualities or spiritual insight. God designates Gideon a mighty warrior not because he has potential that no one has noticed but simply because that is the way God intends to use him.

Gideon's requesting a sign is a further indication that he lacks spiritual insight. Yet even this does not make God decide to abandon him and get someone with more obvious potential (perhaps there was no one). God simply gives him the sign. It is then that Gideon realizes he has actually been in conversation with Yahweh's aide, and thus in effect with God, which is a frightening fact, but God reassures him he has nothing to be afraid of. "*Shalom* to you," God says. "Everything is fine; all is well." And Gideon builds an **altar** there and calls it "Yahweh *shalom*," Yahweh is **peace**," "God makes things well."

109

JUDGES 6:25–40

How to Be a Mixed-up Person

[25]That night Yahweh said to him, "Get the young bull belonging to your father and a second bull of seven years. Pull down the Master's altar belonging to your father and cut down the sacred column by it, [26]and build an altar for Yahweh your God on the top of this refuge, in proper order. Get the second bull and sacrifice it as a burnt offering with the wood of the sacred column that you cut down." [27]So Gideon got ten men from among his servants and did as Yahweh had told him, but as he was afraid to do it by day because of his father's household and the men of his city, he did it by night.

[28]Early next morning the men of the city got up: there, the Master's altar was demolished, the sacred column by it was cut down, and the second bull was sacrificed on the altar that had been built. [29]One person said to another, "Who did this?" They inquired and investigated and said, "Gideon son of Joash did this." [30]The men of the city said to Joash, "Bring your son out: he must die, because he demolished the Master's altar and cut down the sacred column by it." [31]But Joash said to all those who stood against him, "Do you defend the Master or do you deliver him? The person who defends him should be put to death by morning. If he is a god, he should defend himself because [Gideon] has demolished his altar." [32]That day they called him "The-Master-Contends," saying, "The Master must defend himself against him, because he had demolished his altar."

[33]When all Midian, Amalek, and the easterners gathered together, crossed over, and camped in the Jezreel Plain, [34]Yahweh's spirit clothed itself in Gideon. He sounded the horn, and the Abiezrites let themselves be summoned to follow him. [35]When he sent aides through all Manasseh, they also let themselves be summoned to follow him, and when he sent aides through Asher, Zebulun, and Napthtali, they came up to meet [the Manassites]. [36]Gideon said to God, "If you are really going to deliver Israel by my hand, as you said: [37]there, I am placing a wool fleece on the threshing floor. If there is dew on the fleece alone but on all the ground it is dry, I will acknowledge that you will deliver Israel by my hand as you said." [38]So it happened. Early next day he got up, squeezed the fleece, and wrung out

dew from the fleece, a bowlful of water. [39]Gideon said to God, "May your anger not flare against me if I speak just one more time. May I test with the fleece just one more time. May there be dry on the fleece alone but on all the ground may there be dew." [40]God did so that night. There was dry on the fleece alone but on the ground there was dew.

This week I asked a group of students what impressions their Christian background had given them about prayer. One of the recurrent themes was that we need to be a bit careful how we talk to God. You don't complain to God, question God, or ask God for things that God hasn't already encouraged you to ask for. Now, I admit that when I ask God for things, God sometimes doesn't grant them, and when I question God, the response is sometimes, "Shut up." But at least that suggests the relationship is real, with give and take. It's like the relationship of parents and children; I would not have wanted my children to hesitate about asking me things and also asking me *for* things because they were afraid of how I might react. Or it's like the relationship of teacher and students; while some students ask for extra time to write their papers and get a positive answer, and some ask and get a negative answer, the ones who don't even ask certainly don't get it.

Gideon asks and gets it. First we are given a more specific picture of the waywardness that characterizes people in Gideon's area. Each of these stories in Judges relates to a particular geographical area; we need not assume that the wrongdoing directly involved the people as a whole, and neither does the trouble that follows. Gideon belongs to the part of Manasseh that settled west of the Jordan, and his home is not far from Shechem. There in Israel's heartland Gideon's city (really only a village) is given over to the worship of the **Master**. So the sanctuary in the village is dedicated to him, and there is the kind of sacred column alongside the **altar** that you would regularly have in a **Canaanite** sanctuary. The word for a sacred column is actually *asherah*, which came in Judges 3:7 as the name of a goddess; the idea is likely that the column is a wooden image that represents the goddess who stands alongside the god as an object of worship.

What Gideon is challenged to do is destroy these objects of worship and replace them by ones "proper" to people who are committed to **Yahweh**. He continues to be a somewhat mixed-up person. He does exactly what Yahweh says but makes a point of doing it when no one is looking, even though Yahweh seems to want a very public action: the new altar is to be built on top of the "refuge," the place where the people hid from the Midianites. It will be a public demonstration of the dethronement of the Master and the recognition of Yahweh. In the event, trying to be discrete doesn't stop Gideon's being discovered, as when Moses tried to kill a man secretly but got found out. His fear is quite reasonable; his whole family and his whole community are committed to the Master.

That includes Joash, Gideon's dad, who plays an intriguing cameo part in this drama. The name that Joash's parents had given him (like a name such as Joshua or Jonathan) indicates that they were committed to Yahweh, but the story eventually refers to the fact that Gideon's other name is Jerubbaal, "The Master Contends." When people's names refer to God, this God is regularly the God to which they are committed. It is difficult to imagine Gideon's being given a name that refers to the Master at this point, just after he has issued his challenge to the Master. The people's comment that the name signifies "The-Master-Contends" will be a comment on a new significance that they now see in his name (as happens to the place name Gilgal in Joshua 5). If Gideon's parents named him Jerubbaal, that will imply their commitment to the Master. Yet Joash now comes good in the story. It is natural for a father to want to protect his son, but somehow his son's action drives Joash into abandoning his commitment to the Master and challenging the village to do so.

Now comes the next political crisis for the community and for the wider clan of Manasseh when Midian invades again. This time God's **spirit** "clothes itself in Gideon." Some translations have God's spirit coming on Gideon as if the spirit is the clothes, but it is Gideon who is the clothes. You can't see the spirit; what you can see is Gideon behaving like someone who has new power and dynamic inside, transformed from someone too scared to take on his village into someone who will take on Midian, Amalek, and the easterners. Yet the real, natural Gideon remains alive and well, and it is this Gideon who asks God for another sign of God's involvement with him, this time a sign that his sense of being taken over by God and his starting to do things that he could never have imagined doing is not just his imagination. Indeed, when God grants that sign, and Gideon realizes it need not have been so miraculous, he asks for a third sign, and God (with a sigh, or a grin?) grants that one, too.

Gideon knows that we don't have to hesitate over asking outrageous things from God, things we shouldn't need. By all means be deferential to God; Gideon reminds us of Abraham praying for Sodom in Genesis 18. By no means assume that God will grant your outrageous request. There's no guarantee that God will. But God might. So it's a shame not to ask. Gideon's action also points to another Old Testament assumption. Its attitude to doubt is that what ultimately matters is not whether you are doubting or believing in God but whether you are doubting or believing in the real God. It's okay that Gideon is doubting Yahweh; the important thing is that it is Yahweh he is doubting, not the Master. Even in his doubt he is turning to Yahweh, not to the Master.

JUDGES 7:1–25

How to Increase the Odds against Yourself

[1]Early next day The-Master-Contends (that is, Gideon) and all the company with him camped above the Spring of Harod; the Midianite camp was north of him at Teacher's Hill, in the plain. [2]Yahweh said to Gideon, "The company with you is too big for me to give Midian into their hand, lest Israel takes glory for itself, saying, 'My hand delivered me.' [3]Will you now proclaim in the ears of the company, 'Anyone who is afraid and trembling is to go back and fly from Mount Gilead.'" Twenty-two thousand of the company went back; ten thousand remained. [4]Yahweh said to Gideon, "The company is still big. Get them to go down to the water and I will sift them for you there. When I

say to you, 'This one will go with you,' that one will go with you. Everyone that I say to you, 'This one will not go with you,' that one will not go with you."

⁵So he got the company to go down to the water. Yahweh said to Gideon, "Everyone who laps from the water with his tongue as a dog laps, you are to place on his own, and [likewise] everyone who bends down on his knees to drink." ⁶The number of people who lapped with their hand into their mouth was three hundred. All the rest of the company bent down on their knees to drink water. ⁷Yahweh said to Gideon, "By means of the three hundred men I will deliver you and give Midian into your hand. All [the rest of] the company are to go to their own place, each one." ⁸So they got the company's provisions in their hand, and their horns, and every [other] Israelite he sent off, each one to his tent, but kept hold of the three hundred men.

The Midianite camp was below him in the plain. ⁹That evening Yahweh said to him, "Get up, go down to attack the camp, because I have given it into your hand. ¹⁰If you are afraid to go down [to attack], you yourself go down to the camp with Purah your boy ¹¹and listen to what they say, and afterwards your hands will be strong enough to go down against the camp." So he himself went down with Purah his boy to the edge of where the men organized into companies were in the camp. ¹²Now Midian, Amalek, and all the easterners were lying in the plain like a locust swarm in quantity, and there was no counting their camels, like the sea on the seashore for quantity. ¹³Gideon came, and there: a man was recounting a dream to his neighbor. He said, "Here, I had a dream. There, a loaf of barley bread was rolling against the Midianite camp. It came to a tent and struck it down, and it fell. It rolled it over and the tent fell." ¹⁴His neighbor answered, "This is nothing but the sword of Gideon the son of Joash, the Israelite. God has given Midian and the entire camp into his hand."

[In verses 15–25 Gideon gives his three hundred men the horns they got from the others, and also a jar and a torch. In the middle of the night they surround the Midianite camp, sound the horns, smash the jars, and wave the torches, which makes the Midianite army panic. They either run for it toward their homes beyond the Jordan or fight anyone handy, which means fellow Midianites because the Israelites have stayed outside the camp. The rest of

*the twenty-two thousand now join in pursuit of them, joined by
some Ephraimites who capture and kill the Midianite generals.]*

Two weeks ago a man tried to blow up a plane going from
Amsterdam to Detroit, and one week ago when I came back
from London to Los Angeles after Christmas, it took two hours
to board the plane rather than the usual half hour because of the
extra security arrangements that had led to. The United States
and European powers are involved in a battle with forces that
have their center in Afghanistan and Pakistan but are spread
around the world, and we are expending huge amounts of
resources trying to win this battle. It seems we have no choice
but to do so, even if we fail and the attempt bankrupts us. At
the same time, we decline to intervene militarily in some other
contexts, such as Sudan, not because the moral issue is very
different but because we recognize the limit to what we can
realistically reckon to achieve. Christians talk about whether
wars are just, but decisions about war are made on the basis of
whether they are practical (though that is one of the criteria for
deciding whether a war is just).

God's way of deciding whether and how to fight battles is
quite different. You couldn't blame Gideon for thinking it was
rather crazy. Given that this man has no problem telling God
what he is thinking, it is somewhat surprising that he does not
say so. The battle takes place on the southern side of the fer-
tile central plain that divides the main mountain chain where
Gideon lives from the mountains of Galilee, and thus not far
from where Bee and Lightning fought their battle. The spring
where Gideon camps comes out of those mountains, so his
camp is on the slopes of the mountains, while the Midianite
camp is in the main plain.

Excusing from battle the men who are scared of fighting fits
with the rules for war laid down in Deuteronomy 20. Person-
ally, I would hightail it away as the twenty-two thousand do.
God's own image is that they are to wing it away (this particular
Hebrew word for *fly* comes only here, but it is related to a word
that denotes a small bird). The procedure for reducing ten thousand to three hundred seems to involve distinguishing between

people who simply crouched in order to reach down into the water with their hands, so that they then use their hands to lap in the way a dog uses its tongue, and people who knelt right down to do so. It's an arbitrary distinction, just a way of dividing people into two groups, so that the big group can be sent home even though they are looking forward to a fight.

God anticipates that you couldn't blame Gideon if any confidence that the signs have given him now dissipates. God thus offers him another sign. Like us, traditional societies such as Israel know that dreams can be important, but they locate this importance differently. Dreams can be a means of God's telling you something that is going to happen, and maybe this dream does so. Or maybe the dream is more like one of ours in that it simply reveals that the average Midianite is scared stiff. Presumably he doesn't know about the nonsense in the hills whereby nearly all the Israelite army has been sent home, and thus he isn't aware of the contrast between the small number of men Gideon now has and the size of his own army, to which the story draws attention again. Either way, the dream is an encouragement to Gideon.

Many previous stories in the Old Testament picture God's giving Israel victory in one of two ways. On some occasions God simply puts people down, and the Israelites just watch, as happened at the **Reed Sea** and at Jericho. On other occasions there is a regular battle with a surprising result, as happened when Bee and Barak took on Jabin. God's reducing Gideon's army to three hundred obviously means it will take something like a miracle for them to dispose of the huge Midianite army, but God does involve them in bringing it about. Yet they carry no weapons, only the means of performing a silly trick. They shout, "The sword for **Yahweh** and for Gideon," but the only literal swords employed in the battle are the ones the Midianites use on one another.

Later, Jesus will turn a few fish and loaves into food for thousands of people; he could have started from scratch. Sometimes God works through ordinary human means, but there is no miracle involved; sometimes God acts without human means; and sometimes God does a miracle that uses human means. Further, sometimes God gives people instructions on what to

116

do, and sometimes God leaves it to them to work out. There is no indication here that God tells Gideon what to do with the horns, jars, and torches, and no indication that his stratagem is not one God would approve of. He works out the plan for himself, revealing himself to be less clueless than we might have inferred from earlier parts of his story.

JUDGES 8:1–35
I'm Not the Hero; the Hero Is God

[Verses 1–21 relate further aspects of the battle's aftermath. First, the Ephraimites express their dissatisfaction with not having been summoned to join in the main battle, but Gideon manages to get them to calm down. He himself pursues the two Midianite kings and eventually captures them and kills them. On the way, he is refused provision by the people of Succoth and Penuel, on whom he takes redress on the way home.]

²²The men of Israel said to Gideon, "Rule over us, you and your son and your grandson as well, because you delivered us from the hand of Midian." ²³Gideon said to them, "I myself will not rule over you and my son will not rule over you. Yahweh is the one who will rule over you." ²⁴But Gideon said to them, "I will make a request of you. Each man, give me the earring that was his plunder" (because [the enemy] had gold earrings, because they were Ishmaelites). ²⁵They said, "We will indeed give them." They spread out a coat and threw there, each man, the earring that was his plunder. ²⁶The weight of the gold earrings that he had requested came to one thousand seven hundred gold [shekels], apart from the crescents, pendants, and purple robes on the Midianite kings, and apart from the collars on their camels' necks. ²⁷Gideon made it into an ephod and placed it in his city, in Ophrah. All Israel acted immorally in going after it there. It became a snare to Gideon and his household.

²⁸So Midian subjected itself before the Israelites and did not again raise its head. The country was quiet for forty years in Gideon's time. ²⁹The-Master-Contends, son of Joash, went off and returned home. ³⁰Gideon had seventy sons who issued from his own body, because he had many wives. ³¹His secondary wife in Shechem also bore him a son; he named him

117

Abimelek. ³²Gideon son of Joash died in a good old age and was buried in his father Joash's tomb in Ophrah of the Abiezrites.

³³When Gideon died, the Israelites again acted immorally in going after the Masters, and they made the Covenant-Master into a god for themselves. ³⁴The Israelites were not mindful of Yahweh their God who rescued them from the hand of their enemies around them. ³⁵They did not keep commitment with the household of The-Master-Contends/Gideon in accordance with all the good that he had done in Israel.

One of my fond memories of our sons' childhood is of reading Bible stories to them at bedtime, stories that had been rewritten and illustrated for children; I have now passed on the set of books to the son who has children of his own. My favorite was a version of the Gideon story turned into poetry. It was feeble poetry, to be sure, but it ended with a profound piece of theology. My sons would wait for this line and knew how to complete it. Gideon refuses to become a permanent ruler, and explains,

> For though it seems odd,
> I'm not the hero,
> The hero is GOD.

When Gideon makes that declaration, it is the highpoint of his story. Gideon knows that having a human ruler doesn't fit with the idea of God's being Israel's ruler. Neither the Israelites nor Gideon talk about his being "king"; the idea of having a king will arise only in connection with the continuation of the Abimelek story in the next chapter. No one is suggesting that they compromise the idea that God is Israel's king; Gideon can be someone who rules on the real king's behalf. That might make the suggestion even more tempting. So it is impressive that Gideon declines. He knows that God is the hero; and his insistence on this fact makes him a hero. It is fitting that he eventually retires and dies in a good old age and joins his family in the family tomb. It is the way a hero's story should end.

Other aspects of the story compromise that refusal and leave us with a thoroughly ambiguous impression of mixed-up Gideon. Most obviously there are all those wives and the

seventy sons. That is a king's lifestyle. The Old Testament recognizes that fact and doesn't express explicit disapproval, but it
portrays the trouble that tends to follow and thus leaves people
to draw the obvious inference. Having multiple wives no doubt
has something to do with sex, but it also has a lot to do with
status, as does having many sons (not so much with daughters!). It is what people such as David and Solomon do. Many
of Gideon's other wives may have been **secondary wives**; the
reason for mentioning Abimelek and his mother will become
clear in the next chapter.

Then there is the ephod. An ephod is usually a type of
priestly garment, but the use of fifty pounds of gold suggests
something more substantial, so here the term perhaps implies
a statue clothed in an ephod, and this fits with the way it could
become something that led people astray in their worship.
More literally, it led to their acting immorally; the word is one
that literally refers to sexual immorality, which is an image the
Old Testament often uses in speaking of people being unfaithful to **Yahweh**.

What was Gideon thinking? Again, the story doesn't explicitly blame him for Israel's going astray after his death (the
"Covenant-Master" was the way they think of the **Master** in
their community, maybe as guaranteeing **covenant** relationships in some way). Explicitly, it rather draws attention to
their having failed to keep **commitment** with Gideon himself
in response to all he had achieved for them. Yet their "acting immorally" is an example of the pattern running through
Judges, though here alone does the summary of their action
use this verb "act immorally" to describe their going astray, and
it is the same word used of their "acting immorally" in relation
to the ephod. That invites readers to see a link. Yes, Gideon has
some responsibility for what happened.

The ambiguity running through Gideon's story is summed
up by the ambiguity of his names. It's quite common for Old
Testament figures to have more than one name. Here (as happens elsewhere) the names are used in a jerky way that suggests
that some versions of stories about him used one name and
some used the other and that these have been combined without the compilers of Judges feeling the need to tidy them up. The

result is to raise the question whether he is really Gideon or The-Master-Contends. Alternatively, it raises the question, which meaning of Jerubbaal (see the comment on 6:25–40) is more significant? It's both a question about who he really thought he was and about what his long-term effect on Israel was.

At the beginning of the chapter, the **Ephraimites'** complaint again draws attention to an aspect of the dynamic of the stories. Gideon is from Manasseh, whose territory dominates the northern part of the main mountains. The battle happens on the northern edge of its territory where it meets Zebulun, with Asher and Naphtali being just beyond. As usual, although you could call this a crisis and a battle involving "Israel," only some of the clans are involved. The complaint by Ephraim (Manasseh's neighbor to the south) works with the bigger concept of Israel; they should have been involved in the battle even if they were less affected by the crisis. (Maybe they also thought they might have gotten a bigger share of the plunder!) The subsequent unwillingness of Succoth and Penuel to provision Gideon when he is in pursuit of the Midianite kings suggests the other side of the coin to the Ephraimites' resentment. When some of the clans wanted to settle east of the Jordan, Joshua was afraid that they would not really be committed to the rest of the people's destiny (see Joshua 1). Here Joshua's fears are realized. Maybe they have the opposite kind of practical concerns in their minds to those of the Ephraimites. Across the Jordan, they live much closer to people such as the Midianites. For one reason or another, they don't feel a commitment to Gideon that reflects a sense of belonging to one people.

JUDGES 9:1–57

The Man Who Would Be King

¹Abimelek son of Jerubbaal went to his mother's brothers in Shechem and spoke to them, and to the entire kin group in his mother's paternal household: ²"Will you say in the hearing of all the notables of Shechem, 'Which is better for you, seventy men ruling over you, all Jerubbaal's sons, or one man ruling over you? Bear in mind that I am your own flesh and

blood.'" ³His mother's brothers said all these things about him in the ears of all the notables of Shechem. They were minded to follow Abimelek, because (they said), "He is our brother." ⁴They gave him seventy silver [shekels] from the house of the Covenant-Master, and with these Abimelek hired good-for-nothing and wild men, and they followed him. ⁵He came to his father's house in Ophrah and slaughtered his brothers, the sons of Jerubbaal, seventy men on one stone. But Jotham, Jerubbaal's youngest son, survived because he hid. ⁶All the notables of Shechem and all [the people from] the Fortification House assembled. They went and crowned Abimelek king by the oak at the pillar at Shechem.

⁷People told Jotham and he went and stood on top of Mount Gerizim. He lifted his voice and called to them: "Listen to me, notables of Shechem, so that God may listen to you. ⁸The trees once went to anoint a king over themselves. They said to the olive tree, 'Do reign over us.' ⁹The olive tree said to them, 'Have I run out of my rich product, I by whom people honor God and human beings, that I should go and wave above the trees?' ¹⁰So the trees said to the fig tree, 'You come and reign over us.' ¹¹The fig tree said to them, 'Have I run out of my sweetness, my nice fruit, that I should go and wave above the trees?' ¹²So the trees said to the vine, 'You come and reign over us.' ¹³The vine said to them, 'Have I run out of my new wine, which makes God and human beings rejoice, that I should go and wave above the trees?' ¹⁴So all the trees said to the thornbush, 'You come and reign over us.' ¹⁵The thornbush said to the trees, 'If you are truly going to anoint me as king over you, come, shelter in my shade. If not, may fire come forth from the thornbush and consume the cedars of Lebanon.'"

[In verses 16–57 Jotham goes on to interpret his parable, then runs for it. After a while conflict arises between Abimelek and the Shechemites and in due course Abimelek massacres the people. Later he besieges another city, Tebez, and dies when a woman throws a millstone on his head.]

In connection with Joshua 20, I mentioned a woman in my class who apparently had a brain tumor. In an e-mail a couple of weeks ago, she talked about ways God had been speaking to her through classes she had taken over the summer and fall as she was thinking about marriage and about the mysterious symptoms she had. Jeremiah, Lamentations, Daniel, and other books had been speaking to her in ways I could not have guessed or planned. A couple of nights ago she and her husband came to dinner, being now married for four weeks, and we talked some more about the fruitfulness of that Old Testament study. For ten years I was in charge of a seminary, but after that I wanted to get back to being an ordinary professor. Oftentimes I think that my teaching doesn't make the slightest difference to anybody, but sometimes God sends someone to put me right and remind me that the study I get people to do can be worthwhile.

On those days I agree with Jotham. Being in charge of the seminary was the right thing for those ten years, but teaching is more worthwhile than being in charge. Maybe there were all sorts of considerations that led to Abimelek's proposal and to its acceptance. Maybe he resented the difference between his status as the son of a **secondary wife** and the status of the people Gideon treated as his "real" sons. The strange reference to his mother's paternal household may link with this. Perhaps the fact that her husband is an absentee means his mother is in charge of her own household, which might seem fine in the modern West but seems pretty deviant in a traditional society. Or perhaps she is still part of her own father's household, which would also seem odd in that context as in a Western one, though for different reasons. Maybe Abimelek just liked the idea of being the big guy around there; maybe being a secondary son of Gideon was a big deal in Shechem even though he would be small fry if he ever went to Ophrah. Maybe the Shechemites resented being under the rule of those guys from Ophrah.

What the Shechemites sadly have in common with the other Israelites is that they are committed to the Covenant-Master who was mentioned at the end of the Gideon story. There is a grievous irony about worshiping the **Master** under this name at Shechem. Joshua 24 recounts how the Israelites assembled at Shechem and made a commitment to **Yahweh**, and how Joshua made a **covenant** for them that solemnizes that commitment, but Judges 2 notes that the pattern of life the book introduces is one that involves Israel's transgressing this covenant. To put it concretely, at Shechem (of all places) the Master has become the covenant figure in their lives. The people of Shechem turn the Covenant-Master into the sponsor of their plot to massacre Gideon's family. (Maybe the "one stone" is in effect an **altar**, so this is a kind of sacrifice to the Master; Samson's father offers his sacrifice on a rock in Judges 13.)

Jotham then declaims his cheeky parable from the same spot near Shechem where half the clans had stood declaring Yahweh's blessing when the Israelites first arrived in the country (see Joshua 8:33: it is the only other connection in which Gerizim is mentioned in the Old Testament). But his words end up with a curse, not a blessing. Nobody who has a worthwhile job wants to be a leader, and anyone who wants to be a leader is a great danger to the people he (or she) leads. That is particularly so (Jotham goes on to imply) when the leader shows himself to be someone capable of acting with the ruthlessness Abimelek shows and when the people associate themselves with that ruthlessness. They couldn't call this acting in good faith in light of what Gideon had done for them, could they? How can their action not backfire on both the leader and the people? Jotham prays that it may. The rest of the story shows how right he is and anticipates what often happens in Israel, in the church, and in society.

God answers Jotham's prayer and sends a "bad **spirit**" between Abimelek and the Shechemite "notables," the leading citizens of the city, the heads of the families (the people of the Fortification House are apparently another such group). They then "broke faith" with Abimelek. To speak of God's sending a bad spirit could sound as if it implied God intervened to do something that would never naturally have happened, but I have already implied that it will not be at all surprising if an alliance rooted in ambition and violence falls apart. The story's way of making that point is to say that by this breaking of faith the violence done to Gideon's seventy sons "came," as if it had been waiting and had eventually arrived to do its further work. In other words (it says), their blood was "put on" Abimelek and the Shechemites. There is a sort of natural process whereby such terrible wrongdoing brings about terrible consequences for the people who do it. So the Old Testament can describe things as involving the ordinary processes of cause and effect but also as something God is involved in. My story of the student with the disappearing brain tumor may well give a more positive illustration of that; the medics have no clue what happened, but if one day they can explain it in medical terms, this will not make us stop thinking that God did something wondrous for her.

While Abimelek is out of town, the Shechemite notables psych themselves up by means of a religious festival in the city and plan a coup d'état, but the mayor (presumably Abimelek's appointee) gets word to him. He returns with his private army and conducts a massacre in the city. He subsequently attacks a nearby city called Tebez (perhaps they had taken part in the rebellion), whose citizens take refuge in the tower that a city often had for precisely this purpose. This does not faze Abimelek; the Shechemites had done the same, and he had just set fire to their tower. But before he can do so, a woman drops a millstone onto his head and cracks his skull. He gets his arms bearer to finish him off because he doesn't want people to say he was killed by a woman, but the story survives to tell us that this is more or less what happens to him, as it happened to Sisera.

JUDGES 10:1–11:29

When God Finds It Hard to Be Tough

[Judges 10 begins with brief accounts of two further deliverers called Tola and Jair, then relates how Israel again gave itself to serving other gods, which leads to God's subjecting it to the Philistines on the west and the Ammonites on the east.]

[10]So the Israelites cried out to Yahweh, "We have done wrong against you, because we have abandoned our God and served the Masters." [11]Yahweh said to the Israelites, "Yes, from the Egyptians, the Amorites, the Ammonites, the Philistines—[12]and the Sidonians and Amalek and Maon, they oppressed you, and you cried out to me, and I delivered you from their hand. [13]But you—you abandoned me and served other gods. So I will not deliver you again. [14]Go and cry out to the gods you chose. They must deliver you in your time of distress." [15]The Israelites said to

Yahweh, "We have done wrong. You yourself—deal with us in accordance with what seems good in your eyes. Only do rescue us this day." [16]They removed the foreign gods from their midst and served Yahweh, and his heart was overwhelmed by Israel's misery.

[17]The Ammonites summoned themselves and camped in Gilead, and the Israelites assembled and camped at Mizpah. [18]The company (the officers of Gilead) said to one another, "Who is the man who will be first to fight the Ammonites? He will be head over all the people who live in Gilead." [11:1]Now Jephthah the Gileadite was a powerful warrior, but he was the son of an immoral woman. Gilead had fathered Jephthah, [2]but Gilead's wife had born him sons, and when his wife's sons grew up, they threw Jephthah out and said to him, "You will have no share in our father's household, because you are the son of another woman." [3]So Jephthah ran away from his brothers and lived in Good Country. Dishonorable men gathered around Jephthah and went out [fighting] with him.

[Verses 4–28 relate how, in light of Jephthah's reputation, the Gileadites invite him back to lead them against the Ammonites, who claim that the Israelites took from them the land Gilead occupies; Jephthah denies that this is so.]

[29]Yahweh's spirit came on Jephthah and he crossed to Gilead and Manasseh, crossed to Mizpeh in Gilead, and from Mizpeh in Gilead crossed to the Ammonites.

In my prayers each day (well, most days, to be honest), I pray either for the nation or for the church in our nation. I do so against the background of the fact that nations grow and triumph and then decline and fall, and that churches do the same. I come from a continent where the church once flourished but is now virtually nonexistent. I live in a country where the church once flourished and is now in decline, and might be on the way to the same fate. If I were God, I could indeed be tempted to let the church fall. Yet in contexts where God has announced the intention to bring a people down, the Old Testament sets before us examples of people preaching and also praying against the odds, and of God having a change of mind about putting the people down. That shapes the way I pray for the nation and the church. I ask God to resist the temptation to decide, "That's it" and bring us down. One of my encouragements in doing so is that God has a hard time being tough. It's not so difficult to persuade God to let people have one more chance.

Once again the Israelites abandon **Yahweh** and worship other deities. Once again they pay for it politically. Once again they **cry out** to God. On this occasion, for the first time, God says, "I've had enough." The trouble is that God isn't tough enough to maintain that stance, and perhaps the Israelites suspect that this is so. When God has said, "We're done. I'm not rescuing you again," one might have expected that they would say, "Okay, no good turning to him, then." In fact, they turn back to God even though God has told them of this intention to let them stew in their own juices. Perhaps they indeed suspect God lacks the strength of character to do so. Or perhaps they turn back because they know it is the right thing to do even if it gets them nowhere.

One context in which it is worth reading these stories is that of the **Judahite** people in **exile**, at the end of the story that runs through Judges, Samuel, and Kings. God's eventually letting Jerusalem fall to **Babylon** is the ultimate expression of God's saying, "I'm through." Yet in that context the story in Kings and the prayers in Lamentations represent the people's casting themselves on God and saying, "Yes, we have done terribly wrong. We have no claim on you. All we can do is throw ourselves on your mercy." Then all they can do is wait. These stories in Judges might be an encouragement to them. Maybe God will not be able to maintain the tough stance. . . .

So it was in this story. God's heart is overwhelmed by their misery. More literally, God's soul or person or spirit is "short" at their misery. Usually the word implies being ineffective or feeble or impatient. It can suggest not having the inner resources to put up with something any longer. God lacks the inner resources to put up with Israel's suffering, even though they deserve it. God cannot resist the temptation to act on their behalf. Admittedly, how things turn out makes that seem less wonderful than you might have expected. Perhaps this again shows the way God works with the potentials of the people in a situation.

Like the other crises in Judges, this one affects a particular part of the country and affects particular clans. In this case it is Gilead, the area east of the Jordan where Reuben, Gad, and half of Manasseh live. It is thus an area especially vulnerable to people such as the Ammonites, who live south of Gilead. The man to whom the clans turn is a complicated person with a background rather like Abimelek. The translations describe him as the son of a prostitute, but the words require only that he be the son of a woman who breaks the society's sexual codes, and he may thus simply be a boy born of an affair between his father (who is also called Gilead) and a single girl in the village. Either way, he has a status not so different from Abimelek's. His father accepted responsibility for him, but everyone knew he was illegitimate, and when all Gilead's sons were grown up, they threw him out. Maybe experience and exclusion drove him to achievement as it drove Abimelek, and he became an outstanding warrior whom the Gileadites therefore call back to lead them against the Ammonites.

"Good Country" is a place farther northeast of Gilead; the striking name suggests he was doing well, but the men he got involved with were the opposite. That begins to illustrate Jephthah's ambiguity. It emerges further in his initial negotiations with the Ammonites, which involve him in giving them a long lesson in relations between Israel and the peoples east of the Jordan, largely as these are recounted in the **Torah**. The Ammonites accuse the Gileadites of appropriating their land; Jephthah argues that they did no such thing. They made a point of seeking to avoid encroaching on any territory east of the Jordan. They did end up taking over land belonging to the **Amorites** (not Edom, Moab, or Ammon), as a result of the Amorites' insistence on attacking the Israelites. But anyway (he goes on), what about the statute of limitations? This all happened three centuries before.

When the Ammonites are unconvinced, the **spirit** of God comes on Jephthah as it once came on Gideon (though not on Abimelek). He is inspired to race through the area east of the Jordan (presumably gathering forces) as he prepares to face the Ammonites, like Elijah racing King Ahab back to Samaria when the hand of God comes on him (1 Kings 18). Then comes

127

the most fateful moment in his story. After Abimelek, we might think Judges cannot reach any lower points. We would be wrong.

JUDGES 11:30–12:15

The Man Whose Promise Makes the Blood Run Cold

[30]Jephthah made a promise to Yahweh: "If you do actually give the Ammonites into my hand, [31]whoever comes out of the doors of my house to meet me when I return in peace I will offer as a burnt offering." [32]Jephthah crossed to the Ammonites to do battle with them, and Yahweh gave them into his hand. [33]He struck them down from Aroer even to when you come to Minnith, twenty cities, even to Abel-cheramim, a very great defeat. So the Ammonites subjected themselves before the Israelites.

[34]Jephthah came home to Mizpah, and there was his daughter coming out to meet him with a tambourine and dancing. This very girl was his only child. He had no son or daughter apart from her. [35]When he saw her, he tore his clothes and said, "Oh no, my daughter, you have brought me low, brought me low, you yourself have become one to bring calamity on me. I myself opened my mouth to Yahweh. I am not able to go back [on it]." [36]She said to him, "Father, you opened your mouth to Yahweh. Do to me as it came from your mouth now that Yahweh has brought great redress for you from your enemies, the Ammonites." [37]But she said to her father, "May this thing be done for me. Leave me alone for two months so that I can walk and go down on the mountains and weep for my maidenhood, I and my friends." [38]He said, "Go," and let her go for two months. She and her friends went and wept for her maidenhood on the mountains. [39]At the end of two months she came back to her father, and he fulfilled the promise he had made in connection with her. She had not slept with a man. It became a rule in Israel: [40]each year Israelite girls would go to commemorate the daughter of Jephthah the Gileadite, for four days in the year.

[Chapter 12 tells of the Ephraimites' complaint that Jephthah had not involved them in the battle with Ammon, which leads to fighting between the two groups and the death of 42,000 Ephraimites; the story incidentally tells us where the word shibboleth comes

128

from. It also gives a brief account of three other deliverers, Ibzan, Elon, and Abdon.]

There was a story in the news recently about a man who was reversing his car in his drive and accidentally ran over his child who was playing there. Another story related how a mother who had apparently been drinking and taking drugs drove the wrong way onto a freeway, collided with another car, and killed herself, her children, and some other children who were traveling with her. A few months earlier in the summer there was a story about a man who left his daughter in the car when it was very hot; the child died. Any parent's blood runs cold on hearing such stories because we know it could have been us. Just one apparently simple act of stupidity issues in a tragedy with which a person lives for the rest of his or her life.

It is an extraordinary feature of the story of Jephthah and his daughter that it resolutely refrains from telling us what to think about what went on. It offers no expressions of approval or disapproval with regard to what happened. That is not uncharacteristic of Old Testament stories, as it is not uncharacteristic of Jesus' parables. The price it pays is that people come to very different conclusions about the meaning of the story (or the parable). But refraining from incorporating judgments has advantages. Whereas the Bible sometimes works on us by telling us exactly what to think and what to do, sometimes it works on us by making us think things out for ourselves in light of the kind of things it says elsewhere. That may have a more powerful result.

Here are some questions the story doesn't give the answer to. Was Jephthah's promise a result of God's **spirit** coming on him? Who or what did he think would come out of the house to greet him? Did Jephthah's promise work, causing God to give him victory? Why aren't we told his daughter's name? Is it not monstrous that he blames her for what happens and sees her as bringing calamity on him? Why didn't she resist the implementation of her father's promise? What is she weeping for when she weeps for her maidenhood? Why didn't God intervene as God did when Abraham was about to sacrifice Isaac?

Some of these questions are unanswerable. Here is how I would expect an Israelite to answer some of them in light of the rest of the Old Testament. It's impossible to imagine that God intended Jephthah to sacrifice his daughter, since that contravenes the **Torah**. Presumably Jephthah should have known that; it is ironic that earlier he showed such a close awareness of the Torah's story about how the Israelites came to be in control of the land east of the Jordan. If Israel were working properly, his daughter and her mother and other people in the community would also know that human sacrifice contravenes the Torah, but evidently everyone is following the assumptions of other peoples who did sacrifice their children. The Old Testament in general shows that promises to God tend to backfire. Further, if Jephthah had been better acquainted with the God of the Torah, he would also have known that you can renegotiate an unwise promise. God didn't intervene for the same reason that God doesn't usually intervene when (for instance) fathers abuse or kill their children; God leaves us as human beings to exercise our responsibility and does not go in much for intervening.

In light of the way the story in Judges as a whole is developing, it makes sense to see the story as an aspect of the steady degeneration of Israel's life that will eventually issue in the closing judgment that people in general were doing what was right in their own eyes (Judges 21:25). It is a degeneration that especially affects the position of women in Israel; the present story is sickening, and succeeding stories will be at least as much or more so.

Whereas modern readers can be appalled that the Old Testament tells stories like this, it is actually part of its greatness that it does so. It is not a book that provides us with a way of escaping the reality of how the world is but one that rubs our noses in the reality of how the world is. Its lack of explicit moral judgments ("Jephthah did evil in the eyes of the Lord") focuses our attention on the story itself and the horror of its implications concerning the stupidity of Jephthah and the suffering of a girl. That might have the capacity to make a difference to our lives and to our concern about men like that and our concern for their victims.

Further, the story gives great prominence to the grieving that Jephthah's daughter does with her friends and the way they establish a practice of commemorating her, and that offers scope to other young women to come together, stand together, and reflect in a conscious way on their situation in a world where men can abuse women as Jephthah did and on the way they handle the realities of their position in that world. A friend of mine just went on a women's retreat, and I am inclined to think, "Why do they have to have women's retreats? I don't want to have a men's retreat. What are they talking about that they don't want me there?" (Apparently some men *do* want to go on a men's retreat; I have just been asked to speak at one.) There are doubtless a number of reasons, but the ease with which we as men can silence if not sacrifice women is one of the answers to the question.

JUDGES 13:1–25

Entertaining Angels Unawares

¹The Israelites again did what was unacceptable in Yahweh's eyes, and Yahweh gave them into the hand of the Philistines for forty years. ²There was a certain man from Zorah from the kin group of Dan, whose name was Manoah. His wife was infertile; she had borne no children. ³Yahweh's aide appeared to the woman and said to her, "Right. You are infertile, you have not borne children, but you will get pregnant and bear a son. ⁴So now, do take care not to drink wine or liquor or to eat anything taboo, ⁵because you are going to get pregnant and bear a son, and no razor is to come up onto his head, because the boy will be a person dedicated to God from the womb, and he will begin to deliver Israel from the hand of the Philistines."

[Verses 6–14 relate how the woman tells her husband, who prays that the aide may appear again; he does so, repeating the message.]

¹⁵Manoah said to Yahweh's aide, "May we detain you and prepare a kid goat before you?" ¹⁶Yahweh's aide said to Manoah, "If you detain me, I will not eat of your food, but if you prepare a burnt offering, you may offer it to Yahweh" (because Manoah did not realize it was Yahweh's aide). ¹⁷Manoah said to Yahweh's

131

aide, "What is your name? When your words come about, we will honor you." [18]Yahweh's aide said to him, "Why is it that you ask my name when it is awesome?" [19]Manoah got the kid goat and the grain offering and offered them up on a rock to Yahweh, and he did something awesome while Manoah and his wife were looking. [20]When the flame went up from the altar to the heavens, Yahweh's aide went up in the altar flame while Manoah and his wife were looking. They fell on their faces to the earth. [21]Yahweh's angel did not appear ever again to Manoah and his wife.

Manoah realized that it had been Yahweh's aide. [22]Manoah said to his wife, "We will die, we will die, because we have seen God!" [23]His wife said to him, "If Yahweh wanted to put us to death, he would not have received the burnt offering and the grain offering from our hand and he would not have let us see all these things or just now have told us such a thing as this."

[24]The woman bore a son and called him Samson. The boy grew, and Yahweh blessed him. [25]Yahweh's spirit began to impel him in the camp of Dan, between Zorah and Eshtaol.

Some friends of mine have just become pregnant. I am not accustomed to using that verb in the first-person plural; when I was young, it was only women who got pregnant, but now it is a joint operation. There is a certain appropriateness in this, because the event requires two people. When a couple cannot get pregnant, the problem may lie with the woman, or it may lie with the man, and presumably Israelites realized this. If a wife did not conceive, and her husband took a second wife in the hope that he might have better luck, but then the second wife did not conceive, presumably they put two and two together, even if they didn't talk about it. These friends of mine went through all sorts of tests and established that the problem lay with the woman, and the doctors did some strange things to her about which I don't want to know too much, and now she is four months pregnant. They are a lovely couple, and she is a loving person who will make a marvelous mother, so for all sorts of reasons I am excited, though no doubt nowhere near as excited as the couple and their parents.

Manoah's wife is going to make a marvelous mother. She too has waited and waited and tried and tried, and each month has been disappointed, but now she is going to have a baby. It is she who gives him his name, which would make people think of sunshine (his name is more literally *shimshon* and the Hebrew word for *sun* is *shemesh*). Some people might think of the sun god, but his mother hardly thought that. Another woman I know who waited a long time to have a baby said that when her baby was born, the sun shone out of his eyes as far as she was concerned. I suspect this was Samson's mother's attitude as well.

More significantly, she is going to make a marvelous mother because of her spiritual insight. If Jephthah had not been taught enough about **Yahweh** and Yahweh's ways to know how to relate to Yahweh and how to relate to his daughter (and if she therefore had also not been taught enough about this), then there is no danger of this woman's son not learning enough from her. On the other hand, her husband needs to learn a thing or two. Yahweh's **aide** knew what he was doing in appearing to the wife rather than the husband.

The story stands oddly in the tension between God's vision of husbands and wives having the same status in relation to God, society, and one another and the patriarchal reality in the world whereby men count for more than women. The story never names the wife as it names the husband; she gains her significance in society from the son she bears and the man she is married to (though it would be an exaggeration to say that this reflects a property understanding of marriage). She also defers to her husband in the way she handle's the aide's appearance to her. Maybe she is naturally locked into the patriarchal way of thinking. Certainly Manoah thinks that way. The aide tells his wife how they are to treat the baby, but that is not enough for Manoah. Can he believe that she got it right? He wants to hear it for himself.

Evidently God is not locked into that way of thinking, because it is indeed to her that the aide appears. Admittedly, it is she who is to have the baby, and it is the potential mother who is commonly the recipient of such revelations in the Bible. But when Manoah asks God to send the aide to appear again to tell him directly what he has told his wife, the aide again appears to her but is then willing to hang about while she fetches Manoah.

Neither man nor wife is to be blamed for not realizing that they are meeting a supernatural figure. An aide or an "angel" does not wear wings or a halo. In Old Testament stories, the aide or angel looks like a human being. Only when something extraordinary happens do you realize it was more than that. On the other hand, when the extraordinary thing happens, Manoah's wife again shows that she is the person with spiritual insight, or even just common sense.

The word for someone "dedicated" to God is *nazir*. Numbers 6 lays down some rules for people who want especially to dedicate themselves to God for a period of time; it doesn't say for what purpose they might want to do that. The story of Samson is distinctive because it implies his nazirite vow will be lifelong. It involves abstaining from alcohol and letting his hair grow; the significance of the latter is not obvious, but we know in Western culture that letting your hair grow or shaving it can be a significant cultural statement. It also means being strict about the kind of taboos concerning what you eat that people such as priests had to observe if their priestly ministry was not to be compromised.

A famous verse in Proverbs promises, "Train up a child in the way he should go: and when he is old, he will not depart from it" (Proverbs 22:6 KJV). Like other such promises in Proverbs, this one works most of the time but not all the time. Alas, you can be the best parents in the world but that doesn't guarantee how your son will turn out. The story we shall read about Samson is a story that would have been painful to his parents. In the meantime, the present chapter comes to a beautiful close with its description of the boy growing up and God blessing him and God's **spirit** beginning to set him going on his vocation. The opening verse of the chapter would make us think this means starting to take action that would **deliver** his people from the **Philistines**. He does so, but not in the way we might expect.

JUDGES 14:1–15:20

Honey, We Solved the Riddle

¹Samson went down to Timnah and saw a woman in Timnah among the Philistine women. ²He went up and told his father

and mother, "I saw a woman in Timnah among the Philistine women, so now, get her for me as wife." ³His father and mother said to him, "Isn't there a woman among the women from your kinfolk or among all my people, that you are going to get a wife from the uncircumcised Philistines?" Samson said to his father, "Get that woman for me, because she is the right one in my eyes." ⁴His father and mother did not recognize that it stemmed from Yahweh, because he was seeking an opportunity from the Philistines (at that time the Philistines were ruling over Israel). ⁵Samson and his father and mother went down to Timnah and came to the vineyards at Timnah. And there: a young lion, roaring as it met him. ⁶Yahweh's spirit thrust itself onto him and he tore it apart as one might tear apart a kid; there was nothing in his hand. He didn't tell his father and mother what he had done.

⁷So he went down and spoke to the woman. She was right in Samson's eyes. ⁸He went back some time later to get her, and turned aside to see the remains of the lion. There: a swarm of bees in the lion's carcass, and honey. ⁹He scooped it out into his palms and went along eating it. He went to his father and mother and gave them some and they ate it. He didn't tell them that he had scooped the honey from the lion's carcass. ¹⁰So his father went down to the woman, and Samson made a feast there, because that was what the young men used to do. ¹¹When they saw him, they got thirty companions and they were with him.

[In 14:11–18 Samson challenges them to a riddle contest; the winning party will give the losing party thirty suits. The riddle concerns the incident with the lion: "From the eater there came out something to eat; from a strong one there came out sweetness." Samson's bride persuades him to tell her the riddle, and she tells them, so they win the contest. Samson is infuriated.]

¹⁹Yahweh's spirit thrust itself onto him and he went down to Ashkelon and struck down thirty of its men. He took what was stripped off them and gave the suits to the men who had mastered the riddle. His anger flared and he went up to his father's house, ²⁰and Samson's wife came to belong to his companion, who had been his best man.

[In 15:1–20 Samson thus finds he cannot claim his bride later, and he takes further vengeance on the Philistines by setting fire to their harvest. They respond by killing the girl and her father;

Samson therefore kills some more of them. The Philistines invade Judah looking for him; the Judahites surrender him to them, but he breaks free and kills another thousand.]

Only trivial things went wrong at our wedding. Admittedly, for Ann and me it was a narrow escape. At one stage her father said he would not come; that was the degree to which he disapproved of me. I had long hair, like Samson (being a theologian also means being good at riddles but not confronting lions). But in her most winsome way Ann told him how much she wanted it to be her father who walked up the aisle with her (read, even if you don't come, we will still get married), and he did. The minister forgot Ann's middle name, which was a shame because her parents were very keen to have it included (I think it was her grandmother's name). And I provoked our first marital spat when I shut the coat of her beautiful going-away outfit in the car door in my haste to escape the possible pranks of my friends (Brits are big on pranks at weddings, as people in the United States are not).

The troubles Samson and his bride experienced need have been no more than that, but Samson does not do things by halves and lacks the capacity to shrug his shoulders. Excess is his middle name. After the winsome nature of the story concerning his birth and its background and the summary statements about his growing experience of God's blessing and the effect of God's **spirit** on him, it comes as a shock when the story fast-forwards to the time when he is presumably getting toward the end of his teenage years (people marry young in traditional societies, so it is difficult to imagine him as a full adult and still single, and he sure behaves like a teenager, with lots of energy but not much wisdom).

Politically, the background is similar to that of the Jephthah story, though the protagonists have changed. The Jephthah story concerned clans to the east, for whom Ammon was the problem. For Dan on the west, the **Philistines** are the problem. Whereas people such as Ammon, Moab, and Edom are all related to Israel, and conflicts between them are family quarrels, the Philistines are simply foreigners. They don't even practice circumcision, like any civilized people (circumcision was a rite to which God gave a special significance in Israel, but it is not a distinctively Israelite rite, though applying it in infancy rather than in puberty is unusual). They are from Europe, for goodness' sake. They and other groups from across the Mediterranean collectively known as the "Sea Peoples" were causing trouble through much of the Middle East, and they were among the people who were gaining a foothold in **Canaan** from the west at about the time Israel was becoming a force to be reckoned with in the mountains (so the story talks often about "going down" to Philistia and "going up" to Israelite territory). The unfortunate Danites are thus under pressure from this more sophisticated people. Judges, however, sees this as not a matter of bad luck but as another instance of God's using ordinary political events to chastise people who are inclined to serve other deities.

Samson is the person God plans to use to **deliver** Israel from Philistine control. So the first thing he does is decide to marry a Philistine girl. In traditional societies marriages are usually "arranged," but this does not mean they are arranged by the parents without consulting the young people, and other Old Testament stories make clear that the initiative may come from the couple. The point is that the society recognizes how marriage concerns and affects the whole community; it is not just a private arrangement between two people. So there's nothing very odd in the young Samson's fancying a girl and asking his parents to start setting up an arrangement. It's where he finds her that is troublesome. Again, it's not merely that she is a Philistine. Other Philistines, including some people from the Philistine city of Gath, get honorable mention in the Old Testament story, but the presupposition then is that they have come to acknowledge **Yahweh**, the God of Israel. The slur about the Philistines in general being "uncircumcised" also relates to this. A man can't be within the **covenant** if he is uncircumcised.

Paradoxically, this is something else that God is involved in. Saying that Samson's fancying this Philistine girl came from God doesn't mean it happened against Samson's will. We noted in connection with Judges 3 how the Old Testament is happy to see several levels of explanation in events. Here too there are two levels of significance in what happens. Samson does

137

what he wants to do; God is using that. God wants to end the domination of the Philistines over the Danites and intends to use Samson to that end. God doesn't insist on having honorable people as agents in bringing things about; we have noted that this might mean waiting forever. God uses people with all their human shortcomings. So when God's spirit comes on someone, its concern is with doing something powerful, not immediately with doing something moral, though an event such as Samson's tearing the lion apart does form part of God's moral purpose in putting down the Philistines. The same is true of his striking down the Philistines in Ashkelon. You could say Samson did something wrong, but that can also contribute to the achieving of God's intention with regard to the Philistines.

Yet Samson is behaving in a fashion that denies his vocation. It is a theme running through his story. Investigating the lion's carcass points to it, because being dedicated to God means avoiding contact with dead things; Samson ignores that principle. Here, too, however, God simply makes this contribute to the fulfilling of that purpose. God will use Samson whether he does the right thing or the wrong thing.

JUDGES 16:1–21

Love Actually

¹Samson went to Gaza and saw there a prostitute and slept with her. ²The Gazites were told, "Samson has come here." They gathered around and lay in wait for him all night at the city gate. They were still all night, saying, "When morning dawns, we will kill him." ³Samson lay in bed until midnight, got up at midnight, seized the doors of the city gate and the two gateposts, pulled them out with the bar, put them on his shoulders, and took them up to the top of the mountain facing Hebron.

⁴After that he loved a woman in the Sorek Wash named Delilah. ⁵The rulers of the Philistines went up to her and said to her, "Charm him and see where is his great strength and how we can overcome him and bind him so as to subdue him. We ourselves will give you eleven hundred silver [shekels] each." ⁶So Delilah said to Samson, "Will you tell me where is your great strength and how you could be bound so as to subdue you?"

[In verses 7–14 Samson first gives her three false answers.]

[15]Then she said to him, "How can you say you love me when your soul is not with me? These three times you have deceived me and not told me where is your great strength." [16]Because she pressed him with her words all the time and begged him, and his spirit was tired to death, [17]he told her everything in his soul. He said to her, "No razor has come up on my head, because I have been dedicated to God from my mother's womb. If my hair were cut, my strength would leave me and I would be weak. I would be like any man." [18]Delilah saw that he had told her everything, and sent and summoned the rulers of the Philistines, saying, "Come up once more, because he has told me everything." The rulers of the Philistines came up to her and brought up the money with them. [19]She got him to go to sleep on her lap, and summoned a man and had him cut off the seven braids on his head, and began to afflict him; his strength left him. [20]She said, "The Philistines are upon you, Samson!" He woke up from his sleep and said, "I will go out as at other times and shake myself." He did not realize that Yahweh had left him. [21]The Philistines seized him and gouged out his eyes. They took him down to Gaza and bound him in bronze shackles, and he became someone grinding grain in the prison.

After the incident a few weeks ago when a man on a plane bound for Detroit tried to blow up himself and the plane as an act of terrorism against the United States and the Western world in general, an extraordinary piece of background to the event emerged. A few months before, his father (a respected leader in his country) had contacted the U.S. embassy and security agencies in his country to talk to them about his son's "extreme religious views" and about his fear that his son was "planning something." A reporter commented, "I almost feel sorry for the Dad." My reaction is, "Almost?" What must the father have felt about the course his son's life had taken? What must his mother have felt? And what must they have felt when the news broke of their son's action and the narrow averting of a terrible calamity?

From a woman's perspective, the entire story of Samson makes gloomy reading. First there was the woman who bore him, who knew God's vision for his life, made her commitment to God and to him, but then had to watch him make a mess of his entire life even while being unwittingly the means of God's will being put into effect. It must have been evident to her that he was never happy, and I imagine her grieving each day and each night about his fate.

Second, there was the wife. I have noted that there is no presumption that she became committed to Samson against her will, and he was evidently a hunk whom many a girl would regard as quite a prize. But the story says nothing of this. She is simply a victim, simply the object of verbs. Samson sees her, asks his parents to get her, speaks to her, and goes to get her. Her countrymen then lean on her to discover the answer to the riddle, which means she effectively loses Samson and is married off to someone else. Samson is not allowed to see her, which leads to another conflict that results in her death. She is even God's victim as God looks for a way of causing trouble to the **Philistines**.

Third, there is the prostitute. We noted in connection with Rahab in Joshua 2 that what commonly drives women into the sex trade are circumstances that mean the only way they can make a living is to sell themselves to satisfy the sexual desires of men, and it is reasonable to reckon that this is what makes this woman available to Samson.

None of these women has a name. At least Delilah has a name. And at least Samson falls in love with her. Does she love him? We are not told. Her perspective is again irrelevant. What matters is the role she is forced to play; she, too, becomes a victim of her fellow countrymen, and as a result he becomes her victim and theirs. His hair is the last symbol of his promise to be someone dedicated to God. The lion and honey incident meant his betraying the ban on contact with anything taboo; the great banquet in chapter 14 will surely have meant his betraying the ban on alcohol; his relationship with a Philistine woman means he loses his long hair, the permanent visible symbol of his dedication.

With some irony, Samson thus ends up as the fifth woman in the story, because he ends up grinding grain. There was nothing humiliating in itself about grinding grain; it was a task like plowing or sewing that always needed doing in Israel. It was an honorable task. But Israel had conventional ways of dividing up tasks in the family: the men plowed while the women ground grain. There isn't much a blind man's captors can make him do. What they make him do is the work of a woman.

On more than one occasion he has done something extraordinary, and it has seemed that he could do so simply because he was a hunk; he was Rambo. But three times he has done something extraordinary because "**Yahweh's spirit** thrust itself on him," and it seems a fair guess that the earlier blanket statement about Yahweh's spirit beginning to impel him (13:25) implies that all his extraordinary achievements reflected that dynamic. So was he not a hunk after all? Was he a little guy who did extraordinary things? Maybe so, but I am more inclined to assume that his "natural" abilities and God's supernatural compulsion worked together. Either way, surrendering the symbol of his commitment to God meant losing God's involvement with him.

JUDGES 16:22–31

But Samson's Hair Began to Grow Again

[22]Samson's hair began to grow when it had been cut off. [23]Now the rulers of the Philistines assembled for the offering of a great sacrifice to their god Dagon and for festivity. They said, "Our god gave our enemy, Samson, into our hand." [24]When the people saw him, they praised their god, because (they said), "Our god gave our enemy into our hand, the one who wasted our country and who multiplied our slain." [25]In accordance with what was good in their thinking, they said, "Summon Samson. He must entertain us." So they summoned Samson from the prison house and he entertained them.

They stood him between the pillars, [26]and Samson said to the boy who was holding him by the hand, "Let go of me and let me feel the pillars that the house depends on, so I can lean on them." [27]The house was full of men and women. All the rulers of the Philistines were there, and on the roof were some three thousand men and women watching Samson entertain. [28]Samson called to Yahweh: "My Lord Yahweh, will you be mindful of me? Will you give me strength just this once, God, so that

141

I may get redress from the Philistines, one redress for my two eyes?" ²⁹Samson grasped the two middle pillars that the house depended on and leaned on them, one with his right hand and one with his left. ³⁰Samson said, "I myself can die with the Philistines," and pushed with all his might. The house fell on the rulers and on all the people in it. The people whom he caused to die when he died were more than he caused to die when he lived. ³¹His brothers and all his father's household came down, lifted him, and took him up and buried him between Zorah and Eshtaol in the tomb of his father Manoah. He had led Israel for twenty years.

The first time I went to Israel, I took part in an exciting archaeological dig. Just next to a tennis club in the big modern city of Tel Aviv on the Mediterranean, where people started playing at 6:00 a.m. because it would be too hot to play by lunchtime, is another tell, Tel Qasile. Like the tell of Jericho but on a much smaller scale, the tell is an artificial hill accidentally constructed out of the remains of a succession of cities built one on top of another (the name Tel Aviv, "Hill of Spring," thus suggests a combination of the old and the new). As with Jericho, we sought to discover the history of the city by digging down (with a trowel, not an earthmover) through the layers of the tell as through the layers of a cake, mapping carefully where we found anything but mud. We started doing this, too, at 6:00 a.m. because it would be too hot to dig by lunchtime. Tel Aviv is in the area originally allocated to the clan called Dan; that is the name of the local bus company. In Samson's day it was therefore part of the area occupied by the **Philistines**, and Tel Qasile was a Philistine city. One of the great excitements of the year I dug there was the discovery of its sanctuary. It was not a large or impressive building, but an exciting feature of it was the discovery that its roof was supported by two central pillars (the pillars themselves would be wooden and would have rotted; what we actually found were their stone bases). A big guy could stand and brace himself against them. If he were able to bring them down, he would bring the temple down. I could stand in the middle of this sanctuary and imagine the climax of the Samson story.

Reading the exotic, larger-than-life, daredevil stories about Samson makes you wonder whether they really happened. I don't think there is any way to decide whether they did. On one hand, I assume God would have no trouble making it possible for Samson to undertake these exploits. On the other, they are told more like Wild West stories than like sober history, and I know God likes fictional stories as well as factual ones. My working assumption in this regard applies to most Old Testament stories. On one hand, these stories read as though they are indeed meant to entertain as well as to instruct. They look larger than life. On the other hand, when people tell stories like them, I think it more likely that they start from some events that really happened and from someone who really did some extraordinary things than that they are simply pieces of fiction. They are more like stories about Robin Hood or Calamity Jane than like historical studies of Abraham Lincoln or Queen Victoria; that is, they are not simply factual history. They are also more like stories about Robin Hood or Calamity Jane than stories about Rambo or Lois Lane; that is, they are not simply fiction.

Standing in the Philistine sanctuary at Tel Qasile encouraged me in that assessment. Here was just the kind of architectural device that would have made it possible for someone like Samson to bring the house down (is this the origin of that phrase?). It's a distinctively Philistine way of constructing a building; it's not the way Israelites built sanctuaries. It provides circumstantial evidence that the story reflects an actual event. Yet the size of this sanctuary was nothing like the size you would need to get the whole population of Gaza inside or on the roof (which would surely collapse long before Samson tried to bring it down).

So I imagine that behind the stories is a guy who indeed did some extraordinary things and did get into messes and did take on the Philistines, and a mother and some women who were the victims of the patriarchal ways of their culture; but there is no way to get to "the real facts" behind the stories. That is OK, because what their authors apparently wanted us to have were the stories with their entertainment value and their human interest value, and they were what God was happy for us to have as part of the Bible, what the Jewish community who let the Bible accumulate took on, and what the Christian church took on in reaffirming the Jewish community's decision. The stories' excitement and their sadness invite our reflection on the way men (and women) can betray their vocations and on the way women (and men) can be the victims of cultural expectations and assumptions, and they ask us to look for the way we, in our very different contexts, might suffer from the same forces.

Samson's hair began to grow again. In itself that would mean nothing, but the story knows that there is a link between the physical and the spiritual, and it knows that Samson's hair's growing could be read as a sign that his vow as a dedicated person is not done. This doesn't need to imply that Samson has got his act together spiritually. We know already that God's using Samson doesn't depend on his having done so. Maybe more significant is the way the Philistines gave credit for **delivering** Samson into their power to their top god, Dagon (their equivalent to the **Master**, Baal). **Yahweh** sometimes has a hard time being tolerant when sidelined like that and has a hard time just looking on when a servant like Samson is treated the way he is. The fact that Samson deserves it is neither here nor there; he is still Yahweh's servant, and Yahweh is humiliated through his servant's humiliation.

Maybe Samson actually has moved on an inch or two. In Dagon's sanctuary, Samson is praying to Yahweh. You might think it's not much of a prayer, but then God isn't always too concerned about how proper our prayers are. Judges doesn't even actually say that God answered his prayer; you could wonder if he brought the sanctuary down by his own strength. But I would have thought that the story's comment on how many Philistines he disposed of at the cost of his own life implied that he was at this last moment fulfilling his vocation to deliver Israel from the Philistines.

His story comes to a peaceful end, the kind of peaceful end that anyone in the Old Testament looks for. His family collect his body and take him back home, back to Israelite territory, back to his own town, back to where the family tomb is, back to join his father and the rest of his family there, to rest in peace.

He appears once more in Scripture, in the list of the heroes of faith in Hebrews 11, where the writer expresses regret at not having time to tell of people such as David and Samuel—and Samson (not to say Gideon, Barak, and Jephthah). That always excites me, because if there is room for Samson in the New Testament's list of the heroes of faith, there is surely room for me.

JUDGES 17:1–13

They All Did What Was Right in Their Own Eyes

¹There was a man from the mountains of Ephraim whose name was Micah. ²He said to his mother, "The eleven hundred silver [shekels] that were taken from you and you swore, and also said it in my hearing: well, the silver is with me. I am the one who took it." His mother said, "May my son be blessed by Yahweh." ³He gave the eleven hundred silver [shekels] back to his mother, and his mother said, "I hereby definitively consecrate the silver to Yahweh from my hand to my son, to make a statue and a cast image. So now I give it back to you." ⁴Thus he gave the silver back to his mother, and she took two hundred silver [shekels] and gave it to a smith. He made a statue and a cast image, and it was in Micah's house. ⁵The man Micah had a house of God and had made an ephod and effigies and installed one of his sons, who became a priest for him. ⁶In those days there was no king in Israel. Everyone did what was right in his or her own eyes.

⁷There was a young man from Bethlehem in Judah, from the clan of Judah. He was a Levite and had been residing there, ⁸but the man went from the city of Bethlehem to reside wherever he could find [a place] and came to the mountain country of Ephraim as far as the house of Micah, as he made his way. ⁹Micah said to him, "Where do you come from?" The Levite said to him, "I am from Bethlehem in Judah but I am traveling in order to reside wherever I can find [a place]." ¹⁰Micah said to him, "Stay with me. You will be a father and a priest to me. I will give you ten silver [shekels] a year, a set of clothes, and your living." So the Levite went. ¹¹The Levite agreed to stay with the man; the young man became to him like one of his sons. ¹²So Micah installed the Levite, and the young man became a priest for him. He was in Micah's household. ¹³Micah said, "Now I

> know that Yahweh will be good to me, because the Levite has become priest for me."

I am an Episcopalian/Anglican priest, but I don't really believe in priesthood. One of the first things God pointed out at Sinai was that the whole people of God is a priesthood (see Exodus 19), and the New Testament reaffirmed the principle (see 1 Peter 2). God doesn't want some clique claiming to control everybody else's access to God. The trouble is, this arrangement doesn't work. Within the church that was designed to be a priesthood, congregations were already going off the rails within New Testament times and needing someone to exercise some authority to get them back on track. Soon after New Testament times the church was inventing the "monarchical episcopate," the idea that one "bishop" (like a senior pastor or rector) had the key leadership position in a congregation. The trouble is, this only relocates the problem. What if senior pastors go off the rails, as they often do?

The last five chapters of Judges are increasingly troublesome; it is tempting to skip them and move onto the more Hollywood-like story of Ruth. They rub our noses in the reality of how things are within the people of God and in the world. Four times they comment that in those days there was no king in Israel, and at the beginning and end they add that everyone was (thus) doing what was right in his or her own eyes. Israel needs kings to get a grip on the collapse of religion, morality, and social order in Israel. Yet that's just one side to Judges' attitude to kings. The book has noted how a mixed-up guy like Gideon on a good day refuses to be king, and only an irresponsible fool like Abimelek wants to be. The later story of the kings will make clear that they are both a blessing and a curse, like pastors. Judges gives a mixed message about kings. That's not a weakness. There's no way the question it raises can be answered. Kingship just is ambiguous.

Micah, his mother, and the Levite in this story are a bit mixed up, like Gideon. First there is the fact that Micah had stolen all that wealth from his mother. It looks as if his father is dead, and maybe thus Micah is the eldest son and is head of the family and in charge of its assets, so this would facilitate

146

his action. Perhaps he had a rationalization: "It will be better if I make sure Mother doesn't do something silly with that silver, like making an image or something." His mother scared him into coming clean by means of a curse. Was the curse like one of Paul's curses? Was it an expression of faith? Did it bring Micah to his senses and to repentance? Or was her curse an expression of superstitious belief in the power of such words, something that has nothing much to do with God? Was Micah's response the calculated reaction of someone who knows it will be unwise not to come clean? Does he share her suspicious belief in the power of a curse? What should we make of her consequent prayer that Yahweh may bless her son?

Micah's mother wants to give the eleven hundred shekels to God, as the Israelites gave their silver to God in order to make the rich wilderness dwelling for God, as described in Exodus 25–31. But she does indeed want to use it to make an image or two (it's difficult to be sure whether the story is talking about one image overlaid with silver or two separate images, and also why the amount changes from eleven hundred to two hundred). Perhaps her promise to do so was bound up with her curse ("Lord, if you get the silver returned to me, I will make an image with it"—or "with part of it"). She is not someone who worships other gods, like some people we could mention. She and her husband had named their son "Micah," which means "Who is like Yahweh?" But worshiping Yahweh by means of an image is not much of an improvement on worshiping other gods. It implies thinking about Yahweh in just the way other people think about their gods, and in effect that means having turned Yahweh into another god.

It may also be surprising to find that Micah has a sanctuary in his house, though there is some logic to it. The Israelite sanctuary will be located somewhere in the midst of the clans, but by definition it's a long way away from where most people live. Maybe people make pilgrimage there from time to time, as the **Torah** says. But how are they to relate to God for the rest of the year? It doesn't seem inherently objectionable to have a sanctuary in the village or in the homestead. Micah's "house" or "household" will be the home of a large extended family, as is again the case in the Gideon story; it would involve a number of actual "houses." Further, it makes sense for Levites to be spread around the country as sanctuaries are. The Levites are experts in matters relating to God and worship and the way God expects people to live. Micah's expectation that God will be good to him when he has a Levite living in his house is not so far off the mark; he should be in a better position to see that the life of the household is lived according to God's expectations. Yet it becomes apparent that the Levite colludes with the assumptions of Micah and his mother about images and the like.

The Torah makes clear that Levites are in a vulnerable position. They have no land and thus cannot grow their own food, so they are dependent on other people's providing for them (like orphans and widows, with whom the Torah brackets them) or on getting a permanent post somewhere. The word for "residing" is the Torah's word for a resident alien, any foreigner or any Israelite not living on his own land for some reason. They are groups in that same vulnerable position, and the use of the word underscores the vulnerability of a Levite's circumstances. He must have thought he had won the lottery when Micah offered him a permanent position with his keep and a salary. There is a sense in which he will be a father to the household, because he will give it a father's guidance (is it a coincidence that Micah's actual father is perhaps dead?). In another sense, Micah is his father; Micah is going to treat him like a member of the family in the way he provides for him, not treat him like an employee.

It is this that raises the problem about supervision, about people doing what seems appropriate and natural to them; Micah and his mother are doing that, all right. To the image or images Micah adds an ephod (perhaps a robe for the image), which was the way Gideon got Israel into trouble (Judges 8). And he adds "effigies." A plausible theory about these is that they were images of family members who had passed, a little like our family photographs, whom living members of the family would seek to consult on the assumption that they might know things (for instance, about the future) that their relatives who were still alive might not know. It's another example of the practices that other peoples went in for but that were forbidden to Israel, not because they didn't work but because Israel was in a position to relate directly to God and needed to be satisfied with what God deigned to tell it.

JUDGES 18:1–31

Desperate Dan

¹In those days there was no king in Israel. In those days the clan of Dan was seeking a possession for themselves to live in, because until that day there had not fallen to them any possession among the clans of Israel. ²The Danites sent five men from their kin group, able men, from Zorah and Eshtaol, to investigate the country and explore it. So they said to them, "Go and explore the country." They came to the mountains of Ephraim, as far as Micah's house, and spent the night there. ³When they were near Micah's house and recognized the speech of the young Levite, they turned there and said to him, "Who brought you here? What are you doing in this place? What are you here for?" ⁴He said to them, "Micah did thus and so for me. He hired me, and I became priest for him." ⁵They said to him, "Will you inquire of God for us so we can know if the journey on which we are going will be successful?" ⁶The priest said to them, "Go; do well. The journey on which you are going is under Yahweh's eye."

[Verses 7–16 tell of how the men find a plausible place to settle, then return home for six hundred men by way of reinforcements, and once more arrive at Micah's house.]

¹⁷The five men who went to investigate the country went up, and when they came there, they took the statue, the ephod, the effigies, and the cast image. The priest was standing at the gate entrance, as were the six hundred men equipped with weapons of war. ¹⁸When these men came to Micah's house and took the statue, the ephod, the effigies, and the cast image, the priest said to them, "What are you doing?" ¹⁹They said to him, "Quiet. Hold your tongue. Come with us and be a father and a priest for us. Is it better for you to be a priest for the household of one man or to be a priest for a clan, a kin group in Israel?"

[Verses 20–29 relate how, after they leave, Micah pursues them; they point out that there are more of them than there are of him.

They continue north, dispose of the unsuspecting and vulnerable people of Laish, rebuild that city, and settle there.]

[30]The Danites set up the statue for themselves, and Jonathan son of Gershom son of Moses and his sons were priests for the clan of Dan until the time of the exile of the country. [31]They established for themselves the statue Micah had made, all the time that the house of God was at Shiloh.

When we were in the midst of agreeing to come to California for me to teach here, one of our students at my seminary in England sensed God saying to her one day in chapel, "Tell John, 'Judges 18:6.'" "I don't know what it says," she replied. "Never mind," God said, "Just tell John 'Judges 18:6.'" So she did. "That's the story of the Levite and his concubine, isn't it?" I said to her. Actually that's Judges 19. We looked up Judges 18 and found the verse that appears in the translation above. It came as a wondrous confirmation that I could take the risk of bringing my disabled wife to this strange setting without knowing how a number of aspects of life would work out. I still have the little scrap of paper on which the student wrote down that Bible reference.

The reassurance God gave me through that text has virtually nothing to do with the text's inherent meaning. God likes to do that with texts, and who am I to argue? In its original context, the text is an element in another ambiguous story, or rather in the continuation of the ambiguous story that began in chapter 17. As with many Old Testament stories, you will gain something through reading it from the end backward. One aspect of its significance for later Israel is that it explains how the Danites came to be in the far north of Israel. We have noted in connection with the Samson story that the land allocated to Dan was in the southwest, in the area of modern Tel Aviv, not so far from Bethlehem (hence perhaps their recognizing the Levite's accent). But this was territory that the more sophisticated **Philistines** had come to occupy. The Danites were never going to be able to settle there.

It is as a result of these dynamics that Dan comes to be in the far north of Israel. When the Old Testament talks about the length and breadth of the promised land, it sees the country as extending "from Dan to Beersheba." Even today Dan is right on the border of Israel, Lebanon, and some territory belonging to Syria that Israel occupied in 1967. You can thus see three countries when you stand on the tell at Dan, surrounded by lush greenery as it is watered by magnificent flowing streams that emerge from Mount Hermon, visible to the northeast. As you walk over the tell, you keep coming across trenches dug by Israeli soldiers defending the area in the years before the 1967 war. It was the destructive nature of this necessary trench digging that stimulated archaeological investigation of the tell. Israeli archaeologist Avraham Biran dug there for over thirty years. He explained that when people asked him when he was going to stop, he would reply with an old Jewish story of a guy desperately fighting with a bear. His friends keep yelling at him to let go of the bear. "I want to," he says, "but the bear won't let me go." It is not surprising that this impressive bear would not let Biran go.

As well as being a geographical and political marker, Dan was of huge religious significance. While it paired with Beersheba geographically, it paired with Bethel religiously. As the Old Testament tells the story, when the nation of Israel split into two after Solomon's time, and the northern kingdom of **Ephraim** cut itself off from the temple at Jerusalem in **Judah**, King Jeroboam set up two alternative sanctuaries, at Bethel in the south of Ephraim and at Dan in the north, and set up images there. Deep in his heart, Biran says, he kept hoping that they might find the "gold calf" that was set up at Dan.

The story ends with a reference to the country going into **exile**, when **Assyria** terminated Ephraim's political independence and transported many of its people. When people subsequently listened to this story, it resonated with that history. One can imagine people saying, "Well, given the origin of the city of Dan, it's not surprising what happened to it." People might sympathize with the Danites for not being able to settle in the area allocated to them, but really! The fact that the Old Testament is not usually sympathetic to the former inhabitants of their country highlights the sympathy this story shows for the poor unsuspecting people of Laish. There they are, getting on with their lives peaceably, minding their own business, and—boom—they have suddenly been overwhelmed by Desperate Dan, which on the way has simply stolen the wherewithal to set up a sanctuary and has made a priest an offer he can't refuse.

Then at the end it transpires that the unnamed priest who tends the image(s) at Micah's house and then at Dan is actually a descendant of Moses, who is presumably turning in his grave. (In horror and disbelief the mainstream Hebrew text of the Bible changes the name of Gershom's ancestor from Moses to Manasseh, which is only one letter different in Hebrew, but the original reference to Moses is preserved in some versions of the story. And there was a sense in which Gershom was a son of Manasseh—the king Manasseh who will later lead Judah in apostasy.)

"Go; do well," Gershom had told them, and they did. "The journey on which you are going is under **Yahweh's** eye," he went on. In some sense no doubt he was right, but did Yahweh really rejoice in what they did and in how they did it? "God has **delivered** the country into our hand," the five spies reported when they went back to Zorah and Eshtaol. In some sense they were right, but did God really rejoice in what they did and in how they did it? Yet once again God is complicit in the results of their action, with its unprovoked violence. Once again, this all shows the kind of thing that happens when there is no king in Israel (verse 1).

JUDGES 19:1–30

The Story Reaches Its Lowest Point (I)

[1]In those days, when there was no king in Israel, a certain Levite residing in the remote parts of the mountains of Ephraim married a woman as a secondary wife for himself from Bethlehem in Judah, [2]but his wife was unfaithful to him and went from him to her father's household in Bethlehem in Judah. She was there for a full four months. [3]So her husband set off and went after her to win her over and get her to come back. His boy and a pair of donkeys were with him. She let him come into her father's house, and when the girl's father saw him, he was glad to meet him. [4]His father-in-law, the girl's father, prevailed

over him, and he stayed with him for three days. They ate and drank and spent the night there.

[Verses 5–22a relate how eventually they set off for home late on the fourth day and reach Gibeah at nightfall, where a man offers them somewhere to sleep for the night.]

22bThen men from the city, worthless men, surrounded the house, pounding on the door. They said to the man who was the owner of the house, an old man, "Bring out the man who came to your house so we can have sex with him." 23The man who was the owner of the house went out to them and said to them, "No, brothers, don't do wrong, will you, after this man has come to my house. Do not commit this outrage. 24Here is my teenage daughter, and his wife. Let me bring them out to you. Use them. Do to them whatever is good in your eyes. But to this man you will not do this thing that is an outrage." 25But the men would not listen to him. So [the Levite] seized his wife and made her go outside to them. They had sex with her and abused her all night until morning, and let her go as dawn broke. 26So the woman came back toward morning and fell down at the entrance of the man's house where her master was, until daylight. 27When her master got up in the morning, he opened the doors of the house and went out to go on his journey. There was the woman who was his secondary wife, fallen at the entrance of the house, her hands on the threshold. 28He said to her, "Get up; let's go." There was no answer, so he put her on the donkey. The man set off and went to his place. 29When he reached home he got a knife and took hold of his wife and cut her up limb by limb into twelve parts and sent her through all Israel's territory. 30Everyone who saw it said, "Such a thing has not happened or been seen from the day the Israelites came out of Egypt until this day. Apply yourself to this. Take counsel. Speak."

One of the Oscar contenders at the time I write is the movie *Precious*, the story of a teenager whose life is characterized by systematic abuse in the context of her family, including rape and incest on the part of her father and physical and emotional abuse by her angry mother. It's a movie that forces people to face hideous truths about what some people's lives can be like.

Although made in Hollywood, in terms of genre it's not really a Hollywood movie. While it contains glimmers of hope, it's more about survival than about triumph. It doesn't undo the horrific nature of its story by having Precious emerge triumphant against all the odds of her background and experience. In this sense it's not a "feel good" movie, and reviewers commented that therefore it might not work at the box office or in the Oscars race (though it did win an Oscar). We don't go to the movies to have our faces rubbed in reality. We get that outside the theater. We go there to escape reality.

We go to the Bible for the same reasons, and therefore we don't like the kind of story that Judges 19 tells. Yesterday I read a memoir by a woman whose mother had been horribly murdered when she was a child. The woman needed eventually to discover the real story about what had happened to her mother. "The truth, no matter how ugly, was necessary," she said. She had to know the truth about her mother because that was part of the truth about herself.

Why do we need to know the truth about the Levite's nameless wife? Some of the reasons are practical. The story begins with that mantra "There was no king in Israel." The mantra implies that it was the case in Israel that having some governmental authority did lessen the prevalence of the social and moral chaos the story describes. There would be at least two ways in which this was so. One is that the kings had responsibility for knowing the **Torah** and for seeing that the people knew it. The Old Testament portrays them sending teaching teams around the country to see that people know the Torah. Their other responsibility is to take action to see that the vulnerable are protected, the weak are supported, the afflicted are **delivered** from their oppressors, and the oppressors themselves are put down (see Psalm 72). It is a magnificent vision of government as having as its primary responsibilities be teaching and protecting.

In a social context like that of ancient Israel, however, there is little scope for "big government." Local communities are necessarily much more self-sufficient and responsible for themselves than is the case in the urbanized West. So the story holds up a mirror to cities and villages and challenges them to see their potential for the kind of abuse the story describes, and it reminds individuals and families of the way communities can develop a demonic corporate personality. Individuals and families need to be wary of that.

The story reminds men of their capacity to act in the way the story describes. After what happened, the Levite's father-in-law, the Levite's host, and the Levite himself were in a position to say, "If only I hadn't acted the way I did. If only I had seen this coming." Her father would perhaps in any case not be keen to have her back; it was odd (not to say socially unacceptable) to have unmarried daughters staying at home, and even more to have a rebellious daughter returning home. The Levite would surely be less willing to stay on just for one more drink. The woman was his **secondary wife.** Did he want her back because he had a "first-class" wife who resented not having her household assistance? The word used to describe him in verses 26 and 27 is significant. When it refers to "his wife" or "her husband," the Old Testament usually uses the ordinary words for "his woman" and "her man" ("Bess, you is my woman now"). These could suggest a mutual, egalitarian commitment. The Hebrew words that specifically denote husbands and wives literally describe the husband as master or owner and the wife as someone owned, and the Old Testament rarely uses these terms, but one of them appears in verses 26–27. It is the same word that is used to describe his relationship with "his boy," his servant.

The story also reminds women of men's capacity to behave the way these men did. The Old Testament provides women with role models of women who were not willing to work within the patriarchal assumptions of their society; Joshua and Judges have told us of some of them (Zelophehad's daughters, Achsah, Deborah, and Jael). Maybe the Levite's wife's willingness to walk out of the door at the beginning of the story (which is what her "unfaithfulness" refers to) indicates that she was that kind of woman; maybe being this man's secondary wife was worse than having to stay in her parents' household or going back there. It would add to this woman's suffering if we were to blame the victim for what subsequently happens to her, but it might take a tiny bit off the edge of it if she inspires other women to refuse to be pushed out of the door.

155

You could gain all that from stories like *Precious*. In this sense, we don't need the Bible to tell us those stories. What does the Bible add to what we can learn from the movies and from our own experience? What it adds derives from another aspect of the significance of its mantra. This story is part of a wider story, and even the book of Judges does not stand alone. It is part of a story that goes back to Genesis and forward into Samuel and Kings. It is thus part of the broader story of God's creating the world and God's involvement with Israel, an involvement that is committed to achieving God's purpose to bring into being a good world. If we leave God out, we have no way of knowing whether the horror of the story of *Precious* or the Levite's wife is the ultimate truth. Humanity is left to its own devices to see that this is not so; and who knows whether we will be up to that challenge? But Judges leaves God in and knows that this woman's story was not and will not be the end of the human story, Israel's story, or the story of women.

JUDGES 20:1–48

The Story Reaches Its Lowest Point (II)

[1]All the Israelites went forth and the community assembled as one person, from Dan to Beersheba and from Gilead, before Yahweh at Mizpah. [2]The leaders of the entire people, all the clans of Israel, presented themselves as the assembly of God's company, 400,000 men on foot, bearing the sword. [3]The Benjaminites heard that the Israelites had come up to Mizpah. The Israelites said, "Explain how this evil thing happened."

[Verses 4–7 relate how the Levite does so and challenges the Israelites to do something about it.]

[8]All the company arose as one man, saying, "Not one of us will go to his tent or return home. [9]This is what we will now do to Gibeah, against it, by lot. [10]We will get ten men per hundred for all the clans of Israel, a hundred per thousand, a thousand per ten thousand, to get provisions for the company in [its] taking action by going to Geba in Benjamin in accordance with all the outrage it has committed in Israel." [11]So all the Israelites gathered against the city, united as one man. [12]The Israelite clans

sent men through all the clans of Benjamin, saying, "What is this evil thing that happened among you? [13]Now give us the worthless men in Gibeah. We will put them to death and consume the evil from Israel." But the Benjaminites would not listen to the words of their brother Israelites.

[Verses 14–34a relate how Benjamin and the other clans prepare for battle. The Israelites seek God's guidance for the battle but suffer a reversal. Then the same thing happens again. It seems to be happening once more, but the Israelites set an ambush for the Benjaminites.]

[34b]They did not realize that disaster was falling on them [35]when Yahweh overpowered Benjamin before Israel. That day the Israelites slew 25,100 men in Benjamin, all men who bore a sword. [36a]The Benjaminites saw that they were overpowered.

[Verses 36b–48 describe how the Israelites pursue the rest of the Benjaminite forces and slaughter all of them except for six hundred who escape, and also kill the noncombatant Benjaminites and destroy their towns.]

For some years now there has been ongoing tension between Russia and Georgia. Sometimes it seems open to being characterized as a little comical; Russia banned the import of Georgian wine on the grounds that it did not meet proper standards, and Georgians said that Russians had no insight about wine anyway. But sometimes it threatened to escalate into military conflict, and this then interestingly caused consternation among Orthodox Christians in the two countries because it opened up the possibility of their fighting each other, which had never previously been a prospect. Christians in the rest of the world, of course, have not usually been troubled about fighting one another; their national citizenship took priority over their oneness in Christ. A "Modest Proposal for Peace" made by the Mennonite Central Committee suggested that the Christians of the world agree that they will not kill one another. Such an agreement would have substantially reduced killing in war in the twentieth century. Surely our oneness in the body of Christ makes it impossible that we should kill one another?

It also seems impossible to conceive of the Israelite clans making war on one another, yet that is what they are reduced to doing. If the story of the Levite and his wife is exceedingly troublesome in some ways, the story of what happens next is troublesome in other ways. The mantra about the consequences of having no king continues to hang over the chapter.

The story illustrates how easily one thing leads to another. Are the Israelites simply to ignore the horror of what the men of Gibeah did to the Levite's wife? Are they to send envoys to Gibeah and protest? If these envoys were lucky, they would merely be humiliated like the envoys David will later send to Ammon (see 2 Samuel 10); quite likely they would mysteriously never return. So the Israelites act with carrot and stick. The army demands that the Benjaminites surrender the guilty men. If they refuse to do so, they are associating themselves with their action and share in their guilt. But one wrong done to one person has now become the reason for all-out civil war. The men of Gibeah, like Achan near the beginning of Joshua, have behaved more the way the **Torah** portrays the **Canaanites** as behaving and are thus deserving to lose their land. They deserve to be treated like the Canaanites, as Achan was. That is exactly what happens. Yet what about the way the Torah limits punishment to an eye for an eye and a life for a life? It is a poetic expression, like Jesus' talk about cutting off your hand if it offends you, but it raises the question of whether the kind of punishment the Israelites go in for is way out of line.

When the Benjaminites decline to turn in the guilty men, surely God will support the other clans in imposing justice on them. It certainly seems as if God is doing so; when they go to the sanctuary to ask for God's guidance about how to undertake the battle, God gives them guidance. So what is God doing in giving them guidance and then not making things work out in accordance with it? Did they not follow God's guidance with enough precision? If this was the problem, one would expect God to point it out to them when they protest and/or one would expect the story to make it clear to us.

Instead, when they come to weep before God and ask God again, why is God once more offering them guidance that will lead to their defeat? Is it because they have been asking the wrong question in presupposing they should make war on Benjamin? And/or is the civil war and the misleading guidance all part of God's judgment on the people as a whole, who have no reason to be acting as they are and who are not so much better than Benjamin? This would be like Jesus' acting to make people morally and spiritually blind as an act of judgment on them (Mark 4). The story offers no answers to these questions. It at least offers us the strange comfort of portraying Israel as living with the same enigmas with which we live when sometimes we do our best to discover God's will and fit in with it and then everything goes wrong, or when we do our best to discover God's will and fit in with it and then discover that God has a quite different agenda to pursue. Yet as with the story of the Levite's wife, we again have to remind ourselves that this is not the end of the story of God's working a purpose out in Israel and in the world.

JUDGES 21:1–25

How Not to Save the Situation

¹Now the Israelites had sworn at Mizpah, "None of us will give his daughter to Benjamin as a wife." ²The people came to Bethel and sat there before God until evening. They lifted up their voices and wept much and loudly. ³They said, "Why, Yahweh God of Israel, has this happened in Israel, that one clan is missing today from Israel?" ⁴The next day the people got up early and built an altar there, and sacrificed burnt offerings and fellowship offerings. ⁵The Israelites said, "Who is there from all the clans of Israel that did not come up to Yahweh in the assembly?" (because there had been a great oath with regard to anyone who did not come up to Yahweh at Mizpah). "He will definitely be put to death."

[Verses 6–17 relate how they identify the people of Jabesh-Gilead as ones who did not show up, and go and kill everyone there except the girls, so that they can give them to the Benjaminites so that the clan does not die out; but there are not enough of these girls.]

¹⁸"We cannot give them any of our daughters as wives," because the Israelites had sworn, "Cursed is the person who gives a wife

159

to Benjamin." ¹⁹They said, "Right. It is Yahweh's annual festival at Shiloh" (north of Bethel, east of the road going up from Bethel to Shechem and south of Lebonah). ²⁰They instructed the Benjaminites, "Go and lie in wait in the vineyards ²¹and look. There: when the girls of Shiloh come out to join in the dances, come out of the vineyards and each of you capture a wife for yourselves from the girls of Shiloh, and go to Benjamin. ²²When their fathers or brothers come to argue with us, we will say to them, 'Be gracious to them, because we did not get [for] each man his wife during the battle, [and] because you yourselves did not give them to them at the time when you would be guilty.'" ²³The Benjaminites did this and carried off wives in accordance with their number from the dancers whom they stole, then went and returned to their possession and built cities and settled in them. ²⁴The Israelites went off from there at that time, each to his clan and his kin group. They went from there each person to his possession.

²⁵In those days there was no king in Israel. Each person did what was right in his own eyes.

The story goes that in 1941, on the eve of the U.S. entry into the 1939–1945 war, two teenage ham radio operators who had joined the U.S. National Guard were enrolled into the army and were trained in "scrambling" messages to try to avoid their being understood by the enemy. This involved the use of random groups of five letters, which for fun the two young men turned into acronyms. One day the letters were SNAFU, which instantly became "Situation normal, all fouled up" (except that the next to last word wasn't actually "fouled"). The word became a standard description of the military situation just before and after Pearl Harbor. It is often the case that in war things do not turn out in the way the best intelligence suggested they would, and you cannot see the implications of the actions you take.

It's a fair description of the situation in Israel following the battle whose story was told in chapter 20. It's as if the Israelites are so dumb they haven't given a thought to the obvious implication of their action in virtually eliminating Benjamin: Israel will be one clan short (duh!). Neither have they thought of the obvious implication of their vow at Mizpah: that they won't be able to redeem the situation by allowing their daughters to marry the Benjaminite survivors. Once again (as in the Jephthah story, for instance), the Old Testament illustrates how vows can get you into a mess. With magnificent obtuseness, the Israelites ask God why things have gone so wrong as to eliminate a clan from Israel. There are two possible answers, and both might be true: because you have been so stupid (duh!) and because God is bringing judgment upon you. Admittedly, when Israelites ask God, "Why?" it is usually not a request for information but an implied plea for God to do something about it (the motif featured in Gideon's story).

So they came to the sanctuary and sat before God all day, lifted up their voices to God and wept, asked the question, built an **altar**, and offered the proper sacrifices as an expression of their seeking and their commitment. Yet there is no statement about whether God was listening and agreed to take action to **deliver** them from the mess they had gotten themselves into, the kind of statement that appears in other stories in Judges. God is absent from the story. Indeed, God has been effectively absent from the story for a long time. The last time God was the subject of a verb was the earlier part of the Samson saga, but God disappeared after chapter 15. Various people have talked to God and reckoned they knew what God was saying, but the story has not told us that God was actually involved in events or that God said anything. The scary exception to the last statement is the way God spoke in chapter 20, where on two out of three occasions God gave direction, but it did not lead to the expected result. It looks as if God has withdrawn from Israel and speaks more as an act of judgment than as an act of grace.

The New Testament warns churches about making the same mistakes as Israel made, and these last chapters of Judges form frightening examples of mistakes we might make as we go through the motions of consulting God but then just do our own thing. It is doubtful if these Israelites have noticed those dynamics of their own experience. Nor do they wait for an answer to their "Why?" whichever way they intend the question to be understood. They simply get on with solving the problem themselves. It's just as well we don't do that. As a result, precisely when you think the story couldn't get any worse in its portrayal of the way men treat one another and the way men treat women, it has one last fling at doing so. It draws our attention to another dubious-looking vow, which leads to the men killing off everyone but the teenage girls in Jabesh-Gilead. Then there is the carrying off of wives from among the girls celebrating a festival in honor of God.

In reacting to what happens to the girls from Jabesh and from Shiloh, we do need to allow for some cultural differences. In Western culture, it is an article of faith that we should be allowed to choose our own partners; we look with horror at the idea of arranged marriages. Yet the testimony of our culture is that this doesn't work very well; half the marriages we choose end up in divorce, though we would still like to make our own decisions. We noted in connection with the Samson story that the custom of arranged marriages does not mean the people involved have no say in the match, and the testimony of people from traditional societies is that arranged marriages can work quite well. For all we know, the girls from Jabesh and Shiloh may have been happy ever after. But how they got there was horrible.

"In those days there was no king in Israel. Each person did what was right in his own eyes." It is the end of a book, but it is just as well that it is not the end of the larger story.

RUTH 1:1–9

How Naomi's Life Falls Apart

¹In the time of the leaders, there was a famine in the country and a man went from Bethlehem in Judah to reside in Moabite country, he and his wife and his two sons. ²The man's name was Elimelek, his wife's name was Naomi, and his sons' names were Mahlon and Chilion, Ephrathites from Bethlehem in Judah. ³Naomi's husband Elimelek died, and she was left with her two sons. ⁴They got themselves Moabite wives; the name of one was Orpah, the other Ruth. ⁵But the two men, Mahlon and Chilion, also died, and the woman was left without her two sons and her husband. ⁶So this woman and her daughters-in-law set off to return from Moabite country, because they had heard in Moabite country that Yahweh had paid attention to his people by giving them bread. ⁷She left the place where she

was, her two daughters-in-law with her, and they went on the road whereby to return to Judah. ⁸But Naomi said to her two daughters-in-law, "Each of you go and return to your mother's household. May Yahweh keep commitment with you as you have kept commitment with the dead men and with me. ⁹May Yahweh grant that each of you find a settled place in the household of her husband." She hugged them, and they raised their voices and wept.

One Sunday in the church to which we belonged in England that story was the set Old Testament passage on a day when I was due to preach. My default instinct is to look to the Old Testament passage as the one on which to preach (someone has to), but on that occasion when I read this story, my immediate reaction was to think there was no way in which this tale about women from the countryside could speak to our inner-city congregation. Then I realized that the difference was superficial. The life issues the story deals with were the pressing life issues in our urban setting. Both contexts involve people handling similar experiences, such as having to move because they have no work, migrating to a foreign country in that connection, losing husbands and coping with widowhood, undertaking cross-cultural and interreligious marriages, and wondering which community they belong to.

Ruth starts where Judges leaves off; we are still in the time of the **leaders**. It starts with things going wrong, but whereas Judges talks about things going wrong because God makes them go wrong when Israel itself goes wrong, there is no suggestion here that the famine is an act of judgment. It's just one of those things, like the famines in Genesis that affected the families of Abraham and Sarah, Isaac and Rebekah, and Jacob and his wives. In a good year there can be a good harvest in Israel, but in a bad year there can be insufficient rain at the right time, or a locust epidemic. The country is always only one step from famine. What is Elimelek to do? His own farm cannot feed his family, and presumably the famine affects everyone else in the area so they cannot simply bail him out (the Ephrathites would be one of the kin groups within the clan of **Judah**, the group living in the Bethlehem area). Somehow he has to provide for his family. Apparently other farmers in Bethlehem are just hoping to get by somehow. Perhaps they have been able to store up some grain from the good years and can now use it to get through the lean years, but evidently Elimelek has not been able to do that. He hears that things are better in Moab. From Bethlehem he can look east across the deep Jordan Valley, with the Dead Sea at the bottom, and see the mountains of Moab rising on the other side. The story of Ehud and Eglon in Judges 3 shows that there is no love lost between Moab and Israel. It would be humiliating and dangerous to move there, but he has to feed his family. He will not just sit there hoping against hope, like some other Ephrathites he could name. So they make the move.

Does Elimelek die of a broken heart, of a sense of failure as the breadwinner, of a sense of shame at having to abandon his farm in the promised land? The story doesn't tell us, partly because this is a woman's story. Elimelek is in it only because he is Naomi's husband. Naomi in turn watches her sons get Moabite wives. Did that threaten to break her heart and impose on her a sense of failure and shame as a mother? What are nice Israelite boys doing marrying Moabite women? We all know about Moabite women. Think about where they came from (see Genesis 19:30–38). Think about the way Israelite men got attracted to them before and ended up serving their gods (see Numbers 25). And what about when the two young men then die? (The story doesn't give us a time frame, but evidently Ruth is still childless, young, and eligible when she and Naomi get back to Bethlehem. So I imagine Naomi being forty or so and her sons being twenty or so and the marriages being quite short.) Isn't that God's judgment? That is what one can imagine some people hearing this story would be thinking.

Naomi's story parallels Job's. Blow after blow has devastated her life. She had married with such high hopes of her and Elimelek's making the farm work and raising a family, and she has lost her farm, her extended family, her homeland, her husband, and her sons, and she is left alone in this foreign country with two foreign daughters-in-law.

Then she hears that the famine is over. For the first time, the story mentions God. Throughout, it will be reticent about doing so. It parallels the way we experience our lives, recognizing the importance of coincidences and of human initiatives that you can see, and believing that God is involved behind the scenes, but it does not usually pontificate on the precise way that is so. The storyteller doesn't know how or whether God was involved in the catalog of negative events with which the story begins— the famine, the leaving, the marriages, the deaths. The storyteller does know how the famine came to an end. God had "paid attention to his people." The King James Bible talks about God's "visiting" his people. It's actually a worrying word, because often God's "visits" are like a visit from the Mafia. They mean judgment. It's safer when God doesn't visit you or pay attention to you, but this visit is different. God has become involved with Israel by giving them bread. The rains have come. The grain has grown and been harvested. The famine is over. Bethlehem is living up to its name again (it means "house of bread"; the area around Bethlehem is good farming country).

So Naomi can go home, and she really has little alternative; otherwise, what are a woman and her daughters-in-law to do? All she can do is go back to Bethlehem where the abandoned family farm still is, with her tail between her legs, as humiliated and saddened when she returns as she was when she left, ready for the women to be whispering, "You see; they thought they were being so clever going to Moab to escape the famine, and see where it got them."

The two young women set off with Naomi to go back to Bethlehem—"back" for her, but they have never been to the land where their husbands came from. The three of them do after all comprise one family, even though an odd one now that the men are gone. Paradoxically, the two daughters-in-law, who might seem to be the symbol of everything that has gone wrong, are actually the two people who might be able to help Naomi find healing. Yet sometimes when trouble hits you, you may be afraid to rely on anything positive that is left in your life. If you have lost your farm, your country, your extended family, your husband, and your sons, it may seem there is a curse on you. If you stay attached to these two girls, will you not lose them, too? Better to anticipate the curse. They have alternatives not open to her. They have Moabite families they can go back to. Naomi refers to them as "your mother's house-hold." It is one of many ways in which the story encourages readers to resist the patriarchal stereotypes that often prevail in cultures. It is not just the men who are in charge of the family's destiny. Naomi was "Elimelek's wife," but he was also "Naomi's husband"; if he "owned" her, she also "owned" him.

What is the tone of her voice and what is going on in her heart as she expresses the hope that God may look after them and that they may find other husbands? It's often hard to "read" Naomi. She will sound deeply depressed and disillusioned with God when she is trying to persuade the two women to stay in Moab and when she herself gets back to Bethlehem. At one level she no doubt means what she says, but does she have much hope that her hopes will be fulfilled? One could hardly blame her if the answer is no.

RUTH 1:10–19a

The Choice

[10]They said to her, "No, because we will return with you to your people." [11]Naomi said, "Return, my daughters, why should you go with me? Do I yet have sons inside me who would become your husbands? [12]Return, my daughters; go, because I am too old to belong to a man. If I said there is hope for me, if I indeed belonged to a man tonight and indeed bore sons, [13]would you then wait for them until they were grown up and would you then hold yourself back from belonging to a man? No, my daughters, because things are much harsher for me than for you, because Yahweh's hand has gone out against me." [14]They raised their voices and wept again, and Orpah hugged her mother-in-law, but Ruth clung to her. [15]So she said, "Now. Your sister-in-law is going back to her people and to her gods. Go back with your sister-in-law." [16]Ruth said, "Do not press me to leave you by going back with her, because wherever you go I shall go, and wherever you lodge, I shall lodge. Your people will be my people, and your God will be my God. [17]Wherever you die, I will die, and there I will be buried. So may Yahweh do to me and so may he do more if [even] death separates me and you." [18]When [Naomi] saw that she was determined to go with

her, she stopped speaking to her, [19a]and the two of them went
on until they came to Bethlehem.

When my wife's multiple sclerosis was first diagnosed, I wrote
to tell her pastor, who had also been a mentor of mine. I
remember reading his reply. He told us how that morning he
happened to have been studying the story of Jesus' making the
water into wine in John 2, which includes the surprised comment of someone at the wedding that the groom has kept the
best wine until last. "God always does that," our pastor commented; it would somehow be true for us. As Ann got more
and more disabled over the years, I often pondered those words
and wondered what they might mean. Of course they are true
in the sense that Ann will rise to new life on resurrection day,
but is there more to them than that? What hope could we have?
They came true in the sense that God gave us an odd but good
life together and that through my having to cope with the experience, God turned me into a less objectionable person than
I would otherwise have been. Could there be more to it than
that? Now that she has died, I know the answer is "No."

What does hope mean? Naomi has lost hope, and you can't
really blame her. It also means she can't take seriously the way
her daughters-in-law reach out to her. In a sense they are offering her hope, but she can't recognize it as that. In the aftermath of bereavement it's impossible to imagine that there will
be any future for you. The way you have always pictured the
future involves this other person—for Naomi it had involved
these three other people, her husband and her sons. In a traditional society you know that your husband may well die in
his twenties or thirties or forties, and you know one or other
of your children may die before you do, but losing all of them,
husband and sons, is a worse scenario than you had reason to
contemplate. Ruth and Orpah are offering Naomi another way
of looking at the future; the three of them will form an ongoing
family. It will be an odd kind of family, but it will be a family. It
has hope. But Naomi can't see it. For herself and for them she
can only imagine one form of family, and there's no way she can
have that form of family again. The two girls could start over,
and they should do so, not stick with her.

"Things are much harsher for me than for you," she says, "because **Yahweh's** hand has gone out against me." The Old Testament often speaks of God's hand being stretched to act. Not far from where Naomi and her daughters-in-law are standing at this moment, God's hand had been stretched out in bringing her people across the Jordan, according to the story told in Joshua. But that hand had also been stretched out in the stories told in Judges, when it was turned against Israel. As far as she and we know, Naomi is like Job in having done nothing to deserve the kind of treatment God gave the unfaithful Israelites in Judges, but that is the way she has been treated. When the Israelites were treated that way because of their unfaithfulness, they could repent and God might forgive them and restore them. When there is no such reason for your life collapsing, there is nothing you can do but protest. Job and the Psalms model the way you go about offering such protest, but Naomi has not reached the point where she can lift her voice and protest to God. She talks quite a bit *about* God in expressing her wishes for her daughters-in-law and her understanding of what has happened to her, but she cannot talk *to* God about it.

Two choices now stand before Orpah and Ruth. They can go back to their mother's households, as Naomi urged, or they can insist on going with their mother-in-law. Orpah agrees to do the first. (By the way, you may have heard of someone called Oprah; the story goes that she was originally called Orpah, but people kept mispronouncing the name so her family gave in and changed it.) That does not mean Orpah made a bad choice and that she is somehow inferior to Ruth. She gave her priority to her own people as Naomi urged. She respected the way traditional family values worked. She is a little like Naaman the Syrian general who goes to Israel to get cleansed from his skin disease and comes to recognize Yahweh but then has to go home to Syria, or like the three wise men who come to acknowledge Jesus but then have to go home to the east where they came from. Admittedly Naomi speaks ambiguously about what this will mean for Orpah. "May Yahweh keep **commitment** with you," she had said. "May Yahweh grant that you find a settled place in the household of a husband." Now she says to Ruth, "Your sister-in-law is returning to her people and to her gods."

If Naomi is mixed up, Ruth seems quite clear, in an extraordinary direction. She will not be put off from going with Naomi. She is committed to Naomi, Naomi's people, and Naomi's God, "till death us do part"—except that she says even death will not part them. Death does not part the members of a family; you are buried with other members of your family in the family tomb, so death does mean going to join your ancestors (as the Old Testament puts it). Ruth expresses a radical commitment to membership in Naomi's family. Indeed, Jewish interpreters have seen the word *commitment* as the key word in the book of Ruth. Naomi herself used the word when she expressed the wish that Yahweh would keep commitment with Orpah and Ruth as they had kept commitment with their husbands and with her. Ruth does not use the word here, but her words to Naomi indicate that she is making a commitment of this kind: there is no obligation for her to do so, but it is what she intends.

It is impossible to guess why she should make this commitment. Naomi herself is pushing her away. Naomi's people is a people that looks down on Ruth's people. Naomi's God is the one Naomi has seen abandoning her and Ruth and Orpah. Yet this God is the one Ruth appeals to in her oath of allegiance to Naomi. As Rahab and Achan confused the distinction between **Canaanites** and Israelites in Joshua, Ruth and Naomi confuse the distinction between Moabites and Israelites. Naomi talks like a Moabite; Ruth talks like an Israelite. In a movie, Naomi might now burst into a different kind of tears because she is overcome by Ruth's commitment. Not so much. She just gives in and stops trying to persuade Ruth. "Whatever," we might imagine her saying.

Ruth does not appear in the list of the heroes of faith in Hebrews like Rahab, Samson, and Abraham, but she is indeed a hero of faith like Abraham, and she does appear with Abraham and Rahab in the list of Jesus' ancestors in Matthew 1. Like Abraham she shows herself willing to leave her own country and make her way to Canaan when she has no basis for knowing that Yahweh will look after her there. Her faith will be justified.

169

RUTH 1:19b–2:9

She's a Moabite, for Goodness' Sake!

19bWhen they came to Bethlehem, the whole city buzzed on account of them and said, "Is this Naomi?" 20She said to them, "Don't call me Naomi [Lovely], call me Mara [Harsh], because Shadday has been very harsh to me. 21I was full when I went. Yahweh has brought me back empty. Why call me Naomi when Yahweh has afflicted me, when Shadday has treated me badly." 22So Naomi returned with her daughter-in-law Ruth the Moabite with her, who returned from Moabite country. They came to Bethlehem at the beginning of the barley harvest. 2:1Now Naomi had a relative of her husband's, a powerful man of wealth, from Elimelek's kin group, whose name was Boaz. 2Ruth the Moabite said to Naomi, "Might I go to the fields and glean among the ears of grain behind someone in whose eyes I find favor?" She said to her, "Go, my daughter." 3So she went. She came and gleaned in the fields behind the reapers, and chance took her to the portion of the fields belonging to Boaz, who was of Elimelek's kin group. 4And there: Boaz was coming from Bethlehem. He said to the reapers, "Yahweh be with you," and they said to him, "Yahweh bless you." 5Boaz said to his boy who was in charge of the reapers, "Who does that girl belong to?" 6The boy who was in charge of the reapers said, "She is a Moabite girl who came back with Naomi from Moabite country. 7She said, 'Might I glean and gather among the sheaves behind the reapers?' She came and stayed from morning until now; she stopped in the house for a little." 8Boaz said to Ruth, "Do listen, my daughter. Don't go to glean in another field. No, you will not pass on from here. Stick here with my girls 9with your eyes on the field that is being reaped. Follow them. I have ordered the boys not to touch you. When you are thirsty, go to the vessels and drink from what the boys draw."

I was just reading the story of a man called Maxo who died in the earthquake in Haiti a couple of weeks ago when his house collapsed on top of him. His cousin in New York called Maxo a hustler, but his story showed how he was always hustling on behalf of other people. The last phone call his cousin received from him three days before the earthquake related to his trying to raise money to rebuild a school in their home village in the mountains. The time before that, he was trying to raise money for a coffin for a neighbor who had died. In 2004 he took his aged minister father to Miami to try to get medical treatment, but they were put into detention, and his father died there. When the earthquake happened, his house was full of people, such as children he tutored after school and parents who were there to talk about their children's schoolwork. People who cared about Maxo dug for days hoping to find him alive, but in the end they found only his body.

Maxo was a man who knew about **commitment**. The story doesn't use that word of Boaz, but Boaz is the same. He isn't a man who needs to hustle, on his own behalf or on other people's. He is a big guy. Paradoxically, there is a suspicious side to his being a big guy in the village. The story in Joshua has related how the land was supposed to be distributed around the clans and families. There were not supposed to be big landowners (the Prophets will inveigh against that), and there were not supposed to be people who were merely the "boys" or employees of other people. Maybe Boaz has done well out of the famine; maybe he was a better farmer or had been better at saving for a time when the harvest might fail and had ended up taking control of the land of other people who were not so efficient or careful or lucky. What his story then shows is that power and resources are things that you can use in a selfish fashion or in a way that shows commitment. There's a hint of that in the opening greeting between him and his workers. Maybe the mutual blessing was a conventional greeting, but I would think it is mentioned here as an indication of Boaz's relationship with God and his good relationship with his employees.

His question about who that girl belongs to might seem more ambiguous. It could seem like a typical guy question; he fancies the new chick he's not seen around here before and wonders whether she is attached. But maybe that's too Western a way of reading it. The story portrays Boaz as a quite honorable man who wouldn't think in those terms. Either way, this raises the question of Boaz's marital status. It would hardly be the case that a senior member of the community like Boaz would simply be single. The family would have arranged a suitable match for him. More likely a prominent man like Boaz would be interested in having an extra wife, because that's a sign of status. But that doesn't seem very romantic to us, so yet another possibility is that he was a widow. In telling us about Elimelek, Mahlon, and Chilion, the story has already reminded us that in a traditional society many people die young, and the danger involved in childbirth makes that even truer for women.

The background to the story is the kind of concern the **Torah** shows for needy people, such as widows like Naomi and Ruth. In our culture we assume everything has to be done with maximum economic efficiency. When economic conditions are tough, companies lay people off, and they have to fend for themselves. What else can the companies do? If they fail to take such action, the companies themselves will fold. The need to take that kind of action is built into the system. It produces growth and achievement but also suffering. The system in a traditional society has the opposite advantages and disadvantages. One aspect is that the harvesters who are reaping the grain don't try to do it too efficiently. They leave something behind for people who don't belong to regular families and don't have fields they can farm and therefore have no way of trying to ensure they have food to eat.

The contrast between Naomi and Ruth that emerged when they were in Moab continues now that they are in Bethlehem. Ruth is the person with the energy and initiative to do something to ensure they have something to eat. Naomi is too disheartened. She has no intention of hiding her bitterness at the way life has treated her—or rather, at the way God has treated her. She again speaks like Job, who also describes God as treating him harshly and badly. Another similarity with Job is Naomi's transitioning here to talk about God as Shadday. Translations often have *Almighty* as the English equivalent. We don't know what the word *Shadday* means, but *Almighty* does convey something of the right impression. Shadday is a name that sometimes comes in Genesis, and it's the name a non-Israelite like Job or Balaam would use. **Yahweh** is the special Israelite name for God; it suggests God's involvement with Israel. Shadday suggests God's power and transcendence; it's a bit less personal than Yahweh. It is therefore suggestive that Naomi transitions to using that name.

In Job, we are given the back story; we know what lies behind his suffering, though Job never does. There is no back story in the book of Ruth. God has just let her life fall apart, and she is not afraid to say so. The Psalms will suggest that it is okay to speak the way she does, though they may also suggest that it is a shame that she is not saying all this *to* God and not just *about* God. A student tells me that I once said in class, "Don't complain to other people. Be sure to complain to God. He's big enough; he can handle it." I hope I said it; it's true.

For Naomi to say that God has brought her back to Bethlehem empty is also something of an insult to Ruth, but Ruth seems to roll with it. Once again the contrast between the two women comes out. The story keeps emphasizing that Ruth is from Moab and is a Moabite, and this section keeps underscoring the fact, notably when the boy says, "She is a Moabite girl who came back with Naomi from Moabite country." It's as if the story says, HAVE YOU GOT IT? SHE'S A MOABITE! It would indeed be easy for Israelites to look down on Moabites. This might especially be an issue in the time of Ezra and Nehemiah when **Judah** was an imperiled little **Persian** colony and was in danger of being overwhelmed by neighbors such as Moab. People such as Ezra and Nehemiah know that Israelites have to be wary of marrying Moabites who would compromise the family's commitment to Yahweh. The Ruth story reminds people that this religious concern mustn't become an ethnic prejudice. Ruth is ethnically Moabite, but she has committed herself to Yahweh, like Rahab.

RUTH 2:10–23

The God of Coincidences

[10]She fell on her face and bowed down on the ground and said to him, "Why have I found favor in your eyes in your paying attention to me when I am a foreigner?" [11]Boaz answered her, "I have been told all about everything you have done for your mother-in-law after the death of your husband. You left your father and mother and the land of your birth and came to a people you had not acknowledged before. [12]May Yahweh

reward your deeds. May your recompense be rich from Yahweh, the God of Israel, under whose skirts you have come for refuge." [13]She said, "May I find favor in your eyes, sir, because you have comforted me and encouraged your servant, though I am not one of your servants."

[14]Boaz said to her at meal time, "Come here and eat some food and dip your piece in the vinegar." So she sat by the side of the reapers, he passed her the roasted grain, and she ate and was full and had some left over. [15]When she got up to glean, Boaz ordered his boys, "She can glean among the sheaves; don't put her down. [16]Actually you can pull some out for her from the bundles as well, and leave her to glean. Don't rebuke her." [17]She gleaned in the fields until evening and beat out what she had gleaned. It came to an ephah of barley. [18]She picked it up and went to the city, and her mother-in-law saw what she had gleaned. [Ruth] took it out and gave her what was left over from when she had been full.

[19]Her mother-in-law said to her, "Where did you glean today? Where did you work? Blessed be the man who paid attention to you." She told her mother-in-law whom she had worked with and said, "The name of the man I worked with today was Boaz." [20]Naomi said to her daughter-in-law, "May he be blessed by Yahweh, who has not abandoned his commitment with the living and the dead." Naomi said to her, "The man is a close relative of ours. He is one of our near kinsmen." [21]Ruth the Moabite said, "He also said to me, 'Stick close to my boys until they have finished my entire harvest.'" [22]Naomi said to her daughter-in-law Ruth, "My daughter, it will be good if you go out with his girls, and the men don't approach you in another field." [23]So she stuck close with Boaz's girls as she gleaned until the barley harvest and the wheat harvest were finished, but she lived with her mother-in-law.

When I was thirteen, I was walking home from school one day and met a teacher from the Sunday school I used to attend but had left two years previously to go to another church. She told me that my old church was about to start a new youth fellowship. She wondered if I would like to go. So I did, and it changed my life, not least because the minister was a keen theologian, and I caught his interest in theology. Maybe I wouldn't be writing The Old Testament for Everyone series had it not been for that accidental meeting. Then seven years later I went to a Christian students' conference and one morning happened to sit by a particular young woman at breakfast and got talking to her, and we ended up married for forty-two years. It was the most influential meeting of my life, and it just happened by chance.

The Ruth story alerted us to the role of coincidence or chance in what is happening when it commented on how chance took Ruth to the part of the fields that belonged to someone related to her father-in-law. The implication of this coincidence is now made explicit. Naomi and Ruth had not prayed that Ruth would be led to the right field, but Ruth simply "happened" to end up in the best field possible. It was not only that she got treated really well and managed to gather a significant amount of grain, though that was so. The amount she carries is almost enough to use up your baggage allowance on a plane, so evidently among her other qualities Ruth is no weakling. Further, that is just the "leftovers," on top of the significant amount she ate for lunch.

It is enough to turn Naomi around. She can pray and praise again. It turns out that after all, God has not given up on a **commitment** to them. It's that word again. It applies not only to relationships within their family and between Boaz and them, but to God's relationship with them. It's expressed in the fact that Boaz is one of their "near kinsmen," which makes him also their potential "guardian," "redeemer," or **restorer**.

All those three ways of translating the Hebrew word convey something of what it denotes. It refers to a person outside your immediate family—your "household," in the way the Old Testament speaks. In the book of Ruth, the household now comprises only Naomi and Ruth. Within your extended family (for instance, among Elimelek's brothers) there will be people who are relatively close to you by birth. When trouble comes, if you are lucky there may be among them someone who is the head of another household that is better off than yours, someone who has gotten along better as a farmer than you have or whose own household is in good health when yours is afflicted by illness or accident in a way that imperils your household's capacity to be self-supporting. Such a person is under moral and social obligation to help you and your household in one

175

way or another—for instance, to avoid your having to give up trying to farm independently and/or having to let your children become someone else's indentured servants for a while. (Ironically, "helping" people by taking their children on as servants is perhaps the process whereby Boaz has done well.) Such a person is a near kinsman or close relative, a potential guardian of your freedom, and a potential redeemer who could use some of his resources to get you out of trouble. The nice man who has been so caring about Ruth turns out to be a person in that position in relation to Ruth and Naomi.

Indeed, (Naomi says) he turns out to be a person in that position in relation to the dead—Elimelek, Mahlon, and Chilion, the people to whom he is directly related—as well as to the living, Ruth and Naomi. Remember that the way the system was supposed to work was that Israel's land was distributed among the clans and families and was thus directly in the trust of the male head of the family who ran the farm. To maintain this system and to avoid the land's coming to belong to big landowners, land had to stay under the control of (in this case) Elimelek, and then of Mahlon and Chilion. There were exceptions; the story of Zelophehad's daughters (see Joshua 17) had established that a man who had no sons could pass on the family's land to his daughters. But Elimelek and Naomi had no daughters. It seems that Elimelek and Naomi had to give over their land to someone else because of the failure of the harvest and the famine with which the story started, and they have no one to claim it back and no means of claiming it back.

As Naomi uses this significant expression to describe Boaz's relationship to their household, Boaz uses a significant expression in explaining his generosity to Ruth. Why do you care about a foreigner like me? she asks. She expects to be treated the way we treat foreigners in Britain and the United States. But the **Torah** lays down expectations about how Israelites must treat foreigners in need who come to take refuge in Israel when Israelites are better off than they are. They are supposed to treat them with respect and care. The way Boaz puts it is by speaking of Ruth's coming for refuge with **Yahweh**, under Yahweh's skirts. The Hebrew word for the "skirts" of a robe is also the word for the "wings" of a bird (which are like its skirts), so one can imagine chicks hiding behind their mother hen's feathers as well as children hiding behind their mother's skirts. Translations usually assume that Boaz means "wings," but in the next chapter Ruth turns his words back on him, and there she uses the word to mean "skirts."

Like Ruth, Boaz assumes a link between a relationship with Israel and a relationship with God. A resident alien in Israel is not someone who simply accepts asylum there and makes the most of Israelite generosity; it is someone who joins the community and shares in its relationship with God. If you just want the refuge and the practical support, you stay simply a foreigner who is working there; you do not become a kind of associate member of the community. The former was never Ruth's intention. She had said, "My people will be your people, and my God will be your God." Boaz has heard about the way she has committed herself to Naomi and knows that she has taken refuge under Yahweh's skirts as well as under Israel's skirts. It is what Israelites themselves do: they pray, "Will you hide me in the shadow of your skirts/wings" (Psalm 17:8; the expression recurs in the Psalms).

RUTH 3:1–18

How Not to Leave the Initiative to the Man

[1]Her mother-in-law Naomi said to her, "My daughter, I must indeed seek a home for you where things may be good for you. [2]So now, Boaz is indeed our close relative. You have been with his girls. So. He is winnowing barley on the threshing floor tonight. [3]Have a bath, put on your makeup, put on your best clothes, and go down to the threshing floor. Do not make yourself known to the man until he has finished eating and drinking. [4]When he lies down, note the place where he lies down. Go and uncover his feet and lie down. He will tell you what to do." [5]She said to her, "All you say to me, I will do."

[6]She went down to the threshing floor and acted according to all that her mother-in-law had told her. [7]Boaz ate and drank and his spirit was good. He went to lie down at the edge of the heap. She approached quietly, uncovered his feet, and lay down. [8]In the middle of the night the man gave a start and twisted round:

there, a woman lying at his feet! [9]He said, "Who are you?" She said, "I am your servant Ruth. Spread your skirt over your servant, because you are a near kinsman." [10]He said, "May you be blessed of Yahweh, my daughter. You have made your last act of commitment better than your first in not going after the young men, whether poor or rich. [11]So now, my daughter, fear not, all that you say I will do for you, because all the elders of my people acknowledge that you are a woman of worth. [12]But now, because it is true that I am a near kinsman but there is also a kinsman nearer than me, [13]stay the night, and in the morning, if he will act as kinsman, fine, let him act as kinsman. But if he does not want to act as kinsman, I myself will act as kinsman, as Yahweh lives. Lie down until morning."

[14]So she lay at his feet until morning but got up before one person could recognize his neighbor. He said [to himself], "It should not be known that the woman came to the threshing floor," [15]but he said, "Bring the shawl that you have on and hold it." She held it and he weighed out six [measures] of barley and put it on her. He went to the city [16]and she went to her mother-in-law. [Naomi] said, "How was it for you, my daughter?" She told her all that the man had done for her, [17]and said, "He gave me these six [measures] of barley, because he said, 'Don't go to your mother-in-law empty-handed.'" [18][Naomi] said, "Stay here, my daughter, until you know how the matter turns out, because the man will not relax unless he has dealt with the matter today."

I was talking to a young man who had been dating someone for a long time, but she had then ditched him and broken his heart. For a while he had stayed out of relationships. He had gone out with a number of women friends, some mutual friends; they knew his story, and both parties knew these were not dates. Then his heart had pretty much healed, and he was ready to start again. More than one of the women were people he could imagine dating, but feeling he was ready didn't translate into having the courage to ask one of them, "What do you think about turning this 'friend' relationship into something else?" What he said to me was, "It's not fair that the man has to take the initiative." It seems that in this connection we mostly still adhere to stereotyped gender relationships. Many men and women expect the man to take the initiative, and eventually it is the man who proposes. I know women who wish it were otherwise, but they don't very often break with tradition.

Such attitudes would have been stronger in a traditional society like Israel's, but Naomi and Ruth decide not to be bound by them. Evidently there is more than one person in Naomi's kin group who could be doing something to secure Naomi's future, Ruth's future, and the future of the land that is still in the name of Elimelek, Chilion, and Mahlon. Given that none of them is taking any action, Naomi decides to initiate something. It is also evident that Naomi has come a long way from the justified gloom with which she returned to Bethlehem. She has got her groove back. Her actual words suggest she has also moved on in her attitude toward Ruth. A while ago she was shrugging her shoulders about the silly young woman's insistence on accompanying her to Bethlehem and speaking of God's having brought her back to Bethlehem empty, thus implying that Ruth counted for nothing. Somehow Ruth's "coincidental" meeting up with Boaz and Boaz's kindness have thrown a switch in Naomi's spirit. One result is her concern for Ruth to find a "home," more literally a place of rest. In other words, she speaks not of the destiny of the family land or of her own security, but of Ruth's own destiny and security. You could say that she is starting to be a person of **commitment**, like Ruth and Boaz.

The fields where the crops grow are outside the "city" (which was only what we would call a village, maybe a hundred people who might belong to two or three kin groups). They might be one or two hour's commuting distance, given that you didn't have a truck, and at harvest time people would sometimes camp out in the fields. That also made it possible for them to keep their eyes on their barley and prevent the rogues from the next village stealing it; hence the fact that Boaz sleeps next to his heap of barley, shotgun in hand, so to speak.

Naomi's plan depends on the assumption that there is no custom whereby she or Ruth can breeze up to Boaz in the village coffee shop and inquire about a date, but the plan and Ruth's execution of it look risky. There are lots of ambiguities about the way the story is told that reflect the ambiguity in what Ruth was to do. Dressing yourself up the way Ruth does could mean making it look as if you are a bride on her wedding day, but

179

it could mean trying to look seductive. Uncovering someone's feet could mean what it says, but "uncovering someone's nakedness" is a euphemism for having sex with them, and "feet" can be a euphemism for genitals. If a man wakes up in the middle of the night and finds a woman lying next to him, he could hardly be blamed for thinking she is offering herself to him, though he would be wise also to remember that accepting the offer might mean he will have a hard time avoiding marrying her. To put it another way, sleeping with an unattached woman might imply a marriage commitment. As far as we know, in Israel there is no such thing as a marriage service or a registrar of marriages. Such things belong in urbanized and mobile cultures. So even if Ruth is offering herself to Boaz sexually, she might seem by that act to be proposing and not merely propositioning. Simply offering him a one-night stand would be prejudicing her future with any other man. And what we know about both Ruth and Boaz would make it unlikely that either of them would just be interested in a one-night stand with someone.

Indeed, Ruth makes it clear that she is proposing. She is taking the initiative not merely in approaching him but in talking about marriage. Boaz earlier talked about her seeking to find protection under Yahweh's skirts. She is pointing out that human life works on the basis of our also finding protection under the skirts of another human being. That is what marriage involves. Yet Ruth's going on to refer to his being her kinsman reflects the way a particular obligation to take a person under the wings of his protection applies to a man like Boaz, with his position in the community. Ruth is appealing to Boaz to become her protector, given his position as a close kinsman. But making herself look nice like someone going on a date shows she is not merely appealing to his sense of moral and social obligation. She wants to be someone he is attracted to as well as someone he is under obligation to. It is another indication of the way marriage customs that are very different from those of the urbanized West do not preclude sexual attraction and sexual love.

In any decent romantic comedy, however, there have to be threats to whether the couple do end up together; otherwise the movie will end too quickly. Here the plot device to maintain suspense is the existence of another kinsman who has the same moral and social obligations as Boaz and has first rights to take on Ruth, Naomi, and the family land. The gift of six measures of barley is another sign of Boaz's honor and generosity, but more significantly at daybreak he goes off to the city to initiate the process whereby it can be decided who will get Ruth. Naomi is right that he is a man who can be trusted to take action when action is needed. The women can do what they can to maneuver around the patriarchal assumptions of the culture, but they also have to work within them. Wait for next week's thrilling episode.

RUTH 4:1–10

How Not to Get Overextended in Real Estate

¹So Boaz had gone up to the gate and sat down there. And there, the kinsman of whom Boaz had spoken was passing. [Boaz] said, "Come over, sit down here, so-and-so." He came over and sat down. ²[Boaz] got ten men from among the elders of the city and said, "Sit down here," and they sat down. ³He said to the kinsman, "The share in the land that belongs to our brother Elimelek: Naomi, who has come back from Moabite country, is disposing of it. ⁴I myself said [to myself], 'I must apprise you and say, "You can acquire it in the presence of the people who are seated here, in the presence of the elders of my people. If you will act as kinsman, do so. If not, tell me, so that I may know, because there is no one to act as kinsman apart from you, but I am after you."'" He said, "I will act as kinsman." ⁵Boaz said, "When you acquire the land from the hand of Naomi and from Ruth the Moabite, you will have acquired the dead man's wife, to establish the dead man's name over his possession." ⁶The kinsman said, "I cannot act as kinsman for myself, or I will risk my own possession. You act as kinsman for yourself with regard to my kinship position, because I cannot act as kinsman."

⁷Now formerly in Israel, in connection with acting as kinsman and with transfer, to establish any matter a man took off his shoe and gave it to his fellow. This was the attestation process in Israel. ⁸So the kinsman said to Boaz, "You may acquire it for yourself," and took off his shoe. ⁹Boaz said to the elders and

> the entire people, "You are witnesses today that I have acquired
> from the hand of Naomi everything belonging to Elimelek
> and everything belonging to Chilion and Mahlon. [10]I have also
> acquired Ruth the Moabite, Mahlon's wife, for myself as wife, to
> establish the dead man's name over his possession, so that the
> dead man's name will not be cut off from among his brothers
> and from the gate of his place. You are witnesses today."

The end of the first decade of the twenty-first century saw a
collapse in housing prices in the United States, Britain, and
elsewhere, and an increase in the number of people "walking away" from property they "owned" but could not pay the
mortgage on; such people would also be aware that the total
amount they had to pay came to considerably more than their
homes were now worth. At first, this chiefly involved people who simply could not make their payments, sometimes
because they had lost their jobs. This week, the newspaper has
commented on the way it increasingly involves people walking away even though they have the money to make the payments and are not behind on them. Strategically, it just does
not make sense to stay. A man in Miami Beach had contracted
to buy a small apartment for $215,000 but knows that similar
apartments now sell for $90,000. He would be better off walk-
ing away and renting a nicer home at the beach. So he finds
himself with an ethical dilemma: because he made a commitment, he should surely keep it.

Something like this is the kinsman's dilemma. It is nice
that the story keeps him anonymous; it saves his and his family's shame. He is just "so-and-so." The story presupposes the
way matters are decided in the village in a traditional society:
there is no professional lawyer class; everything is sorted out
by the elders in the plaza inside the city gate. The elders will
be the senior members of the households in the village (in the
previous chapter, the phrase "all the elders of my people" was
more literally "all the gate of my people"). At the gate Boaz
manages to bump into the other kinsman; maybe we are to
see another encouraging "coincidence" here as the man's "happening" to show up facilitates Boaz's sorting things out and

shortening the period of Naomi's and Ruth's and our anxiety about whether everything will indeed work out okay. He then gets a quorum from the elders as they happen to be around. Maybe the implication is that the beginning of the day would be a good time to catch people as they were on their way to the fields to get on with harvesting, that is, if they were not sleeping in the fields like Boaz.

For the first time the story refers explicitly to some land belonging to Elimelek, to his "share"—that is, his allocation within the land belonging to his clan. It is not clear what has happened to the land since Elimelek and his family left **Judah** for Moab some years ago, though we may guess that he had surrendered it as collateral or leased it to someone who had made a loan to him at the time of the famine. Apparently it is then in some sort of limbo; its long-term destiny has not been sorted out, but anyone who wanted to take it over on a more permanent basis would have to "redeem" it—that is, pay Elimelek's debt. In the meantime, Elimelek's widow, Naomi, is apparently assumed to be its legal owner, though there is no reference in the **Torah** to widows' being in this position.

It is an important principle of Israelite law and tradition, as of law and tradition in other traditional societies, that land cannot be bought and sold (though this principle will be ignored as the society becomes more developed, and we have noted how the Prophets attack the way some people have managed to become big landowners). The land belongs to God and by God's will comes under the stewardship of families who can farm it and use what they grow. So Naomi will not exactly be "selling" the land, and no one else will be "buying" it, as some translations express the matter. Neither will Ruth be bought and sold; in Israel, wives are not property that can be bought and sold. Naomi does not have the resources to pay back the loan on the land and thus redeem it, so she is undertaking to surrender that right to someone else, who will then gain control of it and decide how to farm it and what to do with the produce.

In this case there is a complication. Like other traditional societies, Israel had a procedure for handling a situation in which a man died without having fathered a son who would inherit control of the family land. It involved the man's brother marrying the man's widow with the hope that this union would produce a son who from a legal angle would count as the dead man's son and could thus be his heir. What happens in Ruth is a variant on the procedure as it is described in Genesis 38 and Deuteronomy 25:5–10. What it has in common with them is the existence of a childless widow. (At first, you might think that the dead man's wife is Naomi, but the assumption will be that she is not going to be having any more children, and anyway the situation is complicated by the fact that Elimelek did have a son, and Ruth is that son's wife.)

For the anonymous kinsman, the trouble is that redeeming the land, taking on Ruth, and fathering a child who will eventually inherit the land will involve him in significant expenditure and no long-term gain. Like people who can afford to pay the mortgage to which they have committed themselves but who know they will lose money by doing so, he is caught in a dilemma. He is not just in danger of failing to make a fast buck. He is in danger of imperiling his own secure possession of his land and thus imperiling the position of the family he already has. He has a clash of responsibilities, so he chooses to give priority to the responsibility he already has. We should perhaps no more criticize that decision than criticize Orpah's decision to go back to her mother's household. It was a judgment call. And in any case, we breathe a sigh of relief because we want the romantic comedy to end the way we have projected.

The rule about brother-in-law marriage in Deuteronomy 25 also involves taking off a shoe, but there the widow removes her brother-in-law's shoe and spits in his face because the ceremony involves shaming the man who has declined to do his duty. There does not seem to be as much shame involved in this situation. "So-and-so" is not Naomi's or Ruth's brother-in-law. In both cases the ceremony symbolizes the man's formal public surrender of his rights or obligations and their "transfer" to someone else, though we don't know why this particular ceremony should do that.

RUTH 4:11–22

How David Got His Grandfather

[11]The entire people at the gate and the elders said, "We are witnesses. May Yahweh make the woman who is coming into your house like Rachel and Leah, both of whom built up the household of Israel. Do well in Ephrathah; make a name in Bethlehem! [12]May your household be like the household of Perez, whom Tamar bore to Judah, through the offspring Yahweh will give you by this girl." [13]So Boaz took Ruth and she became his wife. He slept with her and Yahweh enabled her to get pregnant. She bore a son, [14]and the women said to Naomi, "Yahweh be praised, who has not left you without a kinsman today. May his name be renowned in Israel! [15]For you he will be one who renews your life and sustains your old age, because your daughter-in-law who cared about you has borne him, she who has been better to you than seven sons." [16]Naomi took the child and put him in her arms and became his nurse. [17]The neighbors named him, saying, "A son has been born to Naomi"; they named him Obed. He was father of Jesse, father of David.

[18]This is the family history of Perez. Perez fathered Hezron. [19]Hezron fathered Ram. Ram fathered Amminadab. [20]Amminadab fathered Nahshon. Nahshon fathered Salmah. [21]Salmon fathered Boaz. Boaz fathered Obed. [22] Obed fathered Jesse. And Jesse fathered David.

I was talking to a friend yesterday who has long been interested in researching into her family history, and she told me how she had discovered some time ago that both her parents had been divorced twice before they married each other. A friend of hers had discovered that her own parents had divorced and then remarried each other. That reminded me of another friend who discovered that his father must have been conceived when his grandparents were not yet married. We may well have idealized impressions of our parents and grandparents from the time of their middle age and old age, but it can turn out that their earlier lives were much more complicated or colorful than we realized. It's a risky business investigating your family history. You may have thought your family was respectable and find out that it was not.

On the other hand, you may discover that your family is no less respectable than previous generations. This genealogy of David feeds into the genealogy of Jesus in Matthew 1. People slighted the honor of Jesus' mother, who got pregnant before she was married, but Jesus' genealogy shows that God has long been at work through women who were the victims of prejudice or through women respectable people wouldn't approve of. Tamar is in his genealogy (see her story in Genesis 38). Rahab is there (see her story in Joshua 2). Bathsheba is there (see her story in 2 Samuel 11). And Ruth is there. Jesus has a Moabite ancestor.

The story of Ruth, Naomi, and Boaz ends up as also a story about David. If you were the child of one of David's many marriages, including the adulterous and murderous one, you might be encouraged to find that your father had the story of **Judah**, Tamar, Perez, and also Ruth in his ancestry. More generally, you might well be an Israelite who was inclined to idolize and idealize David, and the close of this book will give you something to think about. It might warn you about making a plaster saint out of David. It would also make you think again about your attitude toward people such as Moabites. You can hardly be as prejudiced as you might otherwise be when you know that David had a Moabite grandmother.

The Bethlehem community, the people in the town where David will be born and where Jesus will be born, are people who pray that Ruth the Moabite will make a contribution to the building up of the household of Israel as a whole that is equivalent to that of Rachel and Leah! (They will have in mind all the twelve clans, and thus everyone who belongs to Israel, because the sons born to Zilpah and Bilhah, the servants Rachel and Leah encouraged Jacob to treat as **secondary wives** when they themselves could not conceive, will also count as Rachel's and Leah's.) They also pray that Ruth will make a contribution comparable to that of the offspring of the incestuous union between Judah and Tamar, which was the origin of the Bethlehemites themselves as part of the clan of Judah. And God answered their prayers.

I don't know whether Israelites also grinned at the last words of the Bethlehem women. I remember reflecting when we got married that it wasn't really our occasion; it belonged to the bride's parents. Well, they were paying. (Everything is a bit different nowadays.) Later I discovered that when your first baby is born, that isn't your occasion either. "A son has been born to *Naomi*." Yet this comment rounds off one important theme in the story as a whole. You could argue that this book should be called *Naomi* rather than *Ruth*. Its first paragraph relates her quadruple family tragedy (the exile and the death of a husband and two sons). The rest of the book is then the story of how her life gets rebuilt through the **commitment** of a daughter-in-law and a kinsman. But long ago, Naomi has already made the best theological statement, the best statement of faith, in the book: God "has not abandoned his commitment with the living and the dead" (2:20), and the woman's comment reflects that this is indeed so.

We could put the point another way. One of the contributions of the book to the Old Testament is its concrete illustration in the person of Boaz of what it means to be a **restorer**, a kinsman, a guardian, a redeemer. The importance of this portrait lies not least in the way Israel took the figure of the kinsman and the action of the restorer as an image for God and for God's action as restorer. The kinsman's vocation was to accept an obligation to care about members of his family in a way that expressed itself in a willingness to spend his energy and resources to make it possible for their lives to be rebuilt when that was needed. That was what God did for Israel, treating Israel as members of the family, asking no questions about whether they deserve to be in the mess they are in, and expending energy and resources to make it possible for their lives to be rebuilt when that was needed. The image surfaces most often in Isaiah 40–55 in the context of the **exile** when Israel especially needs such restoring. The book of Ruth does not explicitly describe God as Naomi's kinsman or guardian or restorer or redeemer, but behind the action of Boaz in fulfilling that role is God fulfilling that role.

The close of the book points to its theological significance by linking Ruth's story to David's. (The names Salmah and Salmon in successive verses are variants of the same name.) Until this closing paragraph, you might think you are simply reading a short story about some ordinary people's ordinary lives and the way God is involved in them. But it is typical of biblical stories about ordinary individuals to show how they relate to God's wider and longer purpose. This is indeed a story about God's involvement in the story of Israel as a whole, the story that comes to a climax with Jesus (as Matthew's genealogy points out). It encourages readers to wonder how God's involvement in their everyday lives relates to a much bigger purpose; it encourages them to raise their eyes to a bigger horizon. It also issues one of the Old Testament's recurrent reminders that God is concerned with the whole world; God's concern with Israel interrelates with that concern. Admittedly it does so in a paradoxical way. God's concern with Israel is not just for Israel's sake but for Moab; and Moab itself makes a contribution to the achievement of God's purpose.

GLOSSARY

aide

A supernatural agent through whom God appears and works in the world. Standard English translations call them "angels," but this term suggests ethereal figures with wings, wearing diaphanous white dresses. Aides are humanlike figures; hence it is possible to give them hospitality without realizing who they are (Hebrews 13). They have no wings; hence their need of a stairway or ramp between heaven and earth (Genesis 28). They appear in order to act or speak on God's behalf, and they represent God so fully that they can speak as if they are God (Judges 6). They thus bring the reality of God's presence, action, and voice without bringing such a real presence that it would electrocute mere mortals or shatter their hearing. That can be a reassurance when Israel is rebellious and God's presence might indeed be a threat (Exodus 32–33), but aides can implement God's punishment as well as God's blessing (Exodus 12).

altar

A structure for offering a sacrifice (the word comes from the word for sacrifice), made of earth or stone. An altar might be relatively small, like a table, and the person making the offering would stand in front of it. Or it might be higher and larger, like a platform, and the person making the offering would climb onto it. This sacrificial altar is to be distinguished from the much smaller altar within the sanctuary, on which incense was burnt so that its smoke ascended to God.

Amorites

The term is used in several ways. It can denote one of the original ethnic groups in **Canaan**, especially east of the Jordan. It can denote the people of Canaan as a whole. Outside the Old Testament it denotes a people living over a wider area of Mesopotamia. "Amorites" is thus a little like the word "America," which commonly refers to the United

189

States but can denote a much broader area of the continent of which the United States is part.

Apocrypha

The contents of the main Christian Old Testament are the same as those of the Jewish Scriptures, though there they come in a different order, as the Torah, the Prophets, and the Writings. Their precise bounds as Scripture came to be accepted some time in the years before or after Christ. For centuries, most Christian churches used a broader collection of Jewish writings, including books such as Maccabees and Ecclesiasticus, which for Jews were not part of the Bible. These other books came to be called the "Apocrypha," the books that were "hidden away"—which came to imply "spurious." They are now often known as the "deuterocanonical writings," which is more cumbersome but less pejorative; it simply indicates that these books have less authority than the Torah, the Prophets, and the Writings. The precise list of them varies between different churches.

Assyria, Assyrians

The first great Middle Eastern superpower, the Assyrians spread their empire westward into Syria-Palestine in the eighth century, the time of Amos and Isaiah, and first made **Ephraim** part of their empire. When Ephraim kept trying to assert independence, they invaded; in 722 they destroyed Ephraim's capital at Samaria, transported many of its people, and settled people from other parts of their empire in their place. They also invaded **Judah** and devastated much of the country, but they did not take Jerusalem. Prophets such as Amos and Isaiah describe how God was thus using Assyria as a means of disciplining Israel.

Babylon, Babylonians

A minor power in the context of Israel's early history, in Jeremiah's time they succeeded **Assyria** as the region's superpower and remained it for nearly a century until conquered by **Persia**. Prophets such as Jeremiah describe how God was using them as a means of disciplining **Judah**. They took Jerusalem and transported many of its people in 587. Their creation stories, law codes, and more philosophical writings help us understand aspects of the Old Testament's equivalent writings, while their astrological religion forms background to aspects of polemic in the Prophets.

Canaan, Canaanites

As the biblical terms for the country of Israel as a whole and for its indigenous peoples, *Canaanites* is not so much the name for a particular ethnic group as a shorthand term for all the peoples native to the country. See also **Amorites**.

chest

The "**covenant** chest" is a box a bit more than a yard long and half a yard wide and high. The King James Bible refers to it as an "ark," but the word means a box, though it only occasionally designates chests used for other purposes. It is the *covenant* chest because it contains the stone tablets inscribed with the Ten Commandments, key expectations God laid down in connection with establishing the Sinai Covenant. It is regularly kept in the sanctuary, but there is a sense in which it symbolizes God's presence (given that Israel has no images to do so), and in that capacity the Israelites sometimes carry it with them. It is sometimes referred to as the "Declaration Chest," with the same meaning: the tablets "declare" God's covenant expectations.

commitment

The word corresponds to the Hebrew word *hesed*, which translations render by means of expressions such as steadfast love or loving-kindness or goodness. It is the Old Testament equivalent to the word for love in the New Testament, the word *agapē*. The Old Testament uses the word *commitment* when it refers to an extraordinary act whereby someone pledges himself or herself to someone else in an act of generosity, allegiance, or grace, when there is no prior relationship between them and therefore no reason why he or she should do so. Thus in Joshua 2, Rahab appropriately speaks of her protection of the Israelite spies as an act of commitment. It can also refer to a similar extraordinary act that takes place when there is a relationship between people but when one party has let the other party down and therefore has no right to expect any faithfulness from the other party. If the party that has been let down continues being faithful, they are showing this kind of commitment. In response to Rahab, the Israelite spies declare that they will relate to her in this way.

covenant

Contracts and treaties assume a quasi-legal system for resolving disputes and administering justice that can be appealed to if someone does not keep a commitment. In contrast, in a covenantal relationship that does not work within a legal framework someone who fails to keep a commitment cannot be taken to court, so a covenant involves some formal procedure confirming the seriousness of the solemn commitment one party makes to another. In covenants between God and humanity, in Genesis the emphasis lies on God's commitment to human beings, and to Abraham in particular. On the basis of God's having begun to fulfill that covenant, the rest of the **Torah** also puts some stress on Israel's responsive commitment at Sinai and in Moab on the edge of the promised land.

cry, cry out

In describing the Israelites' response when they are oppressed by enemies, Judges uses the word that the Old Testament uses to describe Abel's blood crying out to God, the outcry of the people of Sodom under their oppression, the Israelites' crying out in Egypt, and the outcry of people who are unfairly treated within Israel in later centuries. It denotes an urgent cry that presses God for **deliverance**, a cry that God can be relied on to hear even when people deserve the experience that is assailing them.

deliver, deliverer, deliverance

In the Old Testament, modern translations often use the words *save*, *savior*, and *salvation*, but these words give a misleading impression. In Christian usage, they commonly refer to our personal relationship with God and to the enjoyment of heaven. The Old Testament does speak of our personal relationship with God, but it does not use this group of words in that connection. They refer rather to God's practical intervention to get Israel or the individual out of a mess of some kind, such as false accusations by individuals within the community or invasion by enemies.

devote, devoting, devotion

Devoting something to God means giving it over to God irrevocably. Translations use words such as "annihilated" or "destroyed," and that is often the implication, but it does not convey the word's distinctive point. You could devote land, or an animal such as a donkey, and in effect Hannah will devote Samuel; the donkey or the human being then belongs to God and is committed to God's service. In effect the Israelites devoted many **Canaanites** to God's service in this way; they became people who chopped wood and drew water for the **altar**, its offerings, and the rites of the sanctuary. Devoting people to God by killing them as a kind of sacrifice was a practice known from other peoples, which Israel takes over on its own initiative but which God validates. Israel knows this is how war works in its world, it assumes it is to operate the same way, and God goes along with that.

Ephraim, Ephraimites

After David and Solomon's reigns, the nation of **Israel** split into two. Most of the twelve Israelite clans set up an independent state in the north, separate from **Judah** and Jerusalem and from the line of David. Because this was the bigger of the two states, politically it kept the name Israel, which is confusing because Israel is still the name of the people as a whole as the people of God. So the name Israel can be used in both these connections. The northern state can, however, also be referred to by the name of Ephraim, one of its central clans, so I use this term to refer to that northern state, to reduce the confusion.

exile

At the end of the seventh century **Babylon** became the major power in **Judah**'s world, but Judah was inclined to resist its authority. As part of a successful campaign to get Judah to submit to it, in 597 and in 587 BC the Babylonians transported many people from Jerusalem to Babylon, particularly people in leadership positions, such as members of the royal family and the court, priests, and prophets. These people were compelled to live in Babylonia for the next fifty years or so. Throughout this period, people back in Judah were also under Babylonian authority, so they were not physically in exile but were living in the exile as a period of time.

Greece, Greeks

In 336 BC Greek forces under Alexander the Great took control of the **Persian** Empire, but after Alexander's death in 333 his empire split up. The largest part, to the north and east of Palestine, was ruled by one of his generals, Seleucus, and his successors. **Judah** was under its control for much of the next two centuries, though it was at the extreme south-western border of this empire and sometimes came under the control of the Ptolemaic Empire in Egypt, ruled by successors of another of Alexander's officers.

Israel

Originally, Israel was the new name God gave Abraham's grandson, Jacob. His twelve sons were then forefathers of the twelve clans that comprise the people Israel. In the time of Saul, David, and Solomon these twelve clans became more of a political entity; Israel was both the people of God and a nation or state like other nations or states. After Solomon's day, this one state split into two, **Ephraim** and **Judah**. Ephraim was far bigger and often continued to be referred to as Israel. So if one is thinking of the people of God, Judah is part of Israel. If one is thinking politically, Judah is not part of Israel, but once Ephraim has gone out of existence, for practical purposes Judah *is* Israel, as the people of God.

Judah, Judahites

One of the twelve sons of Jacob, then the clan that traces its ancestry to him, then the dominant clan in the southern of the two states after the time of Solomon. Later, as a **Persian** province or colony, it was known as Yehud.

leader

The book of Judges is named after the leaders whose stories appear in the book. The traditional term is *judge*, so that they are people who also give their name to the period of time between Joshua and Saul, the "Judges Period." But these "judges" do not usually operate in connection with sorting out legal cases, and "leaders" gives more the right idea concerning their role. They are people who have no official position like the later kings, but who arise and exercise initiative in a way that brings the clans **deliverance** from the trouble the clans get into. See further the introduction to the book of Judges at the beginning of this commentary.

Master, Masters

The word *baal* is an ordinary Hebrew word for a master or lord or owner, but the word is also used to describe a **Canaanite** god. It is thus parallel to the word *Lord* as used to describe **Yahweh**. Further, in effect "Master" can be a proper name, like "Lord." To make the difference clear, the Old Testament generally uses Master for a foreign god and Lord for the real God, Yahweh. Like other ancient peoples, the Canaanites acknowledged a number of gods, and strictly speaking, the Master was simply one of them, though he was one of the most prominent. In addition, a title such as "The Master of Peor" suggests that the Master was believed to be manifest and known in different ways and different places. The Old Testament also uses the plural *Masters* to refer to Canaanite gods in general.

peace

The word *shalom* can suggest peace after there has been conflict, but it often points to a richer notion, of fullness of life. The KJV sometimes translates it "welfare," and modern translations use words such as "well-being" or "prosperity." It suggests that everything is going well for you.

Persia, Persians

The third Middle Eastern superpower. Under the leadership of Cyrus the Great, they took control of the **Babylonian** empire in 539 BC. Isaiah 40–55 sees God's hand in raising up Cyrus as the means of restoring **Judah** after the **exile**. Judah and surrounding peoples such as Samaria, Ammon, and Ashdod were Persian provinces or colonies. The Persians stayed in power for two centuries until defeated by **Greece**.

Philistia, Philistines

The Philistines were people who came from across the Mediterranean to settle in **Canaan** at the same time as the Israelites were establishing themselves in Canaan, so that the two peoples formed an accidental pincer movement on the existent inhabitants of the country and became each other's rivals for control of the area.

Reed Sea

The "sea" where God finally delivered the Israelites from the Egyptians might be one of the northern arms of what we call the Red Sea, either side of Sinai, or it might be an area of marshy lakes within Sinai. The name designates it as more literally a "sea of rushes" (the word is the one that comes in Exodus 2 where Miriam left Moses in the reeds by the Nile).

restore, restorer

A restorer is a person in a position to take action on behalf of someone within his extended family who is in need, in order to restore the situation to what it should be. The word overlaps with expressions such as *next-of-kin*, *guardian*, and *redeemer*. The use of "next-of-kin" indicates the family context that "restorer" presupposes. "Guardian" indicates that the restorer is in a position to be concerned for the person's protection and defense. "Redeemer" indicates having resources that the restorer is prepared to expend on the person's behalf. The Old Testament uses the term to refer to God's relationship with Israel as well as to the action of a human person in relation to another, so it implies that Israel belongs to God's family and that God acts on its behalf in the way a restorer does.

secondary wife

Translations use the word *concubine* to describe people such as Abimelek's mother and the Levite's wife, but the term used of them does not suggest that they were not properly married. Being a secondary wife rather means that a woman has a different status from other wives. It perhaps implies that her sons had less or no inheritance rights. It may be that a wealthy or powerful man could have several wives with full rights and several secondary wives, or just one of each, or just the former, or even just a secondary wife.

spirit

The Hebrew word for spirit is also the word for breath and for wind, and the Old Testament sometimes implies a link between these. Spirit suggests dynamic power; God's spirit suggests God's dynamic power. The wind in its forcefulness with its capacity to fell mighty trees is an embodiment of the powerful spirit of God. Breath is essential to life; where there is no breath, there is no life. And life comes from God. So human breath and even animal breath is an offshoot of God's breath. The book of Judges relates a series of extraordinary military and political achievements by a series of leaders that issues from God's spirit coming on them in a way that makes them do things that look humanly impossible.

Torah

The Hebrew word for the first five books of the Bible. They are often referred to as the "Law," but this title is misleading. Genesis itself is nothing like "law," and even Exodus to Deuteronomy are not "legalistic" books. The word *torah* itself means "teaching," which gives a clearer impression of the nature of the Torah. Often the Torah gives us more than one account of an event (such as God's commission of Moses), so that when the early church told the story of Jesus in different ways in different contexts and according to the insights of the different Gospel writers, it was following the precedent whereby Israel told its stories more than once in different contexts. Whereas Kings and Chronicles keep the versions separate, as would happen with the Gospels, in the Torah the versions were combined.

Yahweh

In most English Bibles, the word "LORD" often comes in all capitals, as sometimes does the word "GOD" in similar format. These represent the name of God, Yahweh. In later Old Testament times, Israelites stopped using the name Yahweh and started to refer to Yahweh as "the Lord." There may be two reasons. They wanted other people to recognize that Yahweh was the one true God, but this strange, foreign-sounding name could give the impression that Yahweh was just Israel's tribal god, and "the Lord" was a term anyone could recognize. In addition, they did not want to fall foul of the warning in the Ten Commandments about misusing Yahweh's name. Translations into other languages then followed suit in substituting an expression such as "the Lord" for the name Yahweh. The downsides are that this obscures the fact that God wanted to be known by name (see Exodus 3), that often the text refers to Yahweh and not some other (so-called) god or lord, and that it gives the impression that God is much more "lordly" and patriarchal than actually God is. (The form "Jehovah" is not a real word but a mixture of the consonants of Yahweh and the vowels of the word for "Lord," to remind people in reading Scripture in the synagogue that they should say "the Lord," not the actual name.)

CPSIA information can be obtained
at www.ICGtesting.com
Printed in the USA
FSHW01n1302290818
51863FS